MEDFORD EVANS

The SECRET WAR
for the A-BOMB

Introduction by
JAMES BURNHAM

Chicago · HENRY REGNERY COMPANY · *1953*

Introduction ⚖ How Many Atoms in a Good Idea?

Magician. "I can call up spirits when I please."
Bystander. "Yes, but will they come when you call them?"
From a Princeton Triangle Show.

When three atomic bombs were exploded during the summer of 1945, one above the sands of New Mexico and two over Japanese cities, no one expected that to be the end of the affair. If three bombs had been built in a few years, starting from scratch, then presumably many more could be in the future. If two could compel the immediate surrender of a weakened but still mighty empire, it was hard to feel indifferent about who would possess and perhaps use the others that would, or might, come into existence.

There were commentators who believed that in the form of the atomic bomb mankind had brought forth *the absolute weapon:* that is, the weapon to which there could be no counter-measure. This opinion was mistaken. Unless all men are annihilated, to any and every weapon some sort of reply is always *possible*. But in 1945 there was a relative truth in this extreme estimate of the atomic bomb. In that year and for the years immediately following, the atomic bomb went

so far beyond all pre-existing weapons as to give its posses-
sor, so long as he held a monopoly, the military basis for
enforcing his will against any military opposition then
possible.

The sudden intrusion of the atomic bomb as an operative
weapon of warfare was analogous on a world scale to what
would have been the potential regional effect if muskets had
appeared on one side at Agincourt, ironclads at Trafalgar,
or machine guns at Gettysburg.

It was therefore inevitable that any nation which was not
ready to accept military subordination to the United States,
the initial atomic monopolist, should seek to redress the
balance. Germany and Japan, the defeated powers, were
crushed to a level where they could not be heard from for
at least a number of years. Britain, a rooted and close ally,
had been intimately associated in the atomic project. It was
unlikely that she would want to start off on her own, or that
she would be a threat if she did. No other Western nation
and no industrially undeveloped nation possessed the physical premises for large-scale nuclear armament. That seemed
to leave only the Soviet Union to worry about. If expressed
in public, such a worry would have been ungallant in those
days. However, not all Americans are as foolish as most of
them who wrote about Soviet questions then sounded.

For the Soviet Union to redress the balance would seem
to mean, reasoning by normal precedent, that the Soviet
Union should itself acquire a nuclear armament of the same
order as the American. To achieve this, Moscow apparently
had to do two things: (a) acquire, either by theft (espionage) or by the independent labors of its own scientists and
technicians, the scientific and technological data necessary
to a nuclear project; (b) build an adequate nuclear armament industry.

If Soviet counteraction was going to proceed as thus
expected, conventional reasoning further suggested that, in

addition to provisions for direct defense against future enemy nuclear weapons, the principal measures for American protection should be: (a) to safeguard the atomic secrets; (b) to expand American nuclear armament to a level sufficient to guarantee overwhelming superiority even after the monopoly was broken.

This is the pattern of move and countermove, of thrust and riposte, in all those instances where a new weapon of pronounced qualitative superiority has been suddenly introduced into warfare: crossbows and tanks and airplanes as well as muskets and dreadnoughts.

The expectation that Moscow would move in accordance with the precedents was soon confirmed. Only a month after the Japanese explosions, the flight of Igor Gouzenko from the Soviet Embassy in Canada brought word that the systematic theft of data had been going on for at least two years. This meant that the Communists had been taking countermeasures against the atomic explosions long before these had occurred. Reflection on this somewhat paradoxical fact might have led to the conclusion that in this field also, as in so many others, the Communists held the initiative, and that the American nuclear weapons were in historical reality not a thrust but a reply.

Gouzenko's disclosures, though they proved the need to protect the secrets, did not lead to measures which were able to do so. As a matter of fact, no measures based on conventional precedent could have given full protection.

More generally, the conventional expectations about the Soviet reply to the atomic explosions failed to comprehend the complex nature of Communist operations. The Communists, while functioning in the customary manner of all power groupings, were also moving through a quite different dimension.

As any competing nation would have done, the Communists sent agents into and around the atomic energy project.

The agents tried to steal, photograph, or buy the formulas, papers, and objects of various kinds that embody the relevant secrets. Similarly, the Soviet Union tried to organize and build on its own territory a physical plant that would be able to produce nuclear armament.

These were the lesser and non-specific elements of the Communist reply. The principal phase was conceived not in terms of passive physical objects or inert data of knowledge, but dynamically, in terms of men and the minds of men. Of course it was a good thing for the Communists if they got their hands on a piece of paper containing an important formula or if an agent was able to photograph a critical instrument. But more lastingly valuable than possession of any particular formula or object was control over the minds of the men who produced the formulas and the instruments—the scientists and the technicians. Still more decisive would be control, even partial and indirect control, over those whose function it was to decide what was to be done about American nuclear armament—the leaders of government and public opinion.

Conventional but not Communist reasoning tends to forget that a weapon—any weapon—is only a powerless bundle of matter apart from human minds and wills. It is sadly deceptive to repeat the statistic that an atomic or hydrogen bomb is a million or billion or trillion or whatever it is times as powerful as a firecracker. The biggest bomb ever built or building is less than David's slingshot without a mind and will and arm able and ready to use it.

With atomic capability added to its military force already in being, America was in a position, materially speaking, to enforce its views—to reduce the Soviet and any other major threat to manageable proportions, and thus to guarantee for a reasonable future both national security and world peace. This possibility conflicted with the Communist objective of total world domination. The Communists struck back, hard, brilliantly, and successfully. The main impetus of their stroke was directed against the minds and wills of men.

Within the field directly relevant to the production of nuclear armament they had been carrying on major anticipatory operations for at least a decade. With Communist blessing, the American Association of Scientific Workers was started in 1938, along with similarly named sister organizations in the other non-totalitarian countries where advanced scientific work was being done. Five years before that, a broader organization, the Federation of Architects, Engineers, Chemists and Technicians, had begun work in the same and related fields. Still earlier, supporting beachheads had been established in electrical manufacturing, where for many years the Communists were in control of the unionized workers; in the public opinion industry; in the universities where the scientists taught and were taught; and in government.

The Communists were thus in position to counteract the American atomic energy project from its first moment. They did not have to send agents into it, though they did so. Communists or men who had been influenced by Communists were automatically sucked into the project along the prevailing currents of American social life. In order to acquire formulas and blueprints they did not need alien graduates of MVD spy schools to be on location in Oak Ridge, Hanford or Los Alamos. They could get many of the secrets at leisure from Communized technicians and scientists. They could even get, as Medford Evans shows in this book, the essential material of the bomb itself. And after the first bombs had exploded, when for at least a few years the Soviet Union was going to have to act from a military base of decisive material inferiority, they were not limited to external diplomacy in promoting American policy decisions which would sterilize the latent power of the bomb. Communists and those influenced by Communists were already fixed inside the institutions which affect American public opinion and in the agencies of the government itself.

For the Communists it would naturally be desirable if the Soviet Empire could match the non-Communist world in nuclear as in other forms of armament. As they reason, however, this is probably not possible and certainly not necessary. I do not have to fear the threat of a bullet if the man who possesses the gun is unable or unwilling to pull the trigger.

The main thrust of the Communist reply to American nuclear armament is against the men who make the bomb (technicians and scientists) and the men who control it (the leaders of government and public opinion). The primary objective has been to deprive the United States of the benefit of its nuclear armament, to "denature" the bombs not by the physical means referred to in the Acheson-Lilienthal Report, but by political, psychological and moral means. In this field as more generally, the Communists act to confuse and disorient their enemy, to tangle him in contradictory policies, and to destroy his will to resist. If they succeed, a mountain of nuclear weapons will not be worth a molehill.

The Communist action toward and within the American atomic project is only one application of their strategy toward American society as a whole. We discover here the same pattern that has been traced in the public opinion industry, the foreign affairs and intelligence sections of government, parts of the educational system, and elsewhere. It is like a theatrical or cinema style in which the plot is always a variation on a basic fable and the characters the same stock types with changed names and costumes. Those who followed the Senate Internal Security Subcommittee's investigation of the Institute of Pacific Relations will feel at home in Mr. Evans' atomic portrait gallery. Somehow, though, it is more shocking to meet the old gang and the old phrases in these atomic surroundings. In remarks about the atom, we are accustomed to a soothing, sacrosanct tone of white coats and differential equations. We all grasp, moreover, that our lives directly depend on what happens to the atomic project. That being so, we find it almost unthinkable that this project should have been manipulated by those same forces which, after the point is hammered into our heads long enough, we finally recognize to have been active in the U.N. Secretariat, the film industry or the Office of Strategic Services.

I do not mean to suggest that the atomic energy project has been swarming with thousands of Communists. Very few institutions in this country have ever swarmed with actual, conscious, disciplined Communists. The OSS did not, nor the State Department, nor the faculties of the large Universities. Even in Hollywood and the United Nations, where Communists have swarmed pretty heavily, they have been a relatively small minority. That is not the problem. The atomic energy project, like these other institutions, has been played upon, influenced and in some cases controlled by ideas which have been initiated by the Communist and Soviet interests. This has been possible not because of the excessively large number of disciplined Communists, but because of the excessive vulnerability of many sections of the population to Communist influence. The record shows that this vulnerability is especially widespread among the college-educated intellectual "élite" from which the "opinion molders," the writers, editors, preachers, university professors, scientists and upper government employees, are drawn.

Physical scientists, in particular physicists, seem to have, or to have had, a peculiar affinity for contemporary Communism. I remember a conversation I had a year ago with a British writer, himself a pacifist and anarchist, who is acquainted with many of the British physicists. He said that most of them were ideologically pulled one or another degree toward Communism. He attributed this to the attraction exercised by the Communist doctrine of dialectical materialism which, he thought, seemed to the physicist like an analogue in the social sphere of his own neat, ordered scheme of thought in the physical sphere. He cited also the names of well-known pro-Communist physicists in France, India, Germany and Italy.

I do not think that his explanation is sufficient. Many physical scientists who are pro-Communist know little about dialectical materialism, or about politics, society and history. It seems almost an occupational characteristic that they do not apply to philosophy and social life the strict standards of evidence, relevance and adequacy that they use in their specialized field of interest. Vaguer, more irrational factors seem to be at work—a dimly understood but powerfully felt interest in a "social experiment," an arrogant ignorance thinking to know all things because it knows so much about the esoteric mysteries of physical reality, a fascination with the concepts of "social plan" and "social control," a projection of a hidden will to power which is stimulated but not fulfilled by the scientists' role in non-Communist society.

Perhaps I overstate the Communist infection among physicists. Again, it is not a question of a simple listing of numbers. It is not that most physicists have been influenced by Communist ideas, but that many of the most articulate, the most publicly prominent, the most politically active have been. Put it another way: how difficult it is to name any prominently known and publicly talkative physicists, in this or any other country, who are informed, active *anti-Communists!* Or still more bluntly: why don't prominent physicists like, say, Harold Urey or J. Robert Oppenheimer, tell what they know about what went on in the atomic energy project, about such things as Medford Evans writes about in this book?

Once more I insist: we can handle the Communists if we

handle ourselves. It is not so much that they are so intelligent and shrewd as that we have been weak and foolish. Moscow has made its mistakes, many of them and big. We have failed to profit by those mistakes, or to make good use of our own assets.

I do not believe that either Dean Acheson or David Lilienthal or Thomas Finletter is or ever has been a Communist. In the case of all three of these men it is a matter of record that they feared and distrusted the American monopoly of nuclear weapons, that they considered this monopoly a threat against peace and civilization, and that they wanted the United States to give up its monopoly together with its nuclear factories, its secrets, and whatever weapons were in its possession.

This was their view, publicly and aggressively advocated. We, through our duly constituted representatives and leaders, placed these three men—precisely these three—in charge of our atomic project. We stripped the chiefs of our military forces of the physical control over nuclear weapons. We appointed Dean Acheson as the official in charge of our foreign policy as a whole, and thus of the political use of our atomic energy project. We made David Lilienthal chief of the Atomic Energy Commission itself, to which was assigned the entire organization and production facilities for nuclear development. And, as a last full measure of absurdity, after adopting for our air force a military doctrine based on the perspective of strategic bombing with nuclear weapons, we made Thomas Finletter—who did not believe in strategic nuclear bombing—head of that air force.

When I was in India two years ago I met on a number of occasions an Indian who, as many there do, combined in his activity politics with philosophy. We did not get along very well. His conversation was openly anti-American, well over toward the Communist edge of neutralism. Rather late one evening we found ourselves sitting next to each other.

He began talking to me in a voice much quieter, more friendly and more serious than he had used before.

"My negative attitude toward the West," he said in substance, "is really based on my conviction that your civilization is dying. During most of my life, faced with the West's colossal achievements and its apparent extraordinary dynamism, such a view would have seemed to me absurd. But it is the Western achievement that is perhaps most remarkable of all, the atomic bomb, that has convinced me.

"A civilization is dying if it is not able to accept the logical consequences of its own inner nature. Now the atomic bomb is not a casual byproduct of Western life, nor the inspired creation of one or two individual geniuses. It is a logical and inevitable outcome of two of the innermost, essential features of Western culture: mathematico-empirical science and industrial technology. It is a typical, integral culmination of the Western tradition.

"Confronting this brilliant and wholly legitimate offspring, the spokesmen and leaders of the West, turning their eyes away, try to deny and avoid it. They feel a sterilizing conviction of guilt instead of a normal sense of achievement, triumph and power. Instead of the hope that ought to spring from the knowledge that they have unlocked the incomparable resources of nuclear energy, they tremble with fear at their own incapacity. Why should we Indians follow you, if you are afraid to lead? Why should we accept your way, if you yourselves deny it?"

Although I am unable to forget his words, I shall continue to believe that his obituary was premature. I think that he had looked too thinly at the surface of the West, the West as it has been refracted in "journals of opinion," Marxified foreign correspondents both sent and received, exchange professors and professional attendants at international conferences, junior diplomats whose ideas were tacked together out of the dregs of the Depression.

I remembered him when Medford Evans talked to me one afternoon about an incident to which he refers in his book. Evans was in Oak Ridge when the news of the Hiroshima explosion came. There were about 75,000 people there, all of them part of the atomic project. After the 1945 explosions, my Indian friend, or enemy, had heard in Bombay only the voices of those who, beating their breasts, had lamented the imminent end of civilization and their own sinful part in its demise. So far as Oak Ridge was concerned, Evans recalls, this wailing was confined to about 500 of the 75,000— though a noisy 500, drawn mostly from the scientific and upper technical staff.

The others, including many of the more modest scientists and technicians, rejoiced, and looked at each other with pride. Their husbands, brothers and sons would be coming home sooner, and alive. The war would end at once, and in victory. Their country could now lead and guarantee a decent world. And they themselves had had a small but real part in a magnificent, almost incredible creation.

There have been several competent though of course incomplete books written on the scientific side of the atomic energy project. On the political, social and moral phases, this book of Medford Evans' seems to me not merely the best but alone in its class. It is written from the inside, from really inside: Medford Evans was *there,* and there from almost the beginning until he resigned his well-paid, highly-placed job a year ago. He resigned voluntarily, under no pressure, because he believed that he had to try to tell his countrymen what he knew about their most important possession, their atomic energy project.

Evans is not an ideologist. The easy phrases about world government, world federation, United Nationalism, union of East and West and fate of civilization are conspicuously absent from his paragraphs. He seems more anxious to tell the truth than to advertise his own solutions for the problems of earth and Heaven. He writes in an old-fashioned way: as an American to Americans. It's a verbal brand that old-timers used to swear by. It might be worth a re-examination.

JAMES BURNHAM

Kent, Conn.
August, 1953

Contents

Part Three: FUTURE HOPE

Prelude ⟿ Gypsy Music in the Land of Enchantment

Los Alamos.

June 1946.

From Santa Fe 30 miles northwest, and 1,200 feet higher up into the moonlit night of New Mexico.

From V-J Day 10 months.

Those are the rough space-time co-ordinates of one of those events which in my life, as I should imagine in yours, stand ineradicable in the memory, beyond reason. They are the postulates of experience, and we make inferences from them but never to them. They may at the time have no obvious quality of drama, and they are never merely intensifications of pleasures or pains already familiar in kind. They are perhaps as a rule quiet, but they are without precedent, and quite unforgettable.

I was sitting at a table in the PX, which served in the evening as a club for the enlisted men and the rougher civilians. I was a stranger in Los Alamos and quite alone. There was in the air in the PX precisely so much spirit of revelry as may be engendered by the sale of 3.2% beer and Coca Cola to men who know they have to go to work the next day and who are habituated to taciturnity. I was looking at a striking pose of Lizabeth Scott in a picture magazine. The juke box was playing "The Gypsy."

Outdoors in the moonlight on the eastward-tilted mesa were Fuller Lodge and the Big House and the softball diamond and the cottonwood trees. To the east across a great interval were the Sangre de Cristo Mountains, and nearer, behind the lodge, where the forest began, the mesa itself angled up sharply into the western sierra.

Subjectively I registered something between exhilaration and contentment. It was my first field trip out of Oak Ridge as an official representative of the Manhattan District. The run from Chicago to Lamy on "The Chief" defies sophistication, and I am never blasé about trains. I had been received graciously on the Hill by Major Conard, and my room at the Big House if Spartan was scrupulous.

Ten days earlier I had been in Washington as a guest of CBS at the Mayflower, participating in a radio show called "Operation Crossroads" that was broadcast coast-to-coast and included many important people and others like me who felt important on the occasion.

I had just had a raise and bought the children bicycles. My wife had a new hat and was establishing herself as the best gardener on Delaware Avenue next to Vi Warren and Hugh Finley. I was anticipating a week-end drive to Taos with my brother and my parents, who from Las Vegas and El Paso would meet me at the La Fonda Saturday morning.

It was the first full summer of Peace.

What do you want out of life? Los Alamos, in my book, was a great place.

I did not know at all how my enthusiasm was shared by a resident of the bachelors' dormitory who "Living there, high among the pines, in the clear, dry air of the desert . . . began to develop a physical well-being that he could hardly have known before." [1] But like me he was even then preparing to leave Los Alamos—in his case not, so far as I know, to return.

His name was Emil Julius Klaus Fuchs.

✧ ✧ ✧

"But I'll go there again
Because I want to believe the Gypsy."

Yes, I want to believe it, but I don't believe it any more. I want to believe that everybody in the whole United States is true, and especially in the Land of Enchantment that we call New Mexico, because the whole United States depends for its life on what they do there.

But I don't believe it.

That's why I have written this book.

Part One

PRESENT DANGER

Chapter I ✒ Introduction to the Real Situation

The case of Klaus Fuchs dramatized the lie that there was no secret of the atomic bomb. There were many secrets, and there still are. A complex scientific and industrial project generates new secrets daily. As the struggle for world markets may be determined by trade secrets, so the struggle for world hegemony may be resolved by Restricted Data.

Knowledge is power.

But the crucial information that Fuchs and Allan Nunn May and others transmitted to various Soviet agents was, after all, related to a production process, and the end of that process was and is a material product. In that product the information is incorporated. If you have all you want of the product, then from a practical point of view you don't need the information.

By the same token, of course, the information is of purely academic interest unless you have the means of production. As Dr. Ralph Lapp has said, ". . . Fuchs did not give the A-bomb to the Soviets. . . . No one could have given the A-bomb to the Soviets . . . unless he had gone completely mad and had shipped the material for an A-bomb to Russia." [2]

The material that counts is called fissionable material. It would perhaps be more precise to use a few plurals here, since there is more than one variety of fissionable material, and more than one way to produce each variety. The two main varieties produced in quantity so far are ordinarily called U-235 and plutonium.

These are metals. In their pure, or nearly pure, state and in small enough pieces of the right shape, they are not (we are reliably informed) dangerously radioactive, and they will not explode unless two or more such pieces are rapidly assembled. They are heavy metals—half again as heavy as lead—but of course the weight of a small fragment is of no consequence. You have to know a thing or two to handle them safely, but the rules, while important, are simple, and a number of persons are capable of treating them quite casually.

I mention this because a lot of people are apparently not clear that chunks of fissionable material are solid, take up space, can be moved around, and are in general as real as a rock. I have been asked if you can see U-235 and plutonium— the questioner obviously thinking they might be some kind of invisible death ray. If you are in the place where pieces of them are, you can see them plain as a bullet.

They are, of course, worth a lot of money. Just how much is not an easy question. Even—or, I should say, especially—a cost analyst with all the secret data would have a difficult time. Without the burden of detailed knowledge, however, one may find published figures which can be made to yield an estimate of a quarter-million dollars a pound.[3]

That is figuring on a cost basis early in the life of the project. The price in the open market would be something else. It would depend on what you were going to do with the stuff.

If you were going to collect enough of it to stage an atomic bomb raid, and if you believed such a maneuver was the international pay-off, you might mortgage half the world for it.

This, we all hope, is the idlest kind of speculation.

But atomic materials constantly provoke the most intense activity in the most fertile imaginations. The intellectual being cannot abandon this relic of Creation. So much energy concretized in such small compass gives new meaning to Blake's line: "Hold infinity in the palm of your hand." Whether you conceive the ultimate expression to be in terms of kilowatts, dollars, or empire, the potential is enormous. Marlovian man will not let it alone.

Mr. Herbert S. Marks, a keen legal intelligence, friend and adviser of Dean Acheson and David Lilienthal, and first General Counsel of the Atomic Energy Commission, has told how he too was tantalized by the ready negotiability of this suspended violence, according to a report by Daniel Lang in the New Yorker for August 17, 1946.[4]

In company with Mr. Lilienthal, the other members of the Board of Consultants to the Acheson committee on atomic energy control, and Mr. Carroll L. Wilson, subsequently General Manager of the Atomic Energy Commission, Mr. Marks made a tour, early in 1946, of the main atomic bomb installations, then theoretically controlled by the Army's Manhattan District.

The climax of the tour was an inspection of the vault where the capsules of U-235 and plutonium were stored.

The containers were not bulky, according to the New Yorker's report of Mr. Marks' story, and the thought occurred to him with an emphatic expletive that he could walk out with one of them in his pocket.

You cannot, in such a circumstance, restrain such a thought.

To act upon it might be somewhat more complex. There were effective practical checks on such a larcenous impulse, Mr. Marks explained to Reporter-at-Large Lang. They consisted of soldiers. Outside and inside the vault were armed troops on the alert.

This was the year—1946—in which those troops were to be withdrawn from their posts as custodians of the atomic bomb. This was the year in which the chant "civilian control" created such hysteria in the national press and in the Congress that the Honorable Dewey Short of Missouri was moved to say to the House of Representatives on July 17, "I never was so confused and befuddled in all my life. I mean it. Do not laugh—you are too." [5]

Mr. Marks understood that the real control was not military or civilian. It was scientific and technical.

Supposing he had got away with a container of fissionable material, he allegedly told Reporter Lang, he would not as a layman in science have known what to do with it. Yet Mr. Marks was not an ordinary layman, for he seems to have been far enough advanced in atomic technology to be free of superstitious fears of handling properly packaged fissionable material. He was not worried about radioactivity, toxicity, or accidental explosion.

He spoke of two deterrents. One, seasoned troops with clean rifles. Two, the fact that he would not have known what to do with the stuff if he had it.

Mr. Marks' meditation on the ease with which one might ravish the treasures of the final atomic vault, and on the ironic denial of fruition without the key of knowledge, concluded with an eloquent passage which unfortunately cannot be quoted here. In it Mr. Marks reflected upon the inviolable independence of the Manhattan District, considered as an operating complex—an independence amounting to practical sovereignty, capable possibly of dissolving other sovereignties.

It was well put, as Mr. Marks, according to Mr. Lang, put it. It is today not less but more valid.

The Atomic Energy Commission is only a part of the atomic energy project. That project as a whole is, if we may be dialectical for a moment, a synthesis resulting from the thesis of a voluntary association of international scientists and the antithesis of the military requirements of the United States.

Put otherwise, the atomic energy project was begotten by a cosmopolitan group of nuclear physicists on the United States War Department. The Atomic Energy Commission is neither the father nor the mother of this prodigious progeny, but some kind of foster parent—considering the volume and fluidity of the money appropriated, a veritable fairy godmother providing royal furnishings from the resources of us pumpkin-headed American taxpayers. If that portmanteau allusion to Alger Hiss and Cinderella is pondered briefly it may provoke in the minds of some of the atomic scientists a new appreciation of the phrase "Minutes to Midnight."

The Manhattan District, AEC's predecessor in the bureaucratic structure, was also only part of the project, strictly speaking, though not altogether the same part. The War Department once directed the Army's various Service Commands to have nothing to do with the Manhattan District, *except to render all possible assistance when so requested by the Manhattan District.*

Today the industrial, academic, and governmental institutions of the United States have very little to do with the atomic energy project except to support it. We generally presume that in return for this support we shall receive in some remote future marvelous blessings of peace, and that in the meantime we have at hand an unparalleled instrument of war.

But the actual employment of this instrument of war, and the practical development of those blessings of peace, depend alike on the advice and consent of technical experts within the still sovereign atomic energy project.

From one point of view, all we can do about this situation is to acquire more technical knowledge ourselves, for there is no doubt that technical knowledge engenders in some degree its own authority.

But just as there never yet was a philosopher who could endure a toothache patiently, so there is not a scientist without his human qualities of strength and weakness and, specifically, dependence on some kind of society—using that word deliberately to cover both friendly association and formal political organization.

There are scientists who consciously accept the sovereignty of the United States, and there are scientists who do not. The almost inescapable tendency of the latter is to drift into the orbit of Soviet sovereignty, though at first this is seldom their intention.

We cannot compel loyalty, for freedom is of the essence. Nor can we infallibly determine whether any given individual is in fact loyal.

> "There's no art
> To read the mind's construction in the face."

We can, however, do something about the "loyalty of free men." We can by exhortation and the established system of rewards and punishments encourage the free choices we desire. And we can determine more realistically than we have in the past what free choices have actually been made. If we do not do these things about the loyalty of free men, we shall probably lose the freedom of loyal men.

Dr. Walter Zinn, Director of the Argonne National Laboratory, told the Joint Committee on Atomic Energy in June 1949 that, even with fissionable material in a less handy form than items of the final product, ". . . if you cannot have people who you are confident will not do this filching, let us say, your inventories cannot control the situation." [6]

"I worry equally," Dr. Zinn added, "and really much more, about our numbers, the measurements that we ourselves make with these materials. We have skills and ways of making measurements which probably are not current in other places, and numbers when they leave do not leave any trace. . . ." [7]

This is salutary to remember whenever we are tempted to think that Fuchs gave everything away and that secrecy of information is no longer appropriate. Secrecy is indeed essential. But it may be noted that while information may be even more important than materials in a developmental laboratory like Argonne, the materials assume an engrossing importance in the final storehouse.

From the point of view of military utilization, whoever controls storage controls everything. If he is not loyal to the United States, he may use this control position in three general ways:

1. Negative sabotage—inaction.
2. Positive sabotage—destruction.
3. Supplying materials to a foreign power.

The concept of negative sabotage might seem to have little applicability to the final storage sites. So long, however, as custody remains a "civilian" function, action is required to arm the military, and appropriately timed inaction might be fatal to the Air Force or one of the other unarmed services of the United States. Additional possibilities for negative sabotage may occur to the initiated.

Short of the final storage sites there are various opportunities for positive or negative sabotage and for diversion of materials. The selection of personnel is as important to the United States now as formerly to Gideon.

As this is written—August 1953—there is need for great

alarm, but not for despair. Browning has a line about "All that a man may waste, desecrate, never quite lose," and I think the atomic superiority of the United States—the whole military potential of the United States—is like that. We have since 1945 flaunted almost every principle of national security. Yet such is the essential health of the American constitution (with or without the capital), and such also are the weakness and folly of our antagonist, that I think we may hope Representative Short was mistaken when he declared:

"You propose now to hand your enemy a pistol with which to shoot you. Oh! you are a smart people, are you not? We will get it because we asked for it."

We may hope he was mistaken, but it is going to be a close call.

Chapter II ⌒ Where Is the Soviet Sandia?

There has been very little unequivocal truth spoken about atomic energy since 1945. This is due to

(1) The natural difficulty of getting a complex subject straight,

(2) Positive elements of deception introduced into the discussion for partisan reasons, most notably by Soviet agents, and

(3) Well intended notions of giving the public what is thought to be good for it from the point of view of some kind of social psychiatry, instead of the best available approximation of the facts, complete with indications of probable error.

THE TRUMAN HERESY

The classic illustration of the reliability of official U.S. releases was given by Harry S. Truman in January 1953, just one week to the day after he left the White House.

"I am not convinced," the ex-President told an INS reporter in Kansas City—"I am not convinced the Russians have achieved the know-how to put the complicated mechanism together to make an A-bomb work. I am not convinced they have the bomb."

Newsweek (February 9, 1953) headlined this: " 'Ground Zero' in Kansas City; Harry Truman Drops an A-Bomb," and indeed it was a catastrophe for supporters of the official propaganda line. AEC Chairman Dean, Senator Hickenlooper, and President Eisenhower immediately issued statements of contradictory import. This was necessary but almost irrelevant. The news was not that Harry Truman *doubted the Russian A-bomb;* the news was that *Harry Truman* doubted the Russian A-bomb. And there was, of course, nothing that Dean or Hickenlooper or Eisenhower could do about that.

The whole affair was like the apostasy of an archbishop. The lowliest vicar is shaken by the repercussions, no matter how demonstrably in error the apostate may be.

It had been Truman who, speaking officially, had startled the world in September 1949 with an announcement of an "atomic explosion" in the U.S.S.R. The credibility of that announcement depended almost entirely on the assumption that the President of the United States, in such a matter, could not be mistaken and would not be deceptive. To question the statement was to imply the fallibility of the White House—understanding that the whole executive bureaucratic process is involved, not just the integrity and judgment of one man.

To understand calmly the gravity of Truman's offense, one must understand that upon the dogma promulgated in September 1949—the dogma that the Russians had contrived an atomic explosion and, as a corollary, had an atomic energy project of their own—was based:

(1) the justification of a great expansion of the American program of atomic production, and

(2) the cautiously but persistently advanced inference that the American program of "internal security" had been unsuccessful in the past and would be largely an unnecessary impediment in the future.

These propositions were summarized under the slogan "Security by Achievement rather than Security by Concealment," or simply "Security by Achievement."

Much has been staked on this doctrine. It justifies enormous expenditures for the production of fissionable materials, and reckless candor in publication policy. The latter is permitted and the former required by the assumption that the Russians are going great guns in their own atomic energy project.

The slogan "Security by Achievement" appears to have been first introduced into public discussion by Senator Brien McMahon in the summer of 1946.[8] It received fresh impetus when the Majority Report of the Joint Committee on Atomic Energy—published in 1949, three weeks after the Truman announcement of the first Russian explosion—gave an adverse judgment on Senator Bourke B. Hickenlooper's "incredible mismanagement" charges against the then AEC Chairman David E. Lilienthal.[9] At the same time the Congress loosened the purse strings to permit acceleration of the AEC expansion program. (Meanwhile, however, certain enthusiasts for "Security by Achievement" fought tooth and nail in a rearguard action to delay incorporation of hydrogen-bomb development in the plans for Achievement.)

"Security by Achievement" is, of course, spurious rhetoric. There is no more real conflict between "Achievement" and "Concealment" as means of "Security" than there is between the accelerator and the brake as means of secure control of an automobile. Yet this rhetoric—with its implied false dichotomy—was adopted, though the logical ambiguity had been pointed out in an AEC staff memorandum as far back as the summer of 1948. (The author of that memo was later released by "reduction in force" in spite of the "expanding program," and "the difficulty of getting good men in Government." Should I be asked point blank: "Are you implying that he was let go because of that memo?" I should have to reply that obviously the thought had occurred to me, but all I am sure of is that AEC was unfortunate to lose his services, since he was an able man.)

Naturally, the doctrine of "Security by Achievement"— backed by the threat of Russian competition—gained strength daily so long as the fallacious nature of its context was not exposed, for in itself it makes the strongest kind of appeal to an aggressively industrial nation. There is in fact absolutely nothing wrong with such a doctrine *so long as it is not used to exclude or obscure the vital importance of the complementary kind of security represented by prudent concealment and firm exploitation of whatever monopolistic advantages the United States may have achieved or been granted.*

True achievement does not consist of energetically bailing water with a sieve.

A painfully pertinent point is that when Achievement is emphasized not in connection with but at the expense of Concealment, you get an industrial and scientific complex which, being ever larger and looser, is ever more readily infiltrated and milked of the information and materials peculiar to its processes.

More of that in Chapter Four. Meanwhile, what of the credibility of Truman's statement, "I am not convinced they have the bomb"? Will it be all right to examine that on its merits?

I know that in a race you ought to "run scared"; so perhaps we should not do or say anything to lower the common estimate of Russian capabilities, on the ground that it is good for us to believe the Russians are breathing hot on our necks.

How about trying to get the facts straight? There is probably quite enough to be scared about. But wouldn't it be silly, and dangerous, to be scared of the wrong thing?

I submit that the story of Russian competition in atomic

energy doesn't stand up very well, even under such an amateur analysis as I can give it. The following historical notes about Russian industry would probably be stipulated, as the lawyers say, by most persons interested in this kind of discussion:

FACTS ON SOVIET INDUSTRY

1. When the Communists took over in 1917, Russian industry, always backward by Western standards, was badly disorganized as a result of the traumatic experiences of World War I. Four years later the situation was worse. Sir Bernard Pares says that "According to Rykov, Commissar for Industry, factory output had fallen by 85 per cent, and what was produced was looted by the workers, and the plant to boot." [10] This was 1921. "We are a backward country," said Lenin in the fall of 1922 (according to Valeriu Marcu); ". . . our technical efficiency is next to nothing." [11]

2. Russian industrialization began with the first Five-Year Plan, in 1928. At that time, while the United States was producing 5,000,000 automobiles a year, there were in Russia, according to T. Zavalani, Albanian-born graduate of the Marxist-Leninist academy in Leningrad, "no traditions of mechanical production and technical management of a big-scale modern industry." [12]

Nineteen twenty-eight!

Frederick W. Taylor started "scientific management" in America in 1889. Or so they tell me. I can't remember that far back. But I can remember 1928 well enough.

"The Plan," says Pares, "had almost to start from scratch." [13] No wonder that if you take 1928 as a base year you can plot trends and cite percentages which during the succeeding five years make the Soviet Union look good. It had nowhere to go but up.

The American Depression began one year later. The Depression was a trying time, but the Okies went to California by automobile.

3. Obviously the first Five-Year Plan and the second and the others represent work and the work had results. Russia in 1938 must have been a formidable industrial power, *compared to the Russia of 1928,* or compared to India or Afghanistan. But, as a student of baseball might say, it is not just where you stand in the league, it's what league you're in.

Possibly the most dramatically successful program of the Russians was that of "electrification." The Dnieper Dam in 1937 had 600,000 kilowatts capacity, or almost one-fourth the capacity of the Grand Coulee today. Yet with this fabulous advance the Russian output of 36.4 billion kilowatt-hours in the great Soviet year 1937 was about one third that of the United States in the terrible Depression year 1937.[14]

4. In 1941 the Germans blew up the Dnieper Dam. That is only one of the things that happened to Soviet industry during World War II. Total destruction by the Germans, and by the Russians themselves in their "scorched-earth" policy of retreat, has been estimated by the Soviets themselves (according to Zavalani) at about a third of the existing capital. The devastated area originally contained two thirds of the heavy industry.[15]

Much has been made of transfers beyond the Urals, but it is hard to think this can have been very efficient considering how transportation is always a bottleneck in the vast Russian land mass, with one fourth the U.S. railway mileage to serve double the U.S. area, and no help from the highway system worth speaking of in the same breath with U.S. highways.

5. Since World War II there has no doubt been much reconstruction under the fourth Five-Year Plan. And a great amount of goods has no doubt been imported into the Soviet Union from Germany—although there is considerable doubt

as to what shape it was in when it got to its destination, or what productive use was made of it.

At a Cabinet luncheon on April 28, 1947, General George C. Marshall, then Secretary of State, reported on a Moscow conference as follows: "Two underlying motifs ran through all the conversations with the Russians—first, money, and second, reparations out of Germany, *i.e.*, in terms of production. . . . The Russians have found that *the taking of physical assets does not get them the result they want in terms of goods.* [Italics added.] Even taking of management personnel with the plants does not suffice because the trained labor is not available in Russia." [16]

This, from the Soviet point of view, is a sort of bleak picture, don't you think?

In any case the results of reparation and reconstruction combined seem to have left much to be desired as far as putting the Soviet Union in a seriously competitive position with the United States is concerned. For a particularly important example, the Soviet Union's planned electrical production for 1950 was 82 billion kilowatt-hours.[17] This is indeed well over double the Soviet production of 1937, but it is still only about a fourth the U.S. production for 1950.[18]

6. The Muscovites have, of course, resolved to try to do something about their own mess. In August 1952 they promulgated Plan V, focusing on goals set for 1955. According to the editors of *Fortune*, ". . . weaknesses notwithstanding, Plan V makes the Soviet Union a growing military menace to the West." [19] This sounds a bit anticlimactic to ears accustomed to the imagined thunder of Soviet atomic tests three years before Plan V was announced. Let us not minimize, however, the Soviet potential. Let us neither minimize it nor maximize it. Let's try to make some reasoned assumptions about it.

The *World Almanac* for 1953 makes the following summary statement about Plan V:

"The plan, aiming at increased output in nearly every field, set a 10 to 12% yearly increase in average production to attain a general rise of about 70% in 1955 over 1950. Fulfillment of the 1955 goals would make the Soviet Union about ½ as productive as the U.S. was in 1951." [20] But this means that total industry in the Soviet Union in 1949, when we first heard of an atomic explosion there, must have been equivalent to something between a fourth and a third of U.S. industry of the same date.

In view of the historic vicissitudes we have just briefly run over, there seems little reason to argue for a higher estimate of Soviet capacity than this—call it 30% of U.S. capacity. This at the time when they allegedly made an A-bomb.

So far, then, this:

A broad-scale measurement of Russian industry against American does not, of course, reveal whether the Soviets are or are not capable of manufacturing an atomic bomb; but it does reveal, decidedly, a situation where various conjectures are legitimate, where only a crackpot can be sure either way, and where only an ax-grinder will pretend to be sure either way. Unless, of course, he has positive intelligence not available to the public. We cannot argue against the I-know-things-I-am-not-at-liberty-to-reveal line.

But this is where we came in on the Harry Truman story. He knew things he was not at liberty to reveal. Down to January 20, 1953, he was supposed to know more than anyone else. It seems improbable that by January 27 he had forgotten everything, or that President Eisenhower (tied up at least part of the time by the inaugural ceremonies and festivities) had learned everything.

No, the argument from authority is a dead duck. We will reason as best we can concerning probabilities.

THE LIVE ISSUE

Now, let's focus a bit more sharply on the essential problem. The question that counts is not, literally, Do the Russians have an A-bomb? but, Do the Russians have an atomic energy project of significant scope and efficiency?

Put otherwise, we will not agitate ourselves as to whether the United States has a pure monopoly, but will inquire as to whether the United States has in fact atomic superiority. Or, again, has the policy of Security by Achievement been a success?

Actually, there is little doubt that, *within its terms of reference* (i.e., *as far as it goes*), it has been a success. Nor is there likely to be much controversy about that, unless Moscow wants to argue it.

The American atomic energy project has immense superiority over any conceivable atomic energy project within the boundaries of the Soviet Union. This I do believe.

To maintain such superiority was the policy of the Truman Administration, and has continued to be the policy of the Eisenhower Administration. Both Administrations have received co-operation, at any rate since 1949, from every segment of American society. The scientists and the military have reduced public bickering almost to the vanishing point, and the plain citizens have never wavered in their support of more A-bombs, H-bombs, fissionable material—the works!

That is why we are building Savannah River and Portsmouth. That is why we are searing the sands of Nevada, and readying the runways at Groton for the *Nautilus*. That is why we appropriated in one year double the amount invested in the whole Manhattan Project during World War II.[21]

The extent of this superiority, obviously, cannot be measured with precision. Nor does it need to be, for if it were close it would not effectively exist. It is not close. It cannot be.

In order to see how it cannot be, we must examine more closely the startling disparity between American and Russian industrial capacity. The fact is that the most striking differences between American and Soviet accomplishment appear in certain industries which seem to be especially reliable indicators of the technological verve and persistence requisite to a viable atomic energy project.

These industries include the electronics and electric appliance group, the telephone industry, the automobile industry, the chemical industries, including petroleum, and the metallurgical and metal industries, especially nonferrous.

It is not at all unreasonable to assume a significant positive correlation between a nation's atomic potential and its actual performance in the telephone industry.

David E. Lilienthal has explained in some detail how the U.S. Atomic Energy Commission, even though it had inherited the project which had made the Hiroshima and Nagasaki bombs, still faced a shocking problem in establishing a proper organization for "the fabrication of the components, and their assembly into a workable weapon."

"First of all," says Mr. Lilienthal in his book *Big Business: A New Era*, "this task required *industrial* experience. . . .

"Second, what we wanted done required men of a high order of ability in scientific fundamentals. . . .

"Third, this task called for a special kind of operating experience in dealing with the technical characteristics of systems used in these weapons. . . .

"Most important of all, these three capabilities of research, industrial techniques and operation had to be *combined* in the same team. . . .

"To go out and create such an organization was out of the question. There was not time."

Now does anyone seriously think there has been more time for this kind of creation in Russia?

"It was our 'hunch,' " says Mr. Lilienthal, "that there was such an organization in existence—the Bell System. . . .

"A careful analysis confirmed this initial 'hunch.' . . .

"The Bell System took over the Sandia operation (as this part of atomic weapons production is called). . . . It has been responsible for it ever since. The stepped-up production of atomic bombs and the favorable results in the tests of new weapons . . . are, I am sure, in considerable measure due to the unique contribution of the Bell System. . . ." [22]

Now if the industrial giant of the West (that's us, the U.S.) found it in the logic of advantage to petition the services of the Bell (telephone) System, it seems altogether appropriate to inquire whether the infallible guardians of the Workers' Paradise had any comparable organization to which they might turn.

Actually, there are fewer telephones in all of European and Asiatic Russia than there are in Chicago. [23]

As you look at the thing it gets almost ridiculous.

Take the automobile industry. Its record in converting readily from peace to war status and from war to peace status means that its volume of production is at once a symptom of and a factor in industrial and economic strength. By cautious estimate the Soviet Union has one motor vehicle to our fifteen. [24]

A more sensitive barometer is doubtless the electronics and electrical appliance industry. Again from the *World Almanac:* Early in 1952 the United States had 109 TV stations. (Licensing of such stations was "frozen" at the time; shortly thereafter it was unfrozen, and there were 700 applications on file with the Federal Communications Commission by July 1, 1952.) The U.S.S.R. "opened its third television station in Kiev January 15 [1952]. It operates only on Saturday and Sunday." The United States had 21,000,000 TV sets, the Soviet Union 21,500.[25]

The editors of *Fortune* say of Soviet technology in general: "The Soviet Union has developed and produced some equipment as advanced as the best in the U.S. . . . Yet the general technological level remains low. Cold-drawing of nuts and bolts, extrusion in nonferrous metallurgy, and self-recording control devices are still in the pilot stage."[26] Now that is really pretty bad if you are thinking about atomic energy in a big way. And it does not help much if the following report is true: "Inadequate control of heavy-media separation techniques is holding up the beneficiation of marginal ores at Krivoy Rog."[27]

I don't know what ores the editors of *Fortune* here have in mind, but in the judgment of the editors of *Business Week* (as of July 28, 1951) all the uranium ores available to the Russians were marginal.[28]

Mr. Ellsworth Raymond and Mr. John F. Hogerton did a special study for *Look* in 1948 to estimate Russian prospects for making an atom bomb.[29] Mr. Hogerton, who had been chief of the Technical Reports Division of Kellex, the engineering firm that designed K-25, made an estimate of what kind of industrial capacity is required to produce fissionable materials—the recognized crux of the problem; and Mr. Raymond, who had been Adviser on Russian economics to the War Department, took Mr. Hogerton's broad specifications and estimated how soon the Russians might be able to meet them.

"Russian industry," wrote Mr. Raymond, "having neglected the manufacture of precision goods, now finds itself prepared for the wrong type of war.

"In time, of course, Russia can improve the quantity and quality of the output of its precision-machinery factories. But it will take a long time. And no U.S. or England in its right mind will export atomic-plant equipment to the U.S.S.R." [This is the soft spot in Mr. Raymond's reasoning, as, right mind or wrong, we did, in 1947, reportedly make such exports; [30] but Mr. Raymond's argument still has force, both because the quantities of such exports were probably not great enough to furnish a real competitor, and also because, as General Marshall testified, the Russians as a rule do not know quite what to do with advanced equipment when they get it.]

"The Russians," continues Mr. Raymond, "simply cannot hope to have a K-25 plant like the one at Oak Ridge within a few years. This would be physically impossible. The Soviet industries which would have to supply the equipment for such a mechanical monster are too undeveloped."

At this point it should be noted that this physically-impossible-for-the-Soviets K-25 was the only kind of fissionable-material factory that the celebrated Dr. Klaus Fuchs knew very much about. He could not have given the Russians much detailed help on a plutonium plant. And he could not give them the equipment for any kind of plant. At the time of his confession in 1950 he "explained," according to Alan Moorehead, "that it was impossible for him, of course, to do more than tell the Russians the principle on which the bomb was made. It was up to the Russians to produce their own industrial equipment, and he *had been astonished* [italics added] when they had succeeded in making and detonating a bomb as soon as the previous August. He knew, Fuchs said, that scientifically they were sufficiently advanced; but he had not supposed that commercially and industrially they were so far developed." [31]

Mr. Raymond's survey of Russian industrial capacity precluded the possibility of a Soviet K-25, and put a possible Soviet Hanford some years into the future.

"Even if Russian science should be equal to the task, there is still no assurance that a Hanford could be quickly built," said Mr. Raymond. "Soviet scientists successfully worked out the theory of radar some years before its discovery in England. But the Russians were not able to put theory into practice, and did not manufacture radar equipment until long after both England and America had done so."

One thing should be made perfectly clear: Mr. Raymond wrote before anything was known about Klaus Fuchs, and he wrote before President Truman announced that an atomic explosion had taken place in Russia. When his analytical report of Soviet incapacity is read now, the more reasonable inference is not that Mr. Raymond was an unreliable forecaster, but rather that the dramatic and sensational characteristics of the Fuchs case and the Truman announcement blinded most of us to Mr. Raymond's relatively unexciting account. But prosaic as it may be, it is probable. The Russians can hardly be serious competitors with the United States, or with the United Kingdom, in the construction and operation of a complete atomic energy project. Sporadic explosions, perhaps contrived with quantities of fissionable material stolen from the United States, do not alter the general validity of Mr. Raymond's comparison.

His observation of what is apparently a characteristic gap between Soviet science, which everyone knows is occasionally brilliant, and Soviet "industrial construction," which, he says, "is still in the pick-and-shovel age," is especially pertinent, and is supported by other expert testimony.

Dr. J. Robert Oppenheimer, perhaps the most famous of atomic scientists, told the Joint Committee on Atomic Energy in June 1949: ". . . my understanding of the situation in Russia is that even when the basic facts are known, they have, and I think we have cause to be grateful, some difficulty in making practical application of them." [32]

Dr. Irving Langmuir, eminent research director, who visited Russia in June 1945, reported, "The thing that impressed me most was the extent to which they were working on pure science. The Institutes [Institute of Inorganic Chemistry and the Physical Institute] had no connection with industry." [33]

Even the scientists had not progressed very far if what Dr. Langmuir told the McMahon Committee in December 1945 was correct. "When you go to Russia," he said, "and you find that Kapitza, Fersman, Frenkel, and Joffe—all of those men who are working on problems that have nothing to do with atomic energy—when Joffe tells me and shows me the cyclotron started in 1938, work on which was discontinued during the war and is now just starting again, and tells me the cyclotron will be finished in December of this year— and he is the most prominent physicist that has had anything to do with nuclear physics—when you see that, *you are convinced they are not carrying through a Manhattan project.*" [34] [Italics added.] Dr. Langmuir's conviction was presumably based on the evident *rate* of progress on the cyclotron.

Mr. Raymond's instance of radar to illustrate the greater lag normally expected in Russia than in England between theory and production may provoke us to re-examine what we have been asked to believe regarding *atomic* theory and production in the two countries.

The official version has not attempted to deny the pre-eminence of British nuclear science. Kapitza got his start under Rutherford at Cambridge, which was probably the leading pre-war center of nuclear research. All the Manhattan Project scientists known to have given war-time secrets to the Russians were British. But the galaxy of British scientists as a whole was far greater than Fuchs, May, and Pontecorvo. Hence, even with the maximum allowance for the value of the knowledge transmitted by these three, the British resources of knowledge remain far greater than the known Russian resources.

Indeed, the British tradition in the physical sciences and their ingenious practical application is unrivaled. From

Newton to Lord Cherwell, from the steam engine to radar, from the spinning jenny to the jet airliner, the island home of the industrial revolution has produced or attracted a fabulous gallery of scientific and technical genius, including —in the nuclear field—Thomson, Rutherford, Chadwick, Cockroft, Wilson, Penney, and on and on.

Yet in spite of this acknowledged superiority of British nuclear science, in the face of obvious British superiority in access to the raw materials of the Belgian Congo, and ignoring the general superiority of British auxiliary technology, we have been asked to believe that the Russians beat the British by three years in the race to manufacture an atomic bomb independently of the United States, and that they now have an Atomgrad to rival Hanford.

That they have exploded one or two bombs of some kind we can credit if we remember that their entire project was put under the supervision of Lavrenti Beria, chief of their secret police, who might have arranged to smuggle out of the United States enough "nuclear components" for a demonstration or so for the Soviet high command. But that they have an atomic energy project which is serious, complete, and of a magnitude remotely competitive with that of the United States, we cannot lightly accept.

Objection and Rejoinder

There is one objection to concluding quickly that the Soviets cannot have an atomic energy project which amounts to very much. The known occurrence of atomic explosions in Soviet territory is not such an objection, for, as we shall see in the following pages, they have in the past had a very real opportunity to steal fissionable materials from the United States. And as AEC Chairman Gordon Dean has said, "With fissionable material in hand, it is not a difficult technical job to make workable atomic weapons." [35]

But lax as our security system has undoubtedly been, we

cannot suppose that the number of atomic bombs which might have been assembled *in Russia* from items of fissionable material manufactured in the United States can possibly constitute a stockpile seriously competitive with our own. To credit the existence of such a stockpile it is not sufficient to have at hand evidence from the analysis of fission products in air currents and evidence from cryptic intelligence reports that somewhere in the Eurasian heartland two or three nuclear explosions have undoubtedly taken place.

General Groves summarized this point rather succinctly at the time of the commotion over Truman's heresy. "All we know," said Groves, "is there were indications of nuclear explosions." [36]

Dr. Arthur Compton made essentially the same point: "Scientists know," he said, "that there have been two atomic explosions in Russia, but we don't know, of course, whether these explosions are the result of a workable A-bomb." [37] And of course, if we don't know whether these individual explosive devices, whatever they were, were "workable" A-bombs, then we certainly don't know from this evidence alone that the Soviets have a practical atomic arsenal within their own boundaries.

No, the objection to a low estimate of Russian atomic production is almost independent of our knowledge concerning actual explosions, valuable as that knowledge is. The objection lies rather in the well known fact that the Soviet oligarchy may use its executive authority to require an extraordinary concentration of Russian and satellite resources on the struggling Soviet atomic energy project.

James Burnham made this point some six or seven years ago. Having observed that "Soviet industry is for the most part incompetent, inefficient, and qualitatively at a low level," [38] and having pointed out the Communist dependence on and addiction to *loot* [39] (confirmed, as we have noted, by General Marshall), Mr. Burnham proceeded, nevertheless, to warn us how "important, for strategic purposes, is the economic concentration which absolute political control makes possible. This is of great significance in connection with the production of atomic weapons. Deficient as they are in almost all branches of economy, the Communists can concentrate the most and best of what they have both of human and physical equipment on a task which they decide to be dominant. It would, therefore, be a mistake to judge their atomic performance by their general industrial level." [40]

This objection is not to be brushed aside.

Dr. Compton, according to the Associated Press, said, "The difference between the United States and Russia insofar as manufacture of A-bombs is concerned is that the United States is using only one per cent of its industrial capacity in the manufacture while Russia would have to use at least four per cent." [41]

This at once accords with our previous general estimate of the relative magnitude of Russian industry, and at the same time suggests a quantitative paraphrase of Mr. Burnham's point regarding concentration. Granted that the United States ought to be able to stay ahead in an all-out race on both sides (provided the fight was "fair"), what if the Russians chose to devote, say, 16 per cent of their capacity to atomic bombs, while we continued at the one per cent rate? Would they not then have the four to one advantage?

Noting briefly two general points: (1) that no amount of concentration compensates for a single radical qualitative failure (*i.e.*, you have to introduce zero only once into any group of factors to make the product zero), and (2) that even four per cent in Russia cuts far closer to the bone than one per cent in the U.S. (you may trade butter for guns, but not the last bowl of gruel if you are going to have strength enough left to fire the thing), the gravamen of our rejoinder seems to be that the Russians quite evidently are putting great effort into non-atomic military forces. Indeed the commonly accepted and officially encouraged picture is one of hundreds of divisions of ground forces and myriads of MIG's. Those things use up industrial capacity.

The editors of *Business Week*, whose reports on atomic energy have quasi-official authority, stated in their issue for July 28, 1951: "AEC dollars may not bulk large in a $60-billion defense program, but they are spent in very sensitive areas: When its new plants are built, AEC will be the nation's largest single consumer of electricity; plutonium plants compete directly for rare materials with the critical jet-engine program; U-235 plants use the same sort of equipment as refineries and chemical works." [42]

At this point I'm just about ready to pack up and go home, unless you've got some new evidence. If the composition of the atomic materials data sheet is such that the United States can feel the pinch after putting one per cent into this business, then I don't think the Russian Commies are going to make the grade.

"The Soviet Union," says *Fortune*, "has the worst housing in Europe, the shoddiest clothes, the thinnest diet. . . . It also has more jet aircraft than all the NATO nations put together." [43]

Then where are they going to get those directly competitive rare materials for plutonium plants?

There is one other bite out of the Russian economy that is worth considering if we assume an extensive atomic project over there. That is the cost of secrecy. This has been mightily discussed in the conferences of the U.S. atomic energy experts, and there is a copious "literature" on the subject. And, indeed, what we pay for such internal security as we have is not inconsiderable.

But try to imagine, in that line, the drain on the economy

of the Soviets required not only to maintain their whole secret police system, and not only to establish and maintain beyond the Urals all kinds of gigantic industrial installations located for strategic rather than economic reasons—but also to do all this in such thorough secrecy that the President of the United States longest in office during the critical period is not convinced the Russians have a workable bomb!

Put syllogistically, it's like this:

(1) Secrecy is a handicap to progress.

(2) Russia has more secrecy than America has.

(3) Russia is more severely handicapped than America is. With the other handicaps, that may well finish them off as competitors in "Achievement."

Dr. Harold Urey once said U.S. progress involved firing most of our security officers.[44] In Russia the whole project was under the then No. 1 security officer of the world, Lavrenti Beria.[45]

Beria's fall and the detonation of an H-bomb were announced with characteristic incongruity in the summer of 1953. The H-bomb development may end a rumor that Beria's fall was due to failure at Atomsk. On the other hand, perhaps he was purged *because* he made an H-bomb. Several of our own experts have deplored our production of tritium at the expense of plutonium. If Beria diverted scarce materials from A-bomb resources so as to show off before his imperialist friends with H-bomb fireworks, then of course he was open to the charge, among others, of "adventurism."

But speculation on the internal intrigues of the comrades is foreign to a sober estimate of productive capacity. I propose the following as a reasonable working hypothesis: *The United States atomic energy project is today—in the year 1953—overwhelmingly superior in practical productivity to any other atomic energy project known or plausibly conjectured to exist.*

Chapter III ⟶ The Field of Decision

The first consequence of this working hypothesis is to locate the field of decision in the conflict between the Soviet Union and the United States.

It might be supposed that a great nation fighting for its life would know where the fight is taking place. More exactly, it might be supposed that such a nation would have at least a well defined theory on the geographical location of the crucial engagement. If the enemy is clever enough the theory might be wrong, but if there is no theory at all the enemy does not even need to be clever.

The conflict between the Soviet Union and the United States is ordinarily so vaguely defined as to appear somehow unreal. This sensation, we are sure, is one of dangerous euphoria. We shake ourselves awake to the real and present danger. Real, no doubt—and present, no doubt! But precisely where is it?

Conventional warfare between the United States and the Soviet Union is not easy to imagine. There is a marked contrast to the historic situation between France and Germany, for example. This is one reason why the "Peace" offensive of the Communists has had as much success as it has had, in spite of its otherwise preposterous nature. War, like crime,

requires motive, means, and opportunity, and opportunity
includes the existence of an appropriate battleground.

The whole earth is the arena of giants, and American and
Soviet interests seem to clash in one form or another all
over the world. But even the greatest war will not envelop
the globe as evenly as does the atmosphere. A military action may have global antecedents and consequences, but it
will also have a local situation and a name. The repercussions of Thermopylae have not entirely died away even now,
but you can mark on the map where it happened. If the
United States and the Soviet Union fight, they have to fight
somewhere.

It seems ridiculous to say that, and there would be no
occasion to say it except for the paradoxical circumstance
that we find widely prevalent the belief that they will fight,
while at the same time it is hard to select an appropriate
field of decision for the regular armed forces of the two
antagonists. Logical objections appear against the selection
of Europe, Asia, and North America, and of the sea and sky
as places where a showdown might naturally occur or, even,
could be aggressively sought.

The Arctic is about the best we can do if we feel com-
pelled to designate a real area where a decisive battle might
conceivably be fought between air, naval, or ground forces
of the U.S. and the U.S.S.R. Yet it is almost incredible that
either side should commit its main strength to this area.
Considered as sovereign nations, the United States and the
Soviet Union are like mutually incensed duelists with no
place to fight.

Korea is clearly inappropriate except—to shift to the argot
of baseball—as a bull-pen. We are not going into China or
into Russia itself, and the Chinese and Russians are not
likely to come very far out of there either, with one possible
exception.

We (the people of the United States) have been tacitly,

but not imperceptibly, assuming that Western Europe would be the main battleground.

The Western Europeans have viewed this prospect, understandably, without enthusiasm. They are palpably reluctant to offend us by refusing to arm at all, or to offend the Soviet Union by arming punctually and effectively. In Walter Lippmann's apt metaphor, they find themselves between the hammer and the anvil. But the Western Europeans are an astute variety of humanity, not without reasons to regard us and the Russians alike as barbarians, and if they elect to sidestep adroitly the fell incensed pass of these mighty opposites, the odds are on them to succeed. They want Peace. And perhaps Peace is to them quite dear enough to be purchased at the price of limited slavery, since that sort of thing is all in the point of view, don't you think?

No.

The point is, however, that the inhabitants of Western Europe do not want it to be the battleground for the forces of the Soviet Union and the United States, and they will do their able best to insure that if these national behemoths clash they clash somewhere else. The European skill in maneuver will in this instance be reinforced by the so-called isolationist component in the United States, or, put otherwise, by the element of prudence that counsels against overextension of the lines.

The Russians, for their part, surely understand that the beautiful prizes of Western Europe could not be securely theirs while the United States, always restless and unpredictable, retained in its sanctuary across the Atlantic the accumulated fury of a stockpile of atomic weapons.

They will therefore, if they can, remove the retaliatory threat before they collect the prizes.

Through the international Communist organization the Soviet Union was in a position to influence the American atomic energy project from the start. The American project, as has been repeatedly pointed out, was in a very real sense international in origin. The main contributions uniquely American were enormous capital, an engineering tradition of the utmost audacity and resourcefulness, and a plentiful supply of clerical and mechanical personnel in whom the pioneer urges were still vital.

The original scientific cadre was international. It included at the outset Frederic Joliot-Curie, of France, subsequently winner of the Stalin "Peace" prize, and P. M. S. Blackett, of the United Kingdom, subsequently quoted by Andrei Vishinsky in support of the Soviet position on international control.[46] These are scientists of the first rank. Allan Nunn May and Klaus Fuchs would be less famous had they not been convicted of crimes, but they were employed in the project, first in England and later in North America, quite early.

It will be necessary in a subsequent chapter to discuss the problem of Communist personnel in the American project. For the moment the serious nature of the problem may be briefly suggested, first by reference to an address delivered at a Symposium in Oak Ridge in September 1951 by Dr. Lawrence R. Hafstad, AEC Director of Reactor Development.[47]

Discussing an episode in which his having been called a "learned bandit" by the *Daily Worker* had led him to do some spade-work concerning the Communist public-relations merry-go-round, Dr. Hafstad told how he had discovered the identity of one Sol Auerbach, alias James S. Allen (described by a report of the House Committee on Un-American Activities as "a Communist Party literary hack"[48]); he quoted excerpts to illustrate the preposterous nature of the Party line on comparative working conditions for scientists in the Soviet Union and the United States. Then Dr. Hafstad continued:

"Here is another quotation which hits painfully close to home as far as we physical scientists are concerned. I have stated that, as scientists, we have been pretty naive politically and that we have been *used* by the Communists. I cite this as evidence. In his preface [to a book called *Atomic Energy and Society*] Allen says: 'Original material, reprints, and controversies appearing in the earlier issues of the *Bulletin of Atomic Scientists*, of Chicago, have proved useful, but this magazine is now *losing its worth* as an organ of discussion because of its increasing coordination with the official position' (p. 8).

"So the Bulletin was extremely useful to the Communists in the early days but it is no longer useful. So says James S. Allen. . . ." [49]

So says Dr. Hafstad.

The importance of this lies in the fact that the *Bulletin of the Atomic Scientists* (of Chicago) had a relationship to the Atomic Energy Act of 1946 not unlike the relationship of the *Federalist* to the Constitution. Since the influence of the *Bulletin*, exercised both directly and through most of the metropolitan newspapers except the Hearst and McCormick papers, has been uniquely powerful, we may be grateful that a Communist thinks it is "losing its worth." But it is not a trivial matter that this same Communist should have admitted that the *Bulletin* "in the earlier issues" (i.e., the issues appearing at the time the McMahon Bill and the Acheson-Lilienthal Plan for international control were under active consideration) contained material that "proved useful." [50]

This means that what is still the law of the land on atomic energy was shaped in significant measure by Communist pressure.

During the trial of Joseph Weinberg, (late February and early March 1953) Kenneth May testified (under oath and without challenge by either side) that there were in the

Campus Branch of the Communist Party at Berkeley, California (nuclear-science metropolis from which Los Alamos was colonized), in the year 1940—that is to say in the dead center of the period during which Communism was at the lowest ebb of its prestige among intellectuals, because of the Hitler-Stalin pact—one hundred members. And Dr. May testified further that "membership" did not mean general sympathy, but meant action.[51] If you figure turnover there are, of course, more than a hundred persons involved. On the other hand, a majority of them were presumably not scientists. And some would repent and some would flinch. And this was thirteen years ago, this fixed date. As King Claudius said some days before his death, "All may be well."

In April 1951, Judge (then U.S. Attorney) Irving Saypol, who had just completed the Rosenberg case, said, "We have gotten now sufficient information so that we are embarking on a series of prosecutions to stamp out this crime,"[52] apparently in reference to atomic espionage in general. In the two years that have since elapsed, however, no one has been prosecuted. The sanguine will conclude this means that no one except those already convicted has engaged in atomic espionage. Other alternatives will readily occur to those of somewhat more restless intelligence.

Klaus Fuchs, David Greenglass—the Los Alamos machinist who confessed that through Julius Rosenberg he gave the Soviets a schematic drawing of the implosion bomb, and Allan Nunn May, the convicted British scientist who confessed he gave the Soviets a sample of American-made fissionable material, all indicated the existence of still hidden characters in the drama. And, indeed, it would be naive to think that all the actors have been disclosed, or that the plot has reached its dénouement.

Bedell Smith told us last year (1952) that the Central Intelligence Agency assumes, prudentially, it has itself been infiltrated.[53] The CIA credits the enemy with sufficient professional competence for that. In the atomic energy project, as we have recalled, the public record shows that the Soviet Union, through Communist agents, had a firm foothold during World War II.

Quite plausibly, they have retained it. To have dislodged them would probably have required more drastic measures than we have taken, or may yet be ready to take. When the Atomic Energy Commission "cleared" Dr. Edward Condon and Dr. Frank Graham against the recommendation of an Advisory Board headed by former Supreme Court Justice Owen J. Roberts (and including as members Dr. Karl T. Compton, the Honorable Joseph C. Grew, Mr.—now Secretary—George M. Humphrey, and Mr. H. W. Prentis, Jr.),[54] the Commission was quite possibly correct and the Board in error. But a situation in which two such distinguished bodies can disagree about men so much in public view as Dr. Condon and Dr. Graham is obviously a situation in which an obscure and adroit agent should find little difficulty in maintaining a presumption of innocence.

Speaking of the Roberts Board, it has been stated by Professor Walter Gellhorn that the Board "resigned in a body during the summer [of 1948], in large part because of dissatisfaction with the Commission's actions on its recommendations."[55] This view is generally accepted, and "informed sources" add that the dissatisfaction arose less from disagreement over particular cases than from a radical divergence of policy lines.

I have seen what purports to be a letter to the Atomic Energy Commission from the Roberts Board, dated June 30, 1948, which includes the following: ". . . the Board feels that it is of vital importance to have those in positions of leadership, in all capacities, throughout the entire atomic energy program of unquestioned and uncontroversial background. . . ."

But such a "Caesar's wife" policy is counter to the doctrine of Security by Achievement. It may also be construed as counter to the most sensitive solicitude for individual rights and maximum respect for vested individual and professional privileges.

The Commission ignored the counsel of the Board, to such an extent that a year later (June 1949) Senator Hickenlooper could hold the opinion that "the matter of security clearances . . . has become increasingly more unreliable." [56] There are still in the atomic energy project a number of very important persons with highly controversial backgrounds.

To illustrate:

In *The Atom Spies* Oliver Pilat has written: "In the fall of 1947, Fuchs revisited America. He was not included on a list of British scientists originally scheduled to make the trip, but his name was added at the last minute, it is said, on the recommendation of some American scientists." [57] That was published in 1952 and has never been denied as far as I know. In any case I think it is substantially correct. I might add that according to "informed sources" two "American scientists" were particularly involved, and that both of them have occupied positions of the utmost administrative sensitivity, and both of them are—or at least were until quite recently—still in the project.

Perhaps that is as it should be. It is a controversial matter. There are other equally important cases perhaps even more controversial. What seems beyond controversy is that there is a significant statistical probability that some of the controversial cases really are Communists. Certainly, or almost certainly, not all of them. Every controversial case will be defended by the Communists, for they think it better a dozen innocent should go free than that one guilty be convicted. We, unfortunately, cannot go by an equally simple rule of thumb. We must attempt to make a fair decision in every individual case.

But the Atomic Energy Commission went astray, I think, in assuming a burden of proving charges against a controversial case, when it had the legal obligation, the moral right, and the advice of the Roberts Board to lay upon each applicant a burden of establishing his own security qualifications for access to restricted data. No Commission can reasonably hope to bear infallibly the burden AEC assumed, and AEC fallibility means Communists in the atomic energy project.

*   *   *

The field of decision in the conflict between the Soviet Union and the United States is the American atomic energy project.

The American project is fabulous, the Russian project is mythical.

Soviet agents have had access to the American project in the past, and probably still have.

Communist and Communoid authorities deplore this approach to the situation. Joliot-Curie in Paris three years ago "warned his listeners," according to the *New York Times*, "to be 'extremely vigilant' lest they be induced by hostile influences to underestimate the vitality of Soviet science," [58] and P. M. S. Blackett began in 1948 to deprecate "exaggeration of the danger of 'secret war.'" [59]

Nevertheless—or, I should say, accordingly—the danger of secret war is very great, either in lieu of or in conjunction with open war.

If the secret war should be concluded with a theoretically possible atomic coup d'état by the Communists in the United States, then open war between the United States and the Soviet Union would be obviated. Such an outcome might appear desirable not only to Communists everywhere, but also to certain "neutralists," and perhaps to pacifists.

In the presumably more likely event of open war, the Communist forces committed to the secret war might through

negative and positive sabotage deprive the United States of
the use of atomic weapons, and might through diversion of
materials and clandestine assembly of weapons employ
against the United States the product of the American project.

The question whether the Russians have literally no
atomic bombs, or a few, or a considerable number, is almost
irrelevant. The question is whether we have any that are
useful to us. Dr. J. Robert Oppenheimer has said very well
that an "atomic bomb which you do not use is of no use to
you." [60]

If the Communists can prevent our using the weapon in
which we have placed our chief reliance they will have effectively disarmed us. If by a further step they can use that
weapon against us they will be sure in their own minds of
our death and defeat. If the U.S. and the U.S.S.R., considered as sovereign nations, are like duelists with no place to
fight, the people of the United States and the Communist
apparatus are like hero and villain in a Western movie struggling for possession of the gun.

If we get it—and I think we can—we had better look and
see if it's in good shape, if the cartridges are in the chambers, if the percussion caps are dry, etc. Otherwise that light
click when we expect a loud bang is going to be a rather
sickening sound.

Chapter IV ~~~ Dreadful Alternative

It is possible that U-235 and plutonium, the "nuclear components" of the atomic bomb, have been systematically diverted from Oak Ridge, Hanford, and Los Alamos in sufficient quantities to charge perhaps twenty atomic bombs. This material, together with a complement of "non-nuclear components," may be stored here in the United States, waiting the signal for clandestine assembly in a Chicago warehouse or a New York apartment building, the resulting ready-for-detonation A-bombs to be used in whatever manner the conspirators might regard as most "truly revolutionary."

Such tactics would so increase precision of aim and efficiency of delivery that a relatively small number of atomic bombs might be sufficient for a strategic grand stroke.

"Generally speaking," said Lenin, "it is not voting but civil war that decides all serious questions of politics." [61]

Before the "atomic age" a coup d'état in the United States was generally considered impossible. Perhaps it still is, but as Joseph and Stewart Alsop have wisely said, ". . . the whole vast problem of atomic policy requires far closer attention than it has been getting . . . the alternatives had better be examined, no matter how dreadful they may be." [62]

One dreadful alternative is the employment of atomic energy by the Communists to bring the secret war to a climax and establish the dictatorship of the proletariat in the United States. Such a dénouement should not be dismissed merely on the ground that it is alarmist. "The alternatives had better be examined, no matter how dreadful they may be."

When Mr. Chester I. Barnard first heard the news of Hiroshima in August 1945, he said out loud to himself, "Here goes the freedom of the American people," [63] which was certainly a very extraordinary thing for him to do. Since then, atomic energy has had a number of people talking to themselves, and to anyone else that would listen. We have been assured by the most eminent authorities that *Modern Man is Obsolete*, that we must choose—and quickly!—between *One World or None*, that, in fact, it is only a matter of *Minutes to Midnight*. Nothing could be more alarmist than these views, which through repetition have been transmuted from stimulants to sedatives.

Well, we have not got one world on our terms, favorable as we have made them to the Communists. The presumptive reason why we have not got it on our terms is that they still hope to get it on theirs, which would include revolution in the United States and the establishment here of the dictatorship of the proletariat. Communists despise "gradualism." They have great patience, but it is not the patience of the builder; it is the patience of the tiger.

That the Communist conspirators have the motive to seize power abruptly is self-advertised and well known. In addition, we have given them what must look to them like the means and the opportunity. Dr. Robert M. Hutchins once predicted that the next war "will be won by atomic bombs planted by agents." [64] Suppose that were what Lenin would have called a civil war, what is here called the secret war. Almost two years before President Truman made his first announcement of an atomic explosion in Russia, Dr. Hutchins said we would be foolish to assume that Russia was not making atomic bombs. We would also be foolish to assume that international Communism has not strenuously and skillfully exerted itself to infiltrate our atomic energy project, and that it has not succeeded to a dangerous extent. If it has, the use against us of hidden bombs of our own manufacture is simply one of the more melodramatic "alternatives" available to a group that has never shown any aversion to melodrama.

MOTIVE

Would the Communists conquer America through the American atomic energy project if they could?

"It is well known," said Lenin, "that in the long run the problems of social life are decided by the class struggle in its bitterest, sharpest form, namely, in the form of civil war. . . . The more organized, more class-conscious, better armed minority forces its will upon the majority and is victorious over it. . . . The first commandment of every victorious revolution, as Marx and Engels repeatedly emphasized, was: smash the old army, dissolve it and replace it by a new one. . . . Prepare to organize new organizations and *utilize* these so useful weapons of death and destruction *against your own government* and *your bourgeoisie.* . . . He who refuses technically to prepare for the insurrection ultimately rejects the insurrection itself, and transforms the program of the revolution into an empty phrase." [65]

Lenin taught that a well organized, technically prepared minority, having replaced the old army, may and should employ weapons of death and destruction against its own government to win a civil war. Lenin's teachings have always been endorsed, lock, stock, and barrel, by Stalin and by the Communists of all countries, including the United

States. The case could be documented further. The Department of Justice has documented it rather well in the prosecution of Communist leaders. Probably no one wishes to argue seriously that the Communists would not if they could turn our own atomic weapons against us at whatever time seemed to them most propitious.

Our multi-billion-dollar defense program is based on the assumption that Russian Communists would if they could destroy us with atomic weapons, presumably their own. The Communists of the West, more sophisticated, would savor the irony of encompassing America's destruction with bombs made in America.

> "For 'tis the sport to have the engineer
> Hoist with his own petard."

MEANS

Assuming the motive, then, have they the means? Well, the means exists, as Dr. Hutchins has pointed out. The particular adaptability of the atomic bomb to clandestine warfare was observed early by several eminent witnesses. "There is no defense against the atomic bomb," Dr. Hutchins told nearly 2,000 persons attending services in the University of Chicago's Rockefeller Memorial Chapel on October 14, 1945. "There is no method of detecting storehouses of bombs or factories which are making them. There is a defense against the carrier, if it is an airplane, but a carrier, in the ordinary sense, is not needed for atomic bombs . . . the cheapest and surest way of blowing up an enemy's cities is to send agents into them in peacetime to plant bombs in strategic locations, which can be detonated when war is decided on. . . . The conventional reliances of the past—a large army, navy, and air force—are obsolete. They find favor only in the nostalgic dreams of obsolescent generals and admirals. The war will be won by atomic bombs planted by agents . . . and victory will go to the country which lands the most destructive bombs first." Mr. Hutchins renewed his appeal for disclosure of the "so-called secret of the atomic bomb," the weapon that scientists at the University of Chicago helped to create.[66]

Some of this, logically considered, is nonsense—e.g., you cannot disclose a "so-called secret," for unless it is a real secret it has already been disclosed—but the matter should not be lightly dismissed for all that. When Dr. Hutchins, the Federation of American Scientists, and others told us there was no secret of the atomic bomb, there was a dangerous relation between their statement and the truth, as later appeared in the cases of Dr. Fuchs and Dr. May. When Dr. Hutchins tells us of the possibilities of clandestine bomb-assembly, it is well for us to listen thoughtfully.

Two weeks after Dr. Hutchins' meditation in the Rockefeller chapel, *Life* ran an article called "The Atomic Scientists Speak Up," in which Dr. David L. Hill, Dr. Eugene Rabinowitch, and Dr. John A. Simpson chorused: "In order not to leave the results of attack (or the success of retaliation) to chance, the nations bent on securing maximum advantage in a possible 'one-minute war' of the future may seek to substitute preventive mining for bombing from the air." [67]

Dr. H. D. Smyth, author of the celebrated official report on *The Military Uses of Atomic Energy,* and later AEC Commissioner, gave an address at a three-day forum on "The Challenge of the Atomic Bomb," conducted by the Nation Associates at the Hotel Astor in New York December 1–3, 1945. After talking about rockets with atomic warheads, Dr. Smyth said, "The atomic age has made possible still another method of surprise attack. There is no scientific reason why atomic bombs cannot be shipped in trunks or boxes in peace time to key industrial and population centers, and detonated at the moment desired by remote control wireless or other means. Atomic bombs last for a long time after they are made, and can be stored or hidden with slight possibility of detection. As we know from the facts about them which have already been published, they do not explode until properly detonated. Against such secretly planted atomic bombs the only conceivable defense would be an elaborate peace-time system of coast and frontier guards, and continuous X-ray inspection of every item of freight or baggage coming into this country. I do not believe such a permanent defense system could be maintained with anything near complete effectiveness." [68]

Now the question I want to raise is whether the defense system at Oak Ridge, Hanford, and Los Alamos has from the start been consistently better than any system of coast and frontier guards which Dr. Smyth could imagine in 1945. Have the installations always had "continuous X-ray inspection of every item of freight or baggage" leaving the production areas?

Certainly they have not. Dr. Sanford Simons has completed a term in Federal penitentiary because he always liked to collect mineral samples, and in 1946 took a glass vial containing plutonium from Los Alamos as a "souvenir," later burying it under his house in Denver, Colorado, so that his children might not come in contact with it. The FBI arrested him four years after the theft. Dr. Simons apparently did not mean any harm. "It was not alleged," the staff of the Joint Committee on Atomic Energy tells us, "that Simons had any connection with an espionage network, nor was it charged that he was associated with Communist or subversive organizations." [69] If this comparatively innocent young man (he was 24) could make off with such a vial of wrath, and go unapprehended for four years, what shall we conjecture of the activities and success of hardened agents?

Dr. E. U. Condon wrote in *One World or None*, "The atomic explosive, which now can be made only in a large, expensive, and easily identified installation, could be smuggled in little by little by agents, and the rest of the bomb could be built here with the resources of a modest shop. After all, atomic explosives are respectable-looking metals out of which plated cigar lighters, keys, watch cases, or shoe nails can be fabricated." [70] Now, certainly, no one thinks all the cigar lighters, etc. of all the scientists and machine-shop workers leaving Los Alamos have been "inspected in a laborious and sophisticated way," [71] as Dr. Condon says they would have had to be in order to be sure no U-235 or plutonium was stolen. (He presumably means X-ray is not enough, that chemical analysis and isotopic assay would have to be added.)

"The beginning of a new war," says Dr. Condon, "will surely involve not only the launching of the missiles, but the explosion of the mines that have secretly been set near key targets to provide the pinpoint accuracy that long-range weapons may possibly lack." [72] The only thing we have added to Dr. Condon's outline of the shape of things to come is the supposition that the "large, expensive, and easily identified" installations might be our own.

These authorities seem preoccupied with international war, but it is obvious that the method they describe would lend itself still better to sophisticated insurrectionists. Even the maritime variation, suggested first, it appears, by Dr. Einstein, is particularly suitable for conspirators. "A single bomb of this type," Dr. Einstein wrote in 1939, "carried by boat and exploded in a port might well destroy the whole port, together with some of the surrounding territory." [73] Lately, we are told, the U.S. Coast Guard and the Customs Inspectors have been especially alert to prevent, if possible, this kind of intrusion from abroad, not having been discouraged by Dr. Smyth's opinion that their job is pretty hopeless. Incoming ships are said to be checked very thoroughly. It is not clear whether equally strict and similarly oriented inspection is applied to the loading of outbound ships, just in case they never cleared port.

Another expert oppressed with the possibilities of clandestine activities, Dr. Clarke Williams, testified before a Senate committee, "Because of the ease with which an assembled bomb can be concealed, the only way to create a world-wide feeling of security against atomic bomb attacks is to insure that no bombs are being constructed." [74] We have tried, of course, to insure the opposite.

The difficulty in detecting an atomic-age Guy Fawkes was made picturesque by Dr. Oppenheimer in the hearings before the Special Senate Committee. "If you hired me," he said, "to walk through the cellars of Washington to see whether there were atomic bombs, I think my most important tool would be a screwdriver." [75] He was responding to a question directed at the possibility of locating concealed bombs by means of radiation-detection instruments. Atomic bombs, of course, are designed to keep radiation at a minimum until they are detonated. Dr. Oppenheimer was saying he would simply have to open all the fairly large packing cases, piano boxes, etc. in order to be sure they did not contain atomic bombs.

In a somewhat different context Dr. Oppenheimer told the Committee, "The possession of 300 bombs in some vaults around the country is something that I myself don't see any good in." [76] Since Dr. Oppenheimer made that statement, we have presumably increased the number (whatever it was or is) of bombs in some vaults, or somewhere, around the country. We have also passed a law depriving the armed services of the United States of access to any completed atomic weapon except on express direction of the President. We have been unable, however, to use a screwdriver on all the packing cases in all the basements of the metropolitan centers of America. We have also failed to add the known fact of Communist infiltration of the project in the persons

of Klaus Fuchs, Allan Nunn May, David Greenglass, and
others, to the known fact of the theft of fissionable material
by Sanford Simons and others, and come up with any leads
to particular basements where our attention should be centered.

The result is that *the United States of America is the only
country in the world running any appreciable practical risk
of a surprise attack involving atomic weapons manufactured
in the United States of America.* In these circumstances it
is certainly difficult to see any good in any number of atomic
bombs in some vaults around the country.

OPPORTUNITY

Granted the Communists have the motive, and admitting
powerful means exist, it can hardly be supposed that we
have given them the opportunity to get at and eventually
employ such means! Well, it could hardly have been supposed before 1945 that a great nation would be intimidated
by its own victory and, clearly alone in the first rank, would
devote its diplomatic talents to the task of creating a balance of power against itself. It could hardly have been
supposed that the inventors and makers of a revolutionary
weapon would in the very moment of their triumphant discovery betray abruptly such signs of neurasthenia as, without renouncing war, to attempt to renounce their newest
and most powerful instrument of war. The whole atomic policy of the United States since 1945 has been incredible.

In view of the fact that we knowingly and officially tried
to get the Russians to let us build atomic energy plants in
Russia—because "with Hanford, Oak Ridge, and Los Alamos
situated in the United States," as the State Department's
Acheson-Lilienthal report explained, "other nations can develop a greater sense of security only as the Atomic Development Authority locates similar dangerous operations
within their borders" [77]—if we knowingly did that, it is not

at all improbable that unknowingly we have given Communists access to our most secret information and to the bins and shelves of our most remote storehouses.

This is not something you do by turning your head briefly, once. Opportunity in this affair is provided by the existence of long-continued flaws in the systems of physical protection, material accounting, and personnel clearance. What we have done is to permit an organizational arrangement and a physical situation in which no one can be sure the Communists have not gained the leverage to move the world.

We passed a law in 1946 designed to give the Federal government control of what goes on in the American atomic energy project. We could not, however, change by legislative fiat the social and psychological realities of the day. It is all very well to say the Government will operate a laboratory, for example. But if the only people who understand what is going on in that laboratory refuse to work for the Government, then what you say does not mean very much. Of all the ironies in the unfolding of the atomic energy story none is more acid than the headstrong independence of private judgment demanded, attained, and retained by the very group of scientists who campaigned most vigorously for a system of nationalized atomic establishments, to be subordinated as soon as possible to an international authority. A companion spectacle was the inept embrace of socialism by legislators thrown off balance by the atomic blast. "This is too dangerous a force to leave in private hands," the most conservative at once agreed. The awkward fact was that it actually was in the very private hands of a comparatively few scientists.[78]

To be sure, they were powerless, originally, to do very much with it by themselves. They needed the co-operation of a great many other people. But the co-operation they needed could, in the United States, be had with money. "What are you making at Oak Ridge?" was once a popular question in East Tennessee, and "A dollar and a quarter an hour" was a common answer—a tribute to the "security-mindedness" of the workers, but also indicative of the fact that the required skills other than scientific were available in the U.S. labor market even in the days of manpower shortage. "I'm looking," one uninhibited buck is reported as saying, "for that J. A. Jones Consumption Company which pays time and time again." If you can pay time and time again, the scientists can tell you how to make an atom bomb.

What do you do to keep them from telling somebody else as well? After all, they did not part with their knowledge when they sold it to you. Like love, the store of knowledge is not depleted with sharing, and can be shared again, for a price or freely. "We must," said the politicos, "have Government control."

All right. How does the Government control it? Specifically, how does the Government insure that the essential information and the immensely valuable materials are not stolen by the agents of international Communism? This real problem has not received much public discussion, but an analogous hypothetical problem has been thoroughly discussed by experts. That is the problem which an international authority—an Atomic Development Authority (ADA) as it is called in the Acheson-Lilienthal report—would have with relation to the control of atomic energy plants and laboratories "strategically" situated in the various nations of the world.

Under the proposed plan of international control the ADA would have had to insure that no fissionable materials were employed in weapons by any nation at all. Under our existing plan of national control the USAEC is supposed to insure that no fissionable materials are employed in weapons by any nation except the United States. In one respect AEC's job is more difficult than that of the Atomic Development Authority would have been. That is, it is more difficult to prevent diversion of materials from a large establishment legally devoted to weapons manufacture than it is to police effectively almost any number of installations when all production of weapons is illegal. In other words, it is probably easier for the Communists to steal our plutonium under today's set-up than it would have been for the Russians to lay aside their own plutonium under the original Acheson-Lilienthal plan.

In 1946 the U.S. Representative to the UNAEC, Mr. Bernard Baruch, transmitted a report on technological control [79] which made use of studies by two committees, the first consisting of M. Benedict (Chairman), L. W. Alvarez, R. F. Bacher, L. A. Bliss, S. G. English, A. B. Kinzel, P. Morrison, F. H. Spedding, C. Starr, and W. J. Williams; the second of M. Benedict, P. Morrison, J. R. Ruhoff, and W. J. Williams. "All of these men," says the foreword to the report, "were closely associated with the development of atomic energy in this country," [80] which is a very modest statement indeed, for this is a dazzling constellation.

"The best control measures for the prevention of bomb manufacture," says the report, "are not those directed against bomb manufacture itself, but those intended to prevent the accumulation by any means of the essential fissionable materials." [81] This is consistent with the testimony of Dr. Condon, noted above, that once you have the fissionable materials you may continue from there with the resources of "a relatively modest shop." [82] As the report has it, "Fissionable materials which might be diverted would still have to undergo further processing before being converted into weapons, but they would already have been through some of the most difficult and conspicuous operations. For this reason the most stringent control of these materials is particularly important." [83]

Now these materials are, of course, "light" uranium, U-235, and plutonium, Pu-239. The former is produced in "isotope-separation plants," the latter in "chain-reacting piles." Either of these substances may be fabricated into what are called "nuclear components" of the bomb. That is, you can take the right amount of either and make a chunk of metal of a certain size and shape, so that by itself it is harmless, but in conjunction with a similar chunk (if they are brought together fast enough) it contributes to the production of an atomic explosion.

A clandestine organization intent on collecting materials for atomic bombs might divert either U-235 or plutonium at any point in the production process concerned, but, obviously, the later in the process the theft occurs, the more valuable is the product stolen. A chunk of plutonium metal already shaped up is worth more than a corresponding quantity of uranium oxide, even if the latter is "enriched" in U-235. The latter, however, is extremely valuable—quite worth stealing, and in some circumstances perhaps a preferable object. In either case you have to figure in the relative ease or difficulty of making the haul without detection. The report of the experts indicates the nature of the problem relating to each type of material.

"Isotope separation plants," says the report, referring to plants like those at Oak Ridge, Paducah, and Portsmouth, "present some unique problems in preventing the diversion of valuable materials. The small weight of product which is of military significance and the enormous extent of the plant make physical prevention of diversion, by inspection of all outgoing shipments and policing of the process area, of uncertain dependability. This places the principal burden of ensuring the detection of diversion on material accounting, through accurate weighing and analysis of all materials fed to the plant and removed from it, and accurate inventories of material in process. However, the reliability of material accounting in U-235 isotope separation plants is appreciably lower than in conventional chemical plants. The primary reasons for this low precision are:

(1) The relatively inaccurate character of the assay for uranium isotopic content.
(2) The tremendous extent of these plants.
(3) The presence of undetectable but legitimate losses of uranium and U-235 within the process." [84]

All in all, this picture is not encouraging, and, of course, the technical difficulties it describes confront the AEC as implacably as they would an international ADA. W. E. Kelley, formerly AEC Manager in New York, and G. T. Felbeck, Vice-President in charge of the atomic energy division of Union Carbide Corporation, have both stated,[85] based on their wartime experience at Oak Ridge, that the prevention of significant diversion from the isotope separation plants there was possible only through the patriotic co-operation of thousands of varied kinds of employees and officials of the companies actually operating the plants. If for any reason you do not get that patriotic co-operation, you will lose U-235 in significant quantities and never know the difference.

To quote Dr. Walter Zinn again: ". . . if you cannot have people who you are confident will not do this filching . . . your inventories cannot control the situation." [86]

Dr. Manson Benedict, cited above as Chairman of the committee of experts, chief designer of K-25, the first gaseous diffusion isotope separation plant (the only type in active use in the American project today), and subsequently Chief of Operations Analysis for the AEC, once gave a quantitative estimate of what might happen in the kind of process he knows best:

"In the American plant (gaseous diffusion)," he wrote in the *Bulletin of the Atomic Scientists*, February 1, 1946, "one guess is that from one to five bombs per year could be produced from nonaccountable material if one sought to divert material improperly. . . . If we wish to be sure that no uranium 235 is being diverted from uranium isotope separation plants, we had better not build such plants in the first place." Of course, in the United States today we are building such plants as fast as labor-management squabbles permit, and we have trained operators in the layout of such plants prior to FBI investigation of the trainees.

When we come to plutonium the picture at first seems to be more encouraging. Apparently you do not remove plutonium-bearing slugs from a uranium-graphite chain-reacting pile either casually or furtively. The slugs actually stolen at Hanford (as brought out in the Hickenlooper investigation) [87] were valuable, and their theft illustrated a weakness in the Hanford protective system serious enough to warrant a good deal of attention, but those slugs had not been processed in the pile, and contained no fissionable material except the naturally occurring percentage of U-235. Slugs in which plutonium has been generated are highly radioactive because of the nature of the fission by-products, and the plutonium must be extracted by remote control devices.

The plutonium itself, however, is not highly radioactive in its pure state, and in subcritical quantities may be handled with relative facility. As the report of the experts tells us, "At the end of the chemical process, when the material has been 'decontaminated' or freed from radioactive fission products, and concentrated in relatively small volume, there is the greatest danger of diversion from its authorized uses." [88] By way, apparently, of intended consolation, the report adds, "Here the precision of material accounting can be raised somewhat." [89]

Now it is just at this point that a number of people familiar with certain aspects of the history of the American atomic energy project begin to feel queasy in the gorge. Recap: Items of plutonium metal are fantastically valuable and physically they are easy to steal. The *New Yorker*, we recall, reported Mr. Marks as thinking how easy it would be to make off with an end-product container.[90] Embezzlement may be discouraged by a strict system of material accounting, which fortunately seems to be more practicable here than in the early stages of processing.

The general overall flow of fissionable materials in the project—and this is no secret—is from Hanford and Oak Ridge to Los Alamos. The big industrial effort is at Oak Ridge and Hanford. But the product of the effort goes to Los Alamos. Hanford is like Kimberley; Los Alamos is like Tiffany's. Now it is precisely at Los Alamos that the AEC system of material accounting was developed most tardily. It is precisely at Los Alamos that AEC, and the Army before it, have and always have had the most tenuous control. It used to be said of the Sultan that he ruled his remote provinces with a light hand in order that he might rule them at all. That was true of General Groves and Los Alamos. It was far more true of David Lilienthal and Los Alamos.

Groves' authority over Los Alamos was limited by his inevitable dependence on the technical virtuosity of the scientists. Lilienthal was equally dependent in that regard, and in addition he was the political choice of the scientists' lobby. Los Alamos is the one point on the main line of atomic weapons production where the scientists have always dominated not only research and development, and political action on the atom, but also management. Their domination has been equally complete at Chicago, and the political importance of Chicago was probably even greater, but Chicago is not "main line" in the same sense that Los Alamos is.

The point here is not whether the activities of the scientists at Los Alamos have been on the whole good, bad, or indifferent; the point is simply that neither General Groves nor Mr. Lilienthal ever knew or could know in significant detail what those activities were. Particularly, it appears that Los Alamos did not systematically furnish General Groves or Mr. Lilienthal or any of their staff with material-accounting records that were susceptible of significant audit. A layman can have no independent knowledge of whether this was avoidable or unavoidable. It seems to be, at any rate, a fact.

The significant testimony of Dr. Robert F. Bacher on this point is cited in Chapter XIV below (see particularly Note 274). The AEC management staff at Los Alamos stated in July 1950, in a report to Washington on "management improvement," that the procedures for accounting for fissionable materials authorized, and prescribed, by AEC headquarters two years earlier (in "Bulletin GM-95") were, as of the date of the report, in the process of being established. Glancing at the coincidence that this belated adoption of the approved system of controls occurred in the first month after the incidence of the Korean adventure, and in the first month of Mr. Gordon Dean's Chairmanship of the Commission, the point to focus on is that five years had gone by since the bomb test at Alamogordo in the historic summer of 1945. During those five years the kind of material accounting system which the experts then agreed would be necessary for international control was not in operation at Los Alamos. The very place where material accounting was not fully and punctually applied was the place (that is, Los Alamos) where diversion (that is, theft) was easiest to perform and most serious in its consequences. Reverting to the diamond-industry comparison, it is as if you had strict controls at Kimberley and did not bother to keep books at Tiffany's.

There is more. Material accounting, physical safeguards—all the instruments and paraphernalia—would be effective in preventing improper diversion, the experts said, only if the operating personnel in the "dangerous" plants and laboratories around the world were organizationally independent of the nations in whose territories they were situated, and reported directly to the international Atomic Development Authority, or whatever it might be called. This was stressed by the men who knew the American system best, and by the men who took the lead in shaping America's post-war atomic policy. This was the reason given why America could not accept proposals for national operation of "dangerous" activities, with an international inspection force.

Dean Acheson spoke to the American Society of Newspaper Editors April 20, 1946, on this point. The Acheson-Lilienthal report was then new, and the Under Secretary of State was explaining some of its more salient excellencies. A security force without operating responsibility, he said, "would be worse than failure because it would encourage people everywhere to believe that it provided security when in fact there was no security at all." The reason for this was that the technical people "would know far more than those who were trying to police them. . . . You would have what in our discussions we used to refer to as the cops-and-robbers theory of control." [91]

But that cleverly captioned theory is the only one Los Alamos has ever operated on. In fact, Secretary Acheson's whole account of the way a security system ought *not* to be run is in broad outline so much like the way the Los Alamos system always has been run, that it is not difficult to imagine Dr. Oppenheimer, probably the most important member of the Lilienthal Board which wrote the report for the Acheson Committee, drawing on his experience as Director of the war-time Los Alamos Laboratory to make sure that the international security system should be better than the national one had been in his principal area of observation.

But whatever Dr. Oppenheimer may have thought, the representatives of the University of California, which by an interesting legal fiction operates the Los Alamos Scientific

Laboratory, have it in the contract that security is the responsibility of the Federal Government, as represented first by the Army, later by the AEC. In a fundamental sense they are quite right, of course. They are not by this insistence saying they are robbers; they are underscoring the fact that the Feds and not they are the cops. But there is, or was until recently, no one on the Federal rolls at Los Alamos who has professional knowledge of the technical activities he is, in Secretary Acheson's phrase, "trying to police."

Nothing was more surprising to some people—most people who thought about it at all—than the fact that under the Atomic Energy Act of 1946 and under the initial Chairmanship of Mr. Lilienthal the historic policy decision was made to continue a "contractor" method of operation in the atomic energy project. Mr. Lilienthal's friends and foes alike (and he had a number of both at the time) were so baffled by this development that neither group said much about it. Everyone, or almost everyone, had assumed that whether they liked it or not Mr. Lilienthal was going to institute direct Government operation in the atomic energy project. In general the surprise occasioned by his failure to do this (and he not only failed to do it, but everywhere strengthened the hand of the "private" contractors who operated the Government-owned facilities) arose out of the expectations naturally engendered by his widely advertised policy in TVA.

The surprise would have been still greater if more attention had been given to the incongruity between AEC policy on the national level and that recommended on the international level by the Board of Consultants of which Mr. Lilienthal was the Chairman. "The fundamental—and truly revolutionary—idea of the Acheson-Lilienthal Report," says Dr. Eugene Rabinowitch of the *Bulletin of the Atomic Scientists,* "was to break away from the concept of international control as being essentially a system of policing—making sure that certain prohibited activities were *not* being carried out by individual nations. Spurning such 'negative' forms of control, the report proposed instead an 'affirmative' form: control through international *ownership* (or, at least, international *management*) of all installations in the main production line leading from uranium ore to nuclear explosives." [92]

Los Alamos, of course, is at a point further along the main line than this. It is at the point where nuclear explosives are received and incorporated into the latest types of nuclear weapons. The international arrangement would have cut the line off entirely short of this point—at least there was no significant discussion of extending it thus far—but the principles of administration appropriate to an isotope separation plant would apply with even greater cogency to a weapons laboratory. And the astounding fact is that the authors of the Acheson-Lilienthal plan, who could not trust nations, including their own, to be kept in line by "negative forms of control," elected only a short time later to rely entirely on such negative measures in policing an agency of the sovereign state of California. Even an unreconstructed Secessionist would scarcely argue for the legitimacy of giving the state of California decisive military advantage over the Federal Union of which it is a part, and at Federal expense.

But that is by no means the end of the matter. We return to the thought that it is only a legal fiction that the Los Alamos Scientific Laboratory is operated by the University of California. This is pretty well understood at Los Alamos, and one supposes it is at Berkeley and Sacramento as well. Dr. Oppenheimer, during the course of the Congressional investigation into the charges of "incredible mismanagement" leveled against Mr. Lilienthal by Senator Hickenlooper, set the Congressmen right on this point. Some naive assumption having somehow got into the dialogue, that the University of California was responsible for Los Alamos operations, Dr. Oppenheimer said, "My guess is that the directives are agreed to by the laboratory staff and the Commission." [93]

In this matter Dr. Oppenheimer's guess is a good deal better than most people's positive knowledge. What Dr. Oppenheimer failed to bring out, however, though, of course, he did not conceal it either, is that the Commission has no one on its staff at Los Alamos—and not more than a couple in Washington—capable of arguing with the laboratory staff on any technical problem of any substance.

When a directive relating to the main operating procedures at Los Alamos is "agreed to by the laboratory staff and the Commission" you can bet your last dollar that the laboratory staff's agreement is based on their own authorship of the directive, and that the Commission's agreement is based on not knowing any effective or even demonstrably pertinent way to disagree. The result is that the staff of the Los Alamos Scientific Laboratory—"some fellows," as Dr. Oppenheimer calls them—are about as independent as mortal men get to be. The principal role of the AEC is to provide them with money and services. The AEC is in effect their lobby in Washington and their housekeeper in Los Alamos. This is the sort of situation in which one would prefer not to recall Lord Acton's "Power tends to corrupt."

The experts reporting to the UN (Benedict, Alvarez, Bacher, *et al.*) listed six conditions, all of which "imply a very considerable degree of international cooperation," as collectively a *sine qua non* of effective international control. "The degree of security," they said, "is dependent upon the extent to which the . . . conditions are fulfilled." The degree of national security would seem logically to depend on analogous conditions within the national project. Two of the six conditions listed are particularly relevant here:

"The ADA [read AEC] should be staffed with imaginative, technically competent men of the highest integrity," and:

"The Authority [read Commission] should participate actively in research, development, and production, to the end that it will be better informed than any national [read private] group concerning the activities it must control and detect." [94]

We have no reason to suppose the AEC officials at Los Alamos are not "of the highest integrity" or that they are not "imaginative." We know, however, that in the field of nuclear physics they are not "technically competent." This is not their fault. They were not employed to do anything requiring any competence in nuclear physics. The AEC at Los Alamos does NOT participate actively in research, development, or production; and to say that it is NOT better informed than the private group it is supposed to control and, if appropriate, detect is the understatement of the decade.

In brief, the basic administrative set-up of the AEC with relation to the crucial activities at Los Alamos is such as to make impossible any assurance that the most serious diversions of material have not taken place.

The discussion here of the system of protecting and accounting for the materials of atomic energy, of atomic bombs, is admittedly fragmentary. Enough has been observed, however, to suggest that two of the three main-line atomic energy establishments—that is, Oak Ridge and Los Alamos—are, or at least have been, susceptible of being systematically milked by an organization of resolution and ingenuity. This is true at Oak Ridge because of the physical nature of isotope separation plants; it is true at Los Alamos because of the administrative arrangement. Hanford has possibly been less vulnerable. In the total picture it hardly seems to matter.

Relevant official comment from the AEC appears in the Fifth Semiannual Report to Congress, January 1949.

"In 1947," the report reads (page 124), "the Commission's physical security officers were chiefly occupied with surveying installations, taking quick emergency steps to protect those that had serious weaknesses, and planning the full-scale, long-term protection required by the national atomic energy program. They examined identification procedures, studied guarding systems, picked flaws in shipment and storage methods, recommended hundreds of improvements, and set about ordering necessary equipment and construction. The close of 1948 saw most of the needed changes in effect, including the construction of many miles of chain-link fencing set in concrete and topped with barbed wire; the installation of protective automatic alarms using infrared, photoelectric, temperature, proximity, sonic or circuit disturbance detectors; establishment of tamper-proof identification systems; installation of stand-by communications systems, and improvement in the quality, training, and arming of guards."

If there were in 1947 "serious weaknesses" so that one could pick "flaws in shipment and storage methods," and if it was "the close of 1948" that "saw most of the needed changes [and therefore not all the needed changes] in effect," then we have the years 1945 (when production began), 1946, 1947, and 1948 during which random thefts *did* take place (as we know from the case of Dr. Sanford Simons, for example), and systematic thefts *could* have taken place as far as the system of physical protection was concerned.

AEC's comment in the same report on the material accounting system reads (on page 34): "Although satisfactory measurement methods and procedures have not yet been developed for all materials at all stages of production, a fairly comprehensive system was in operation by the end of 1948. Additional refinements and improvements will be adopted as they become available." The author of this last sentence possibly had in mind the hope that one of these days the Commission would be able to persuade Los Alamos to adopt the authorized procedures. And, sure enough, by July 1950 that is just what they did. The trouble is, if Dr.

Benedict's estimate of the possibilities connected with a gaseous diffusion plant be taken (one to five bombs a year), and if we assume a similar range for the rest of the project, including Los Alamos, then we have a not completely uninformed guess that from eight to forty atomic bombs may be stashed away somewhere waiting The Day.

Against some of the residual hopes based on the probability that AEC has greatly improved the system since 1948 (at Los Alamos since 1950) must be reckoned two facts about illegal diversion in general, as noted by the experts: (1) that the risk is cumulative with the age of the project—"small amounts of material accumulated over a long period of time might build up to a real military advantage"; and (2) that the risk increases with increase of plant capacity.[95]

The hypothetical ADA was going to make a great effort to prevent misappropriation of materials for illicit military purposes in a setting where any military purpose was illicit, and where full use could therefore be made of such expedients as "denaturing," which depended on the virtual nonexistence of isotope separation plants. In the actual American project, now in its ninth year of production on a continually expanding scale, there has been, for obvious reasons, no need for "denaturing," and, indeed, the most rapid expansion in both efficiency and capacity, at least as far as public knowledge goes, has been in the system of isotope separation plants.

This illustrates a dilemma of sorts. The very aspects of the atomic energy program which appear most favorable to the military establishment of the United States appear also favorable to the clandestine organization of international Communism. This is simply the old story that it is difficult to feed the host without feeding the parasite. No one is going to suggest treating this cancer by starving the afflicted national body. What is indicated is surgery. But the matter is delicate.

So involved are healthy surface and hidden malignant tissues that international Communism can readily promote in the United States the most efficient production and the most ingenious research and development programs attainable. It will not, of course, promote efficiency in the system of internal security—on the contrary. Less obviously, neither will it promote actual accomplishment in the field (usually called civilian) of economically useful applications. Ideas in this field—yes; practical results—no; leave those for the Russians—they might actually make the grade. But in every other respect international Communism can form a united front with patriotic nationalism.

Both may plan and work zealously for maximum American production of atomic fuels, explosives, weapons, and other militarily useful devices. International Communism, for its own purposes, can go along with and even be enthusiastic about the slogan "Security by Achievement vs. Security by Concealment," promulgated by the majority of the Joint Committee on Atomic Energy in their palliation of the charges made against Mr. Lilienthal by Senator Hickenlooper in 1949.[96] The Communists know the value to them of the specious equivocation involved in this slogan, though patriotic nationalists do not think about it that way. Communist agents may or may not have had to nudge policymakers to get top priority, after weapon manufacture, for submarine development; for certainly an atomic submarine would be very useful to the United States, even if it would be somewhat more useful to the Soviet Union. For the most part, in this situation, the observable activities of the Communist agents and of the patriots will be indistinguishable, but the agents will be exacting a percentage of the material output, as well as practically all the information, as a secret tribute.

We have often been assured, with great plausibility, that the law of diminishing returns affects atomic stockpiles rather quickly. If fifty bombs can destroy what you want to destroy, then five hundred represent nothing but a very expensive excess of four hundred and fifty. You can give your antagonist any number of excess bombs he may fancy, if that enables you to get the number required to destroy him, and if he is paying for all of them anyhow. Ernest K. Lindley said in *Newsweek* May 5, 1952, "Atomic weapons, while we had a monopoly of them, were a deterrent to war. It is by no means certain that our atomic superiority is so much of a deterrent. Both sides must reckon with the power to retaliate."

But our hypothetical Communist agents do not have to reckon with that, for with the run of the project they may wreck the retaliation bases. Of course they are co-operative in the American production program! You cannot distinguish them from their patriotic associates until in some way—you hope not too late—you learn their intent. "What the policeman would be looking for," said Mr. Acheson, "would be a state of mind."

Chapter V ⟶ Los Alamos Alumni

ACTUARIAL APPROACH

So everything comes down to personnel. There are two distinct problems here, which we must be careful not to confuse. One is the detection and conviction of individual spies and thieves. That is not our problem at the moment. We are concerned rather with simply estimating the probability that somewhere in the atomic energy project there are spies and thieves. Insurance companies estimate the death rates of groups set up by age, sex, occupation, medical history, and other stigmata, and adjust their premium schedules accordingly, without attempting at all to say whether any particular person is going to live or die this year or next. Similarly, scientists will calculate a "cross-section" giving the average behavior of a great number of neutrons under specified conditions, without commitment on the behavior of any particular neutron. (Of course the fact that the insurance companies and the scientists have only statistical probability to go on does not prevent them from taking some very practical measures, such as conducting programs of public health and constructing neutron shields, which affect respectively particular persons and neutrons.)

The problem here is similar—simply to figure the odds on there being Communist agents somewhere in the atomic energy project. This means assessing the intensity, direction, and other characteristics of the beam of Communist agents against the density, powers of reflection, and other characteristics of the shields set up by General Groves, Mr. Lilienthal, and their successors and predecessors, and coming up with some kind of coefficient of penetration. It appears the odds are very great that Communists got in in significant numbers.

One would have to be naive to conclude otherwise. The most striking evidence, of course, is the little collection of case histories of Communist operations in the atomic energy project, including the cases of Klaus Fuchs, Allan Nunn May, and David Greenglass. The hackneyed iceberg analogy inevitably comes to mind—the visible part is a small fraction of the whole. All three of these men specifically indicated there were others. Alan Moorehead has told us how Fuchs "said he was certain that there were other scientists besides himself who had been working for the Russians. . . . Fuchs repeated . . . that he was convinced that other scientists were at work for the Russians, and had been all along." [97]

THE LIST

Greenglass, while at Los Alamos, made, according to his sworn testimony, "a list of people who seemed sympathetic to Communism and would furnish information to the Russians." [98] It would be as naive to think Greenglass' judgment of the individuals on that list was invariably wrong as it would be unfair to think him invariably correct. You could not send any particular individual to jail, or even deny him security clearance, merely because his name was on that list, but neither could you escape the conclusion that the existence of the list creates a presumption that people with the sympathies sought by Greenglass did exist. What do you think?

Harry Gold, the courier between Greenglass and Rosenberg, and a more experienced Communist agent than Greenglass, rebuked him for making the list. "At this point Greenglass told me that there were a number of people at Los Alamos that he thought would make very likely recruits; that is, they were also people who might be willing to furnish information on the atom bomb to the Soviet Union, and he started to give me the names of these people, the names of some of these people. I cut him very short indeed. I told him that such procedure was extremely hazardous, foolhardy, that under no circumstances should he ever try to proposition anyone on his own into trying to get information for the Soviet Union. I told him to be very circumspect in his conduct and to never even drop the slightest hint to anyone that he himself was furnishing information on the atom bomb to the Soviet Union." [99]

But if Harry Gold was afraid Greenglass' possible lack of circumspection would get him into trouble at Los Alamos, he was apparently quite mistaken. Greenglass seems to have attracted no more attention than a Dixiecrat in Mississippi.

It seems worth recalling that Harry Gold also testified concerning his Soviet boss, Anatoli Yakovlev: * "Yakovlev at this time told me that I should be very careful, much more careful than ever before. He related to me an incident which had taken place toward the end of 1945. He said that a very important person who had upon him information on the atom bomb had come to New York at the end of 1945 and

---

* Igor Gouzenko wrote in *Coronet*, March 1953 (p. 90): "The directors of the theft of atomic secrets by Dr. Klaus Fuchs and Harry Gold were Anatoli Yakovlev and Semen Semenov, both legitimately accredited to the United States by the Soviet Government."

that he, Yakovlev, had tried to get in touch with that person over a period of time, a period of a few days, but that the man had been trailed by Intelligence men continually, so that Yakovlev had to give up the idea of getting in touch with this source of information." [100] It is, of course, possible to take this as a reassuring anecdote. Did not the Intelligence men frustrate the treacherous interview? What sticks is that they were not able to make an arrest, and that no one yet knows who the "very important person" was.

JOINT U.S.–SOVIET FELLOWSHIP PROGRAM

Less ambiguous in its implications is the following excerpt from the minutes of the Rosenberg trial, as reported in the Joint Committee's pamphlet, *Soviet Atomic Espionage*. David Greenglass is the witness.

In '46 or '47 Julius Rosenberg made an offer to me to have the Russians pay for part of my schooling and the GI Bill of Rights to pay for the other part, and that I should go to college for the purpose of cultivating the friendships of people that I had known at Los Alamos and also to acquire new friendships with people who were in the field of research that are in those colleges, like physics and nuclear energy.

Mr. E. H. Bloch. I am sorry, may I inquire if the witness is now stating what Rosenberg said to him?

The Court. So I understood.

Mr. E. H. Bloch. Are these the words?

The Witness. Approximately the words.

Mr. E. H. Bloch. All right.

Q. [by Mr. Roy Cohn, for the Government] Did he mention any particular institutions which he desired to have you attend?

A. Well, he would have wanted me to go to Chicago, University of Chicago, because there were people there that I had known at Los Alamos and it was a well-known institution and it was doing a lot of good work in the field of nuclear physics.

Q. Did he mention any other institutions?

A. M.I.T., and then later on when N.Y.U. had a nuclear engineering course he wanted me to take that.

Q. Did he give you the name of any scientists with whom he desired you to build up friendships?

A. No; he told me that at Chicago University there were some people that I had gone to school with, I mean, I had been at Los Alamos with, and that I should cultivate their friendships.

Q. Did he specify how much of this money would be furnished by the Russians?

A. He specified that the GI Bill of Rights would pay for my schooling and they would give a certain amount of money for living of the student, and he said the Russians would pay additional money so I could live more comfortably.

Q. Now, did you ever agree to go to any of these schools?

A. I said I would try, but I never bothered.

Q. You never, in fact, did go; is that right?

A. That's right.

Q. Now, did Rosenberg tell you anything about activities of this kind in which he had engaged?

A. Well, he had told me that he had people going to schools in various places.

The Court. Will you fix the time when he told you this.

The Witness. It was during this period of 1946 to 1949.

The Court. All right.

A. (Continuing.) He told me that he had people going to school in various up-State institutions. He never made mention of the institutions, but he said that he was paying students to go to school.

Q. Did he tell you anything else concerning his activities along these lines?

A. He told me that he had people giving him information in up-State New York and in Ohio.

Q. Did he tell you why they were giving him that information?

A. They were giving information to give to the Russians.

Q. Did he mention any particular place in up-State New York from which he was getting information?

A. He mentioned the fact that he was getting information from General Electric at Schenectady.

Q. General Electric in Schenectady?
A. That's right.[101]

It must be emphasized that the preceding is not taken from radio, television, the movies, or pulp fiction. It is sworn testimony in a trial where two persons were sentenced to die. It tells us that during the period 1946–1949 Rosenberg, a Russian agent, had "people going to school in various places," and "had people giving him information. . . . He mentioned the fact that he was getting information from General Electric at Schenectady." (General Electric is one of the more important atomic energy contractors.)

The Russians provided the money—that is, whatever was needed over and above the amount furnished by the Federal government through the "GI Bill of Rights." We need not speculate long on whether the two powerful governments that were (and presumably still are) parties to this joint program of educational support were equally indifferent to the political sympathies of their "fellows." We may fairly suppose that some of the beneficiaries of this program have by now graduated, and that efforts have been made to place them where their knowledge and skill can be most fully utilized.

We shall not attempt here to re-examine all known criminal cases of atomic espionage, or all known cases of Communist affiliation in the project. A systematic and helpful compilation of cases has been prepared by the staff of the Joint Committee on Atomic Energy and published by the Government Printing Office. Several commercially published accounts have appeared dealing with one or more important cases, among them Alan Moorehead's *The Traitors* and Oliver Pilat's *The Atom Spies*. These works focus on the nature and extent of the damage already done by particular agents—the most prominent of whom are now convicts—and on what kind of people these agents were, or must have been, to do what they did. Our concern is rather with the possibility that much greater damage may yet be done and, incidental to this, with the probable rate of incidence of the kind of people that might do it.

It is an interesting psychological problem—the analysis of Greenglass or Fuchs. More directly interesting would be an analysis of the persons whose names appeared on Greenglass' list. Most interesting would be an analysis of the persons of importance who set the style in the atomic energy project—in whose entourages Fuchs and May moved unnoticed.

ROBERT R. DAVIS

Oliver Pilat's *The Atom Spies* should be widely read, as it is a valuable compilation, and no attempt will be made here to paraphrase it or to analyze it comprehensively. Two or three notes, however, ought to be made.

First, the author's usual, high order of accuracy deserts him in his treatment of R. R. Davis. Davis testified before a Congressional committee that G. R. Lomanitz recruited him into a Communist cell at Berkeley, California, before he went to Los Alamos to accept employment there. Pilat leaves the impression that Davis' stay at Los Alamos was brief—practically that security officials met him at the train and sent him packing.

"Robert R. Davis," writes Mr. Pilat, "a Radiation Laboratory [Berkeley] scientist from Idaho, and his wife Charlotte, a native of California, learned to their sorrow how close scrutiny was being kept by CIC [Counter-Intelligence Corps —Army], though at first they did not know what hit them. The Davises were recruited by Lomanitz into the Merriman branch of the Party just before Steve Nelson [important Communist organizer] dissolved it. Davis got an offer of a job at the newly established atom-bomb center of Los Alamos and promptly accepted. His Communist record reached Los Alamos before he did, and he was dismissed on the ground of questionable character and associations." [102]

Actually, Davis was at Los Alamos more than five years—March 1943 to December 1948—more than three years under the Army and two under the Atomic Energy Commission—all, of course, under "the University of California." There is no evidence of espionage or other treacherous activity on his part, which is very fortunate for us, since while he was there he had charge of the library of secret reports and prints. Curiosity is said to have been his motive in becoming a Communist.[103]

DR. DAVID HAWKINS

Another Los Alamos official who left the Communist Party just before departing from Berkeley for the supersecret project in New Mexico was Dr. David Hawkins. Like Mr. Davis, Dr. Hawkins has not been charged with espionage, but like Davis he acknowledges now a record of Communist Party membership.[104]

Dr. David Hawkins, according to his own testimony, worked in three different Communist cells in California—one at Berkeley, one at Palo Alto, and one in San Francisco—over a period of four or five years (right on through the Soviet-Nazi pact, which was often a cut-off point for misguided liberals). He quit just before going to Los Alamos in May 1943. He stayed in Los Alamos through the war, serving as an administrative aide, reporting at first to the Laboratory Director and later to the Director of Personnel. Not a scientist himself, but a philosopher, he associated with the scientists at Los Alamos, apparently having been particularly friendly with Dr. Philip Morrison.

Dr. Hawkins departed from Los Alamos in the summer of 1946, and after a year's teaching at George Washington University in Washington, D. C., joined the faculty of the University of Colorado. In December 1950 he testified before the House Committee on Un-American Activities. Toward the last of January 1951 the Committee released his testimony, and the Denver *Post* published it in full on February 4, 1951. For some reason the story got little play in the Eastern press, though its implications are by no means local to Colorado and New Mexico.

Dr. Hawkins is somewhat prolix, but as a case in the history of polite American Communism his testimony is worth careful study. Unlike Whittaker Chambers, he evinces no signs of melancholy genius. No crises of the soul appear to have attended either his entering or leaving the Communist Party. He seems to have entered because he thought it might be a good thing for the world in general, and he seems to have left because he thought it might be a good thing for David Hawkins. Compared to the case of Chambers it all looks casual, really. But of course really we do not know.

David Hawkins "belonged" in the academic community. He was a Master of Arts from Stanford at twenty-three and a Doctor of Philosophy from California at twenty-seven, having in the interim earned some money and gained experience as a teaching assistant. After receiving his doctorate he taught a year at Stanford, and returned to Berkeley in the fall of 1941 as an instructor at the University. It was here that as a graduate student three years earlier he had joined the Communist Party. No one had recruited him— it was his own idea. "I think more than any other factor," he said, "was the feeling that this drive toward war [of the Nazis] could be stopped by a collective security policy." [105]

As a believer in collective security he had not been greatly disturbed when the Soviet Union formed an alliance with the Nazis. "The German-Russian pact," he said, "seemed to me a sheer act of national self-protection. Later on there was a war against Finland, and I could not accept that *with any happy feeling* [he could, however, accept it], but again you *could say* [and if you could you had to], 'Here is a desperate situation. It may be true that there are secret arrangements that Finland is to be used as a springboard.'"

But his relief that what he was told to think might even be true was short-lived. "I think," he said, "the invasion of Norway and the low countries *gave me a real test* [italics added, here and elsewhere in quotations from the testimony of Dr. Hawkins], because *up to that time* I had felt that the position of the Western Communist parties was *a genuine position of national self-interest.*"

Dr. Hawkins is not impervious to evidence—you just cannot tell what he is going to do with it. He observed the evidence that the French, English, and American Communist Parties were not in the year 1940 exactly cherishing the respective interests of their countries. "In the case of France that was so bad," he said, "that the French Communist Party didn't reverse its position till the actual eve of the invasion of France. That seemed to be a terrifically opportunist position [in the Communist vocabulary "opportunist" is a very bad word], and I was not happy about that, nor was I happy about the position of the American Communist Party at that time, *but I did not withdraw from it.*"

France fell in June 1940, the same lovely season Dr. Hawkins got his Ph.D. He faced two tests about the same time. He could scarcely have forgotten either by the time he went to Stanford in the fall. There he affiliated with a Communist cell at Palo Alto. The chairman of the cell was Dr. Frank Oppenheimer, who must have been given the same test. Dr. Hawkins "held a minor office," in charge of some kind of "educational activities." These two doctors must have found it very educational in the fall of 1940 to study collective security in action as illustrated by the Soviet Union's ally in the air over Coventry.

But by the next fall, 1941, Hitler had already savagely attacked Russia, and it was permissible for American Communists to co-operate with Lend-Lease and other policies of their own nation. Things were looking better for Dr. Hawkins. The new job at Berkeley opened a pleasant prospect which he resolved should not be spoiled by his former Communist associations. "I was beginning a career as a university teacher I hoped, and I didn't want to get reinvolved in the affairs of this branch [of the Communist Party at Berkeley], and I therefore didn't reaffiliate with it. I wanted to have what I thought I deserved and my profession deserved: an independent position in relation to the university at which I was teaching [academic freedom]. . . . *I affiliated with a branch of the Communist Party in San Francisco.*"

Now there is a way to solve your troubles! Put your two lives on opposite sides of a bay. Mr. Pilat has pointed out that too much has been made of Dr. Fuchs' "controlled schizophrenia." [106] Dr. Hawkins put his own case more simply: "A good part of this period I was living in San Francisco and commuting to Berkeley, and this accomplished the separation which I desired."

For two years he seems to have compartmentalized his affairs neatly enough, maintaining in Berkeley the prerogatives of an academically individualistic seeker after truth where it might be found, and in San Francisco, in a cell consisting largely, we are told, of public-school teachers, adhering to the Party discipline, executing the required mental gymnastics, and guiding less agile intelligences in these exercises.

Toward the last of this two-year interval he gradually quit the Communist Party, he told the House Committee, because he "wanted to live in the fuller sense of the word among my colleagues and students." It is not too clear what this means. Perhaps the budding university professor was slowly overcome with ennui among the schoolmarms. It is not even too clear just how anyone could "gradually" quit the Communist Party. Considering the Communist contempt for "gradualism" the thought occurs that in spirit you have to quit before you can do anything gradually. Or perhaps one who quits gradually never really understood Communism in the first place, was never really a Communist at all. Yet Dr. Hawkins had been on the rolls five years, had been affiliated with three different cells, playing a leading role, it seems, in at least two of them, and in the last maintaining a measure of secrecy—oh, well, discretion. He paid dues, of course. Before the Committee he did not recall who collected the dues, or just when he quit paying. It was in February or March 1943—something like that.[107] Two months, maybe three, before he went to the secret mesa above Santa Fe.

The blurred and veiled character of much of Dr. Hawkins' Communist activity and associations tends to modify, to complicate, the fairly widespread opinion that to be a Communist in the 1930's and 1940's (except for the interval of the Soviet-Nazi pact, August 29, 1939, to June 22, 1941) was nothing, that "everybody" was doing it. It is true that a number of intellectuals were Communists and known to be Communists in those days; and it is true that practically all intellectuals held it to be intellectually and morally permissible to be a Communist. "Only, I'm not one myself," they might add.

DR. FRANK OPPENHEIMER

But it is clear that then as well as now open Communist affiliation was a handicap in practical affairs (except the arts), and for this and possibly other reasons a number of Communists were secretive about the connection. For example, when the Washington *Times-Herald* on July 12, 1947, published a copyrighted story on the fact that Dr. Frank Oppenheimer (Dr. Hawkins' Party boss at Palo Alto) had been a "card-carrying" member of the Communist Party, Dr. Oppenheimer was able to make a ringingly indignant denial (reported in the *Times-Herald* July 13, 1947); and no voices from Stanford or anywhere else in the academic world were lifted to defend the *Times-Herald* against the charge that it had deliberately and maliciously lied. The story, said

Dr. Oppenheimer, was a "complete fabrication." And, consistent with professorial responsibility, he read the *Times-Herald* a moral lecture: "The publishing of such false statements can . . . only result in a fear and perhaps a hysteria that will make it impossible for the public to make wise decisions about public matters and in particular about control of atomic energy." [108]

No more was heard of the matter till Dr. Oppenheimer under oath two years later told the House Committee on Un-American Activities that he had indeed been a Communist.[109] Evidently Dr. Oppenheimer had kept his activities as a Communist organizer at Stanford private enough to go unnoticed by the respectable professors with whom he associated. The only alternative is that they were accessories to the deception of the rest of us. Possibly, of course, there were those among them who felt, "Better a lying professor than the *Times-Herald* telling the truth," and whose last word to the Halls of Ivy would always be:

"What so false as truth is,
False to thee?"

Whittaker Chambers has made us aware of the curious paradox whereby in the polite world we are tolerant of our assassins provided they went to a good college, but cannot endure those who warn us in a raucous voice. We are crazier than that. Louis Budenz was not reproached much for being editor of the *Daily Worker* when he was editor of the *Daily Worker*, but after he had been reconverted to Catholicism and began to denounce a variety of Communist agents he was vilified on the grounds that he had been editor of the *Daily Worker*. Ex-Communists are very bad, in the judgment of some of our journalists, but it is not clear whether the obnoxious component here is the *Communist* or the *Ex*.

Dr. Frank Oppenheimer's case suggests that it is neither—it is the act of identifying other persons as Communists. Dr.

Oppenheimer, in the words of the Committee, "admitted former membership in the Communist Party but declined to answer any questions pertaining to the Communist associations of other individuals." [110] This, as we shall see in a moment, was, in the view of Dr. Hawkins, an admirable position for Dr. Oppenheimer to assume.

Moral problems obsess the delicately adjusted inhabitants of this precarious world. Shall I lie to this newspaper man? How much of the truth shall I tell that Committee of the Government? It seems ungracious here to go over this ground again, but these matters are germane to the still unresolved question of our national existence. It is disturbing that Dr. Frank Oppenheimer, after his confession to the Committee in June 1949 that the Communist membership he had denied in July 1947 was actually a fact, still persisted in being less than candid with the press. Following is a statement of his as reported by the Albuquerque *Journal* June 15, 1949:

"My wife and I joined the Communist Party in 1937, seeking an answer to the problems of unemployment and want in the wealthiest and most productive country in the world. We did not find in the Communist Party the vehicle through which to accomplish the progressive changes we were interested in, and so we left it about three and a half years later and never rejoined. Our connection with the Communist Party ended long before the establishment of the Manhattan Project."

Three and a half years onto 1937 gets you into 1940 or 1941. The Manhattan Project, as an Army organizational unit, was established in August 1942. So that would put the separation of Dr. Oppenheimer from the Communist Party before the establishment of the Manhattan Project, all right, and whether you call this "long before" or not we will not worry about. We will give a passing thought, however, to the fact that the establishment of the "Manhattan Project" was a relatively mature development in the life of the atomic bomb project, which began in 1939.

Mr. Pilat has recapped some of the pre-Manhattan-Project atomic history at Berkeley: "It is easy now to see why, of the three great university centers of research in nuclear fission—Columbia, Chicago, and California—California offered such a particularly tempting target for espionage in the summer of 1941. The previous spring—on March 6, 1941, to be precise—a group of young physicists and chemists, most of them in their twenties, working under Dr. Glenn T. Seaborg and Dr. Edward M. McMillan, had bombarded U-238 with neutrons of intermediate speeds and had discovered that these neutrons transformed U-238 into a new element, unknown in nature, called plutonium. . . . The entire atomic project slid into high gear following a report on July 11, 1941, by Dr. Ernest O. Lawrence about the Berkeley discovery to the National Academy of Science, which was studying the uranium problem. Contagious enthusiasm swept the scientists in Berkeley; new miracles seemed to be waiting in every test tube and retort. . . . Dr. Frank Oppenheimer had come from Stanford University in 1941 to work as a research assistant at the Radiation Laboratory in Berkeley. He and his wife retained membership in the Communist Party branch at Palo Alto, but they lived in Berkeley. . . ." [111]

But this must be the time Dr. Frank Oppenheimer had in mind when he said he left the Party. Is it not astonishing that a man who was a Communist organizer throughout the period of the Soviet-Nazi nonaggression pact, remaining loyal to the Stalinist cause during that trying time when such loyalty ran counter to both U.S. national policy and all the liberal doctrines on which he had presumably been nourished, should, just as Communism was re-entering a phase of some kind of respectability (thanks to Hitler's invasion of Russia June 22, 1941), leave the Party he had served three and a half years and throw himself into the work on the atomic bomb, which by a coincidence of fate was itself just coming to life after eighteen months of comparative lethargy? And since all this was going on in 1941, why did Dr. Oppenheimer refer to the "establishment of the Manhattan Project" in 1942 as if that were the beginning of the atomic business?

That is worrisome—it looks like equivocation; but, of course, it may not have been so intended. But the following is a pretty flat statement. To newsmen curious about his relationship with the atomic project, Dr. Oppenheimer said his Communist Party membership was "known to a lot of people. . . . I believe it was known to the Government. *I made no effort to conceal it.*" (Italics added.)

Made no effort to conceal it! What about that statement in July 1947 when he said the *Times-Herald* account of his previous Communist Party membership was a *"complete fabrication"*? Dr. Frank Oppenheimer has not yet established his credibility as a witness.

*　　*　　*

To return to the case of Dr. David Hawkins. Mr. Tavenner, Counsel for the Un-American Activities Committee, has asked him, "Will you tell us the character of your employment in Los Alamos?"

Dr. Hawkins: "I find it difficult to explain the nature of my job. It was called administrative aide. My job was, roughly, to do all of the things that needed to be done and for which there was no regular administrative officer available. I was a sort of handy man or trouble shooter in an administrative capacity." [112]

Mr. Tavenner: "What were some of the fields—you were there from 1943 to 1946?"

Dr. Hawkins: "That is right. My first job, as I well remember, was in connection with the draft deferment of some of the younger members of the scientific staff. When

I got there a man who had been there and who actually preceded me by three weeks had been getting out draft deferment forms, and so on, and set up the routine. Then when I came along I was asked to take the job over, and I formally represented the laboratory in signing letters requesting draft deferments.

"Another job which I had at this time was drafting a book of regulations for people who worked in the laboratory. The rules were established, but they were not codified. For example, we had restrictions on travel at Los Alamos."

Mr. Tavenner: "For security reasons?"

Dr. Hawkins: "Yes. And I did that drafting job. I was in the personnel office of the laboratory in a secondary capacity for quite a long while; and I was kind of representative of the laboratory in terms of the three-cornered relationship that existed between the civilian community of Los Alamos, which was a town that had lots of wives and children and dogs; the laboratory; and the U.S. Engineers. I was a kind of representative from the point of view of the laboratory on some of the problems that arose. If a dog bit a child, and the dog turned out to be the dog of a very important technician, I would have to worry about whether banning the dog would cause the technician to leave and go to another war job. We had a community council at Los Alamos, and I had to meet with the council, together with a representative of the U.S. Engineers."

This homey little sketch of war-time Los Alamos—with its questions of protocol (my dog can bite your little brother because my daddy is a Ph.D.)—is offered to illustrate the *nontechnical* importance of Dr. Hawkins in the community. Dr. Hawkins was not a scientist; he did administrative work. But he was by no means an ordinary administrative worker. He was himself a Ph.D.—in philosophy. There was no reason for him to go to Los Alamos except that they liked him there.

Of course this does not of itself mean they liked the way

he thought, but he is obviously what you would call a thoughtful man—indeed, he is by profession a thoughtful man. It is not easy to imagine any compelling reason for taking him there except the reason that his way of thinking was harmonious with the thinking of the dominant men. Perhaps there is nothing wrong with that in itself, either. If they did not know about his Communist membership, or if they did know it and knew he had quit (it is hard to see how they would know he had quit—he scarcely knew it himself just before he went there), even if they knew it and thought, "Oh, well, he'll outgrow it; it isn't serious" (he was thirty years old, and it was serious enough for him to stomach the Nazis for nearly two years), then you can understand how they might want him as a sort of bridge between the scientists and the rest of the community—academic like the scientists, but like the rest of the community not specifically trained in science. The point here is that a community in which David Hawkins was considered so desirable an employee is a community in which you will have some difficulty in spotting a Communist.[113]

A point of some interest which we can scarcely resolve here is why Dr. Hawkins wanted, or was even willing, to go to Los Alamos. The scientists and the soldiers who had to go complained frequently, and sometimes bitterly, of the living conditions. Today it is a pleasant community, but then water was rationed, and lesser inconveniences abounded. But that is not an issue to pursue; there could have been a number of reasons, including simple love of adventure. At any rate there was some kind of affinity between Dr. Hawkins and Los Alamos, and this concerns us, simply because we are interested in the fact that a man with a documented Communist record, a non-technical man, should fit so easily into that environment. This is, if you like, an ecological approach to the question whether there are likely to be Communists in the atomic energy project.

The search for individual Communists in the project should be continued by the various detective agencies of the Government, and when found such individual Communists should be expelled and, as appropriate, prosecuted. To go, however, into a large hollow-walled, many-partitioned building which you think may be infested with rats, and arm yourself only with a rifle for their extermination, is juvenile. What you have to do is to alter the environmental characteristics of that building in such a way as to make it uninhabitable or at least very unpleasant for rats, while still healthful or at least endurable for legitimate occupants. Then the rats will leave; you may or may not pick them off with your rifle as they go; at any rate you are rid of them.

The environment at Los Alamos in 1945 was clearly one in which Communists could be very comfortable. Since that time individual Communists have departed and been identified (interestingly, they have usually departed *before* they have been identified as having been Communists—R. R. Davis was the exception in this regard), but the evidence is not at hand that the environment has been so altered as to compel Communists to depart. The mere fact that fish have been caught from a stream does not of itself prove the stream is fished out. In fact, if the major characteristics of the stream remain unaltered, or changed only in ways favorable to fish life, then you usually assume that the previous catches are an argument in favor of fishing further in those waters.

The principal changes at Los Alamos since 1945 are the withdrawal of the Army and the very great improvement in living conditions. Communists are not known to object to either of these alterations.

As a genuine Communist, or seemingly unperturbed ex-Communist, who had access to the most sensitive points in the atomic energy project while remaining without any important personal responsibility, Dr. David Hawkins continues to present a case that is tantalizingly enigmatic from the personal point of view, and from the sociological point of view disturbingly clear. What kind of personnel security clearance standards are you going to have in a community where this man was a key administrative aide, where another recent ex-Communist (with no record of an about-face—*ex* only by drifting, it appears) was in charge of secret documents, where another, a former organizer and cell leader who continued to tell demonstrable untruths after superficially confessing, was the brother of the Director? No wonder Dr. Fuchs was inconspicuous! No wonder Harry Gold turned out to be needlessly alarmed by David Greenglass' relatively open solicitation of new members for the spy ring!

Let us be quite clear that it is perfectly possible that Dr. Hawkins, and the others we have mentioned, were perfectly good security risks. After all, General Groves, we are told, cleared Dr. Frank Oppenheimer on Dr. Robert Oppenheimer's endorsement,[114] and who is to say the General was mistaken? But if these men are good security risks, then where do you draw the line?

Dr. Philip Morrison

What would you do, for example, with the case of Dr. Hawkins' friend, Dr. Philip Morrison? Mr. Tavenner, Counsel for the House Committee, questioned Dr. Hawkins at some length (most of this length lying in Dr. Hawkins' replies) about his acquaintance with Dr. Morrison. The testimony suggests certain ambiguities in the status of Dr. Morrison; it reveals more clearly a good deal of ambiguity in Dr. Hawkins' apparent thoughts and feelings.

Mr. Tavenner: "Were you acquainted with Philip Morrison?" [115]

Dr. Hawkins: "I would like to ask at this point if you could ask me a different question from that one?"

After this forthright statement the session was interrupted

for lunch. When the examiners and the witness had returned, the latter resumed his discourse, as follows.

Dr. Hawkins: "I have really no desire to inhibit or impede the investigations of your committee, sir; and if I knew of anything connecting individuals about whom I feel this hesitation [i.e., to say if he knows them] with the Radiation Laboratory [the investigation had for a time centered around the Radiation Laboratory at Berkeley] or with any crimes in which they might have been directly or indirectly involved, I would not feel any hesitation; but not having such knowledge, I feel very deeply—and I am sure you will agree with this proposition—that there are certain fundamental relations of trust which tend to distinguish American society from other societies in the world today; and unless this kind of question is to your knowledge directly or indirectly related to the subjects you are investigating, I would very much like to ask not to be asked such a question. If there is information of this sort that you would like to get, I would just ask whether there may not be more efficient or direct ways to get it, such as asking the question of the individual himself rather than of me."

Representative Moulder asks, "What was the question, Mr. Tavenner?"

Mr. Tavenner: "The question was whether or not he was acquainted with Philip Morrison. I might say [this to Dr. Hawkins] that you gave the information without hesitancy that Mr. Frank Oppenheimer was the Chairman of the Communist Party cell at Stanford University, or at Palo Alto. . . . How can you explain your reluctance to give us the same information relating to Philip Morrison? What distinction do you make?"

Dr. Hawkins: "Because there the relationship of trust is not involved. Mr. Oppenheimer has testified publicly regarding this, and I hope everybody in his position or my position would do the same thing, then there would not be

the difficulty I now feel so deeply." Think it over. Dr. Hawkins feels a personal difficulty because not all the people he
knows to be Communists will admit they are Communists.
If all the hidden Communists would come out in the open,
Dr. Hawkins could heave a sigh of relief and quit worrying about whether he was going to betray a trust which he
feels these hidden Communists have some kind of right to
depend on. But you can see he is beginning to be a bit ex-
asperated at his having to bear this burden of trust while
those whom he is so gallantly protecting are safe in their
retreats.

Mr. Tavenner: "In other words, you mentioned his name
because he had himself made certain statements before this
committee, and you would not have done so if he had not
made that disclosure?"

Dr. Hawkins: "If he had not I would feel about him, as a
man I respect and who I do not feel has been involved in
any criminal activities, the same way."

Mr. Tavenner: "Then your hesitation is limited only by
the knowledge the committee has?"

Dr. Hawkins: "No; it is limited to people about whom I
would find it very hard to believe they are involved in any
way in criminal activities of any kind, and who do not seem
to me to be within the sphere of the investigation you are
conducting. This is a judgment which in the light of later
knowledge I may be willing to modify."

At this point Mr. Fanelli, counsel for Dr. Hawkins, cannot any longer stand the dissertation on the theme *I know
the man so well I could not possibly answer the question as
to whether I am acquainted with him,* and asks, "Mr. Chairman, may I ask for consultation with the witness at this
point?"

Mr. Moulder: "Yes, indeed."

Consultation.

Mr. Fanelli: "Mr. Counsel, put your question again."

Mr. Tavenner: "Are you acquainted with Philip Morrison?"

Dr. Hawkins: "I have conferred with my counsel, and I would like to say that I am acquainted with Philip Morrison."

Communism obviously does something to the mind, to produce testimony like that. For a moment after this dramatic admission Dr. Hawkins answered questions rather simply. He said the circumstances in which he met Dr. Morrison were social—it was somewhere in Berkeley at a party. A social party, not the Communist Party. Then, having answered some questions, Dr. Hawkins started nailing Dr. Morrison to the barn door again by refusing certain answers.

Mr. Tavenner: "Did you ever attend a Communist Party meeting which he attended?"

Dr. Hawkins: "At this point we come back to my deep feeling on this subject of testifying concerning people who I believe have had no connection with the Radiation Laboratory, and to my knowledge he is a very loyal and patriotic citizen, and I would like to ask you if it is necessary that you ask that question of me rather than of him."

At this point Mr. Velde interposed the observation that the inquiry was not limited to the Radiation Laboratory, but was concerned with Communist activity or any subversive activity anywhere in the country. But Dr. Hawkins still seemed to feel that his own duty lay more in the direction of instructing the Committee, rather than co-operating with it.

Dr. Hawkins: "I am afraid that under the conditions which exist today, very different from the conditions which existed ten or eight or nine years ago with respect to American participation in foreign affairs and with respect to the American Communist Party, the publication of information of this kind does the kind of damage which I know is not the intent of you gentlemen in any way, but which is the necessary consequence of your investigations. I hope my position is not misunderstood. I believe that I am completely honest in my statement of it."

Mr. Moulder: "Proceed, Mr. Tavenner."

Mr. Tavenner: "Do you know whether Philip Morrison has ever publicly announced his membership in the Communist Party?"

And to this question, which to the present writer looks as obviously loaded, as elementarily unfair as *Have you stopped beating your wife?* the Doctor of Philosophy in philosophy, who would not say whether he was even acquainted with Philip Morrison till his own counsel told him to go ahead, answers:

"I don't know whether he has made any statements on that subject at all, sir."

At this point we do not know whether Philip Morrison is or ever has been a Communist, but Dr. David Hawkins has certainly made him sound like one.

Mr. Tavenner [obviously satisfied at this point]: "I may come back to the subject of Philip Morrison a little later."

He comes back.

Mr. Tavenner: "I return now to . . . Philip Morrison. . . . I will have to state to you that as far as I am concerned as counsel, I cannot accept your explanation as to why you are reluctant to testify. . . . I will have to insist that you answer." [116]

Dr. Hawkins: "I have asked in turn, might it not be possible that your Committee could find out these matters in a more direct and satisfactory manner, and had hoped you would not press me to answer them."

Mr. Tavenner: "If Philip Morrison be a Communist Party member at this time, would you expect him to admit it?"

Dr. Hawkins: "I believe that is a kind of hypothetical question which is inconsistent with my knowledge of Mr. Philip Morrison."

Mr. Moulder asks Mr. Tavenner to repeat the question.

Mr. Tavenner: "Is Philip Morrison a member of the Communist Party to your knowledge at this time, or has he ever at any time been a member of the Communist Party?"

Dr. Hawkins: "Might I separate those questions?"

Mr. Tavenner: "Yes. I will break it up. Has Philip Morrison been a member of the Communist Party at any time, to your knowledge?"

Dr. Hawkins: "I would prefer to answer the other part of the question if I may."

Mr. Tavenner: "No; I would like you to answer that question."

Dr. Hawkins: "I have conferred with my counsel, and I can say that I know of nothing connecting Philip Morrison with espionage or any other criminal activity. Beyond that I am unwilling to testify. If you insist on more, I must respectfully decline to answer, and, in doing so, claim, on advice of my counsel, all legal and constitutional rights that I might have, including the protection of the First Amendment."

Mr. Tavenner: "Then you refuse to answer the question."

Dr. Hawkins: "Yes, sir."

Mr. Tavenner: "Do you know of any espionage activity on the part of any individual?"

Dr. Hawkins: "No, sir."

Mr. Tavenner: "Is Philip Morrison a Communist today as far as you know?"

Dr. Hawkins: "I believe that he is not."

What does Dr. Hawkins imagine to be the effect of his refusing to answer the question whether Philip Morrison was ever a Communist, and then answering with an opinion the question whether Philip Morrison is now a Communist?

Mr. Tavenner: "What is the basis of your belief?"

Dr. Hawkins: "Mr. Morrison is a man with whom I have discussed political matters at some length, and I believe that his views are incompatible with the views of the Communist Party."

Mr. Tavenner: "When was the last time you talked to him on that subject?"

Dr. Hawkins: "I can't recall the last time I talked to him on that subject precisely, but I believe it may have been last summer [i.e., the summer of 1950]."

Mr. Tavenner: "When was the first time you talked to him on that subject when you gained such an impression?" Mr. Tavenner is a Machiavellian interrogator, is he not? But Dr. Hawkins is also nimble, this time. He does not answer this one directly.

Dr. Hawkins: "I came to know Mr. Morrison fairly well in the period of the war. As I recall, he came to Los Alamos in 1944, possibly; and my conversations with him from that time would very strongly indicate he was not in sympathy with the Communist position."

(Note in passing that this degree of acquaintance with Dr. Morrison, who was an important nuclear physicist, establishes the importance of Dr. Hawkins in the community at Los Alamos.)

Mr. Tavenner: "Would you think that a statement made by him in defense of Eugene Dennis, one of the eleven Communists tried in New York, as reported by the *Daily Worker* on May 5, 1950, would be consistent with his *change* in attitude toward the Communist Party?" (Italics added.)

Dr. Hawkins: "I would have to see the contents of the statement. I believe there are many reasons and many connections in which a man might be defended. I don't know anything about this particular statement."

Mr. Tavenner: "Dr. Philip Morrison, according to information in the hands of the Committee, was a supporter of the world peace appeal in June 1950. Would you think that a person active in support of that particular work would be favoring Communism?"

Dr. Hawkins: "I would think that a person might support —personally, I did not—might support such an appeal as this without being, or without necessarily giving any indication of being, a member of the Communist Party."

(End of Dr. David Hawkins' testimony concerning Dr. Philip Morrison.)

And of course Dr. Hawkins is right. It is exceedingly difficult to tell whether a man is a Communist, unless he confesses that he is. That is one reason why we cannot be sure there are not a great many Communists in the atomic energy project. They are so hard to spot. Here are David Hawkins and Philip Morrison at Los Alamos during the war, while the fissionable material is accumulating and the bomb mechanism is being developed, discussing politics. Later it turns out that for the five years just preceding Dr. Hawkins' going to Los Alamos he was an active Communist. Still later, it turns out that Dr. Morrison also was at one time, in Berkeley, a Communist. In Boston on May 7, 1953, before the Senate Internal Security Subcommittee, in answer to the question, "You were a Communist yourself?" (i.e., around the year 1939), "I did not conceal it," said Dr. Morrison.[117] This darkens the riddle as to why Dr. Hawkins, in answer to such a simple question about such an unconcealed fact as Dr. Morrison's former Communist Party membership, led Mr. Tavenner of the staff of the House Un-American Activities Committee all around the mulberry bush.

Suppose you had been responsible for security at Los Alamos during the war, and suppose you had had the facts then just as they are here now. Would you have cleared Dr. Hawkins for his administrative duties? And would you have cleared Dr. Morrison for his scientific duties? It is not easy, not unless you decide on a kind of Gideon's band, and are willing to let some promising-looking talent go. One question that seems particularly disturbing is how the Atomic Energy Commission and the Joint Committee can have insisted so firmly that there are no Communists in the project, when they are both so well aware of the inconclusive nature of even such more or less startling evidence as that concerning Dr. Hawkins, Dr. Morrison, and Dr. Frank Oppenheimer.

Of course they can say, Well, this was several years ago, and it happened under the Army. The AEC and the Army may take a lot of interest in their competitive standing with each other as custodians of the nation's atomic security, but to you and me it does not make any difference whether the bad security risks got in under the one or the other, particularly since neither has ever had much control over the "University of California" at Los Alamos. Maybe the professional brass-baiters are happy because if we all get blown up they can put part of the blame on General Groves, but that is no consolation for the rest of us.

On July 9, 1947, just three days before the Washington *Times-Herald* broke the story about Dr. Frank Oppenheimer's former Communist Party membership, the New York *Sun* broke a story on Alexander Van der Luft and Ernest Dineen Wallis, two members of the Special Engineer Detachment who on their departure from Los Alamos in 1946 took with them secret papers and photographs.[118] According to Alfred Friendly, of the Washington *Post*, Senator McMahon *and* Senator Hickenlooper hastened to explain that everything was really all right. Senator McMahon congratulated the Atomic Energy Commission (six months in office at the time) "for their vigilance in discovering the incident . . . so soon after they took over the control of the organization." [119]

Why were these people so eager to make it appear (1) that the incident was not serious, (2) that it had come to light only because the newly installed AEC was so sharp, and (3) all subversion had now been discovered and everyone could relax? In the two years to follow, Senator Hickenlooper, at least, was to come to far different conclusions.

The Washington *Post* editorialized July 13, 1947, under the heading *Atom Sideshow:* "There has been no evidence whatever that security precautions of the AEC are not adequate." The equivocation here is possibly not deliberate. There was in the case under discussion no evidence that the security precautions of the *AEC* were inadequate, but there was specific, positive, uncountered evidence that the security precautions of the atomic energy *project* had been inadequate. "It is inconceivable," continues the *Post,* "even assuming the worst, that any very essential part of the atomic secret, which consists largely of know-how and productive capacity, could have been reduced to a simple précis that the sergeants could carry away." It is not, of course, inconceivable at all. It was not know-how and productive capacity that Dr. Klaus Fuchs carried away. Would the editor of the Washington *Post* care to bet that there are not some very important secrets that could be reduced to a précis so simple as to consist of nothing but a number?[120] And others that would consist of a mere schematic drawing? "This current smear," the *Post* observes shrewdly, anticipating President Truman by more than a year in the use of a now celebrated cliché, "smells suspiciously like the same red herring that has been dragged across the path many times before in the effort to defeat effective civilian development of atomic energy." The *Post* and others made much of the fact that the theft took place "while atomic security was *still the job of the Army.*" (The italics are in the *Post.*)

We are not concerned with whether it was under the Army or under the Atomic Energy Commission. What has that got to do with the essential question? In either case it occurred under the same top-level Administration. More important, it occurred under the immediate administration of the atomic scientists themselves. The Army's representative at Los Alamos, called the "Area Engineer," and the AEC's, called the "Manager of Operations," were both respectable butlers. The head of the house was the Laboratory Director.

It is also correct, if uncomfortable, to remember that the pay-off on what happened in 1945 and 1946 may not have come yet. It happens to be the opinion of the present writer that the most dangerous years were four—1945, 1946, 1947, and 1948—and that thus, technically, honors are easy between the Army and the AEC, and that also thus the present situation—this is 1953—is greatly improved. But none of this helps recover those stolen bomb parts, if, indeed, any were stolen during the four years in question, and none of it helps locate the cache where they may now lie in readiness.

The control mechanisms were weak during those four years, and there were Communists in the project during those four years. That much is not just personal opinion.

Two more notes on Dr. David Hawkins, and then we must attempt to analyze the personnel security problem from another point of view. It should be emphasized that for all our dwelling on Dr. Hawkins and some of his friends, we are not here attempting to be thorough in the case-history approach to the personnel problem. Mr. Pilat and the staff of the Joint Committee have assembled far more cases, and more important cases, individually considered. We concentrate rather on Dr. Hawkins because he seems to be so much more typical, not of Communists or spies, but of the whole population of Los Alamos, of the whole atomic energy project, of the United States. Dr. Hawkins is certainly American, in origin, in training, in outlook. The fact that he was a Communist for five years illustrates the inadvisability of approaching the matter of personnel clearance either casually or with any simple rule of thumb.

In July 1946 Dr. Hawkins made a speech at the Episcopal Church in Albuquerque, New Mexico, in which he offered a "probable explanation" of the behavior of Dr. Allan Nunn May, who at that time was the only scientist known to have given atomic information and materials to the Russians. Exactly what Dr. Hawkins said that day is not available, but we have his statements to Mr. Tavenner concerning the episode. He was, he said, possibly a trifle tipsy when he made the speech, since a friend had given him a drink or two to ward off stage fright.[121] To Mr. Tavenner he gave his considered opinion of Dr. Allan Nunn May's conduct.

"It seems strange to me," he said, "that the most romantic kind of wrong-headedness could lead a person to espionage, when from my point of view the whole point of the internationalism of science is that it provides a moral bond between nations, and that people in different countries who give away their countries' secrets are not helping the international movement." [122]

Amen.

We must say for Dr. Hawkins that, however fallacious his reasoning may have sometimes been, he liked to reason on important subjects. He recalled Dr. Joseph Weinberg, a physicist known to the press for some time as "Scientist X," (in March 1953 acquitted of perjury charges) * mainly "as one with whom I had several conversations on subjects very close to my main field of interest, namely, philosophy of science." Dr. Hawkins and Dr. Weinberg discussed the im-

---

* The student of political affairs may be less forcibly struck by the verdict than by the statement of the presiding judge, reported by the *New York Times*, March 6, 1953 (p. 14), as follows: "United States District Judge Alexander Holtzoff, who presided over the seven-day trial, said he did not agree with the jury's verdict. . . . He declared he respected their decision, 'even though the court does not approve of your verdict.' . . . Judge Holtzoff said the testimony had disclosed 'an amazing and shocking situation existing in the crucial years of 1939, 1940 and 1941 on the campus of a great university in which a large and active Communist underground organization was in operation.' "

pact of modern physics on the ancient philosophical question of free will.

If this was a serious discussion it raises again a doubt as to whether Dr. Hawkins was "really" a Communist, for Communists ordinarily avoid getting into fundamental philosophical questions, knowing that all these things are settled for them, and not wishing to incur, unwittingly, any risk of charges of deviationism. When a man does not know what he thinks, and does not know what the boss thinks, but knows he is supposed to think the same as the boss thinks, he usually keeps his mouth shut. That is the way it is with most Communists. Sometimes, of course, they give a boy with an agile intelligence more freedom, not at all for its own sake, or his, but with the hope that it may baffle the bourgeoisie.

Dr. J. Robert Oppenheimer

Obviously no victim of the Communist mental strait jacket was Dr. Hawkins' Los Alamos boss (and celebrated brother of his Palo Alto Communist boss, Dr. Frank Oppenheimer), Dr. J. Robert Oppenheimer, Director of the laboratory that made the bomb, a man endowed with the most extraordinary gifts of intellect and artistry. Reputedly a physicist of the first rank (at any rate, potentially), his abilities as a writer, speaker, and actor are dazzling. Apparently at his best before a relatively select and intimate group, he can hold a seminar or a Congressional committee in the palm of his hand. He is witty or eloquent at will, and his speech is the beam of a searchlight which he can turn illuminatingly on the darkest area or blindingly into the keenest eye.

He was not the dupe of the internationally important Communist organizer, Steve "Nelson" (born "Mesarosh," in Chaglich, Yugoslavia), who in 1942 reportedly made the attempt to enlist Dr. Oppenheimer as a supplier of atomic information to the Soviet Union.[123] It is not difficult to understand why Nelson thought the effort worth while. As an important Communist official on the West Coast he of course knew about Dr. Oppenheimer's brother Frank. He also knew other Communists and fellow travelers who were frequent visitors in Dr. J. Robert Oppenheimer's home, which at this time seems to have been one of those vital, intellectual, private-Bohemian social centers that are so attractive to parasites and so difficult for the host to control. What may have most encouraged Nelson was a sense of having put Dr. Oppenheimer in his debt.

Steve Nelson's checkered past included a chapter in the Spanish Civil War when he rose to the rank of lieutenant colonel in the International Brigade of the red "Loyalist" Army. This was in 1937. During this time he met an American woman, Mrs. Katherine Puening Harrison, who had come to Spain to meet her husband, a volunteer in the International Brigade. It was Nelson's duty to tell the woman her husband had been killed, and his privilege to be of assistance to her. She returned to the United States and three years later married Dr. J. Robert Oppenheimer.

It is said the Communist Party and the Soviet Government knew of this means of entry which Nelson had to the Oppenheimer home, and regarded it as an important advantage. Nelson appears, however, to have had the grace to avoid the direct approach. He worked instead through George Eltenton, a physicist with the Shell Development Corporation, and Haakon Chevalier, Professor of French at the University of California. (This episode occurred at Berkeley, prior to the establishment of the bomb laboratory at Los Alamos.) Peter Ivanov, Russian Vice-Consul in San Francisco, approached Eltenton, who approached Chevalier, who approached Dr. J. Robert Oppenheimer, all presumably set in motion according to a plan by Nelson. Dr. Oppenheimer rejected the proposal.[124]

According to Mr. Pilat, "Dr. Oppenheimer told Chevalier he considered efforts to secure secret information to be treasonable. He would have nothing to do with such a scheme, he said, showing his friend to the door. When he recovered from his feelings of astonishment and shock, the scientist went to General Groves and in guarded terms mentioned the approach which had been made." [125]

The House Committee on Un-American Activities has reported concerning this incident: "An investigation of the aforementioned scientist * disclosed that neither he nor his wife engaged in any subversive activities and that their loyalty has never been questioned by the Government. Nelson later reported that neither the physicist nor his wife were sympathetic to Communism." [126]

The following observation by Mr. Pilat is worth mulling over a bit: "With his NKVD background, Steve Nelson should have realized that failure to corrupt Dr. J. Robert Oppenheimer was bound to kick back and disrupt his atomic net. Instead of decamping in the middle of the night, to save his young American contacts, the Soviet agent decided to stick things out in Berkeley." [127] The point is that Mr. Pilat's armchair theories on the correct technique of espionage, like Harry Gold's professionally learned rules of that game, failed to take account of the opportunities created by the actual attitude of a significant number of the intellectuals at Berkeley, at Los Alamos, throughout the atomic energy project, throughout the academic and literary strata of the United States.

Nelson lived in Berkeley. He knew the people with whom he was dealing, and while he might misjudge one of them,

---

* This Committee Report does not name Dr. J. Robert Oppenheimer. The identification is made from the circumstances of the acquaintance between Mrs. Oppenheimer and Steve Nelson, which are given with particular detail by the Report and which agree with the uncontested account given by Mr. Pilat, and with that in *Coronet*. See also note 125.

he was clearly confident that he could not misjudge all of them. Mr. Pilat's deductive criticism of Nelson's tactics overlooks the reality that Nelson's failure with Dr. J. Robert Oppenheimer did not in fact make further activity impossible. Dr. Oppenheimer's conduct, which to us today seems laudable, if no more than his duty, to Nelson then seemed doubtless merely odd. To be thus rebuffed by Dr. Oppenheimer was a disappointment, but no reason to abandon hope. In a world where David Hawkins, Frank Oppenheimer, Robert R. Davis, Philip Morrison, and many equally enigmatic associates moved easily—some in the Communist Party, some out, and some in and out, whether in or out apparently making little difference—in a world where the proposal to Dr. Oppenheimer had produced no visible official action—in such a world Nelson's chances of continuing operations evidently still looked good to him. This was Berkeley, the mother-city from which Los Alamos was colonized.

It was scarcely possible that either Dr. Oppenheimer or General Groves should be able to exclude Communists from Los Alamos. For two reasons: (1) Russia was our ally 1941–1945, and you could not risk offending her by being too rough with known Communists; (2) liberals and Communists seemed to be similar in so many ways. The principal difference between them—that is, the liberal's renunciation and the Communist's acceptance of violence—was obscured by the fact that the liberals were in power and the Communists were not, which tended, of course, to corrupt the former and chasten the latter. When the Communists get power it is usually no trouble to tell them from liberals. As it was then, however, the atomic energy project had enough on its hands to separate the isotopes of uranium; it could not simultaneously make the effort required to separate Communists from isotopically related liberals.

Chapter VI ⟿ All Clear?

Mr. Raymond Moley has said of Whittaker Chambers' book, "The great importance of this story is the light it can throw on the Washington atmosphere in which such a malign conspiracy as the Hiss 'apparatus' can take root, grow, and in its extremity find support from very high authority." [128] The Los Alamos atmosphere was one in which Klaus Fuchs and David Greenglass lived comfortably. They did not come to any "extremity" till after they had left Los Alamos. Some of the protective coloring against which even an indiscretion on the part of Greenglass was inconspicuous was provided by Frank Oppenheimer, David Hawkins, and Robert R. Davis.

The backdrop, however, was far larger than that, and in the intricacies of its camouflage design were more important persons than these. For example, in 1948 a great many people were in doubt about the relationship between Henry Wallace and the Communist Party. They knew that the Communists, or many of the Communists, were supporting Wallace, and they knew that Wallace was in some sense "pro-Russian." Instinctively, however, one feels that Mr. Wallace is not fitted for conspiracy. Whether he is a "bubble-head" or a workaday saint, he somehow gives the impression that he intends to "be good . . . and let who will be clever"; and the Communists, of course, certainly will be clever, just as often as they can figure out the way.

Today we feel pretty sure Mr. Wallace is not a Communist, principally because today he is willing to admit past error,[129] but we still think that he has from time to time provided aid and comfort to the Communist cause, whatever his purpose. President Truman thought so in the summer of 1946, when Mr. Wallace took it upon himself to criticize—while he was still in Mr. Truman's Cabinet—the official American proposals for international control of atomic energy, the Baruch Plan.[130] Mr. Wallace, like Mr. Norman Cousins and Mr. (later Secretary) Thomas K. Finletter,[131] believed, as did Andrei Gromyko, that the Baruch Plan favored the United States over the Soviet Union (though most of the world seemed to be impressed by the extraordinary generosity of the proposals), and that this would never do.

The late Secretary James Forrestal thought Mr. Wallace was "completely, everlastingly and wholeheartedly in favor of giving [the atomic bomb] to the Russians." [132] President Truman's diary, as reported in William Hillman's *Mr. President,* has an entry concerning "X," who is generally assumed to be Mr. Wallace (certainly Mr. Wallace took it to mean Mr. Wallace),[133] as follows: "X is a pacifist 100 per cent. He wants us to disband our armed forces, give Russia our atomic secrets and trust a bunch of adventurers in the Kremlin Politbureau. I do not understand a 'dreamer' like that. The German-American Bund under Fritz Kuhn was not half so dangerous. The Reds, phonies and the 'parlor pinks' seem to be banded together and are becoming a national danger." [134]

One might gather from this that President Truman, personally, would not clear Mr. Wallace for access to restricted data in the atomic energy project—unless it were on the fatalistic ground that Mr. Wallace having been, when he was

Vice President, a member of the top policy committee on atomic energy, and having been, when he was Secretary of Commerce, the boss of Dr. Edward U. Condon, head of the National Bureau of Standards (which is in the atomic energy project in part)—that Mr. Wallace knew all he was capable of knowing anyway.

Now if, presumably, President Truman would not want to clear Mr. Wallace, and if, presumably, the House Committee on Un-American Activities would not want to clear Mr. Wallace's former Bureau Chief, Dr. Condon (who, by the way, was scientific adviser to Senator McMahon's Special Senate Committee that drafted the Atomic Energy Act of 1946), and if, as alleged, the AEC's Personnel Security Advisory Board under former Supreme Court Justice Owen J. Roberts did not want the AEC to clear Dr. Frank Graham,[135] for example—can anyone doubt that the whole problem of personnel clearance has been, at least until fairly recently, a practically insoluble mess?

In the chapters that follow we shall see how the campaigns to pass the original McMahon Bill and to promote the original Acheson-Lilienthal Report served the objectives of the Communists' secret war. Had the main purposes of these campaigns been achieved there would be no personnel security clearance difficulties today, for there would be no security program; but while these campaigns failed of their primary objective they incidentally served the vital residual purpose of bringing the protective coloring for Communists almost to perfection, so various in origin and conscious purpose were the American groups united in the promotion of these effectively pro-Soviet plans.

The magnitude of the problem of personnel clearance as it faced the Army in 1945 and 1946, and as it has subsequently (but particularly in 1947 and 1948) faced the Atomic Energy Commission, is not to be even approximately assessed except in the light of those campaigns. Imagine yourself in the position of a personnel security officer in, say March 1948. The law (Atomic Energy Act of 1946) says you are supposed to determine that giving persons access to restricted data will not affect adversely the national security, and you are supposed to make this determination in the light of the persons' character, associations, and loyalty. There is no question of "guilt" by association. You are set up to estimate security risk, and the law says you are to make a positive determination that each individual is all right. You have no more legal obligation to prove he will betray security if cleared than a physical examiner for an insurance company has to prove an applicant he rejects for arrested tuberculosis is going to die soon. Unless you are willing to endorse him, you are not supposed to clear him. That is the letter of the law.[136]

At the same time you have to live in a practical world. You know, for example, that Johannes Steel has spoken with approval of "scientists under the leadership of Secretary of Commerce Wallace and former Secretary of War Stimson." You know Mr. Wallace is currently being supported for the Presidency by the Communists, among others. You know C. E. Calkins, administrative assistant to Senator McMahon, has resigned to work for Mr. Wallace's election.[137] The House Committee on Un-American Activities has called Dr. Edward U. Condon "the weakest link in atomic security," and you know that Dr. Condon was scientific adviser to the Committee (Senator McMahon's) that drafted the Bill under which you are operating. You know further that the legal counsel for that Committee, Mr. James R. Newman, has said that the provisions of the Act under which you operate—the security provisions—"are as dangerous as they are confused." [138]

You do not know yet about Klaus Fuchs. But you do know about Dr. Oppenheimer's brother, Frank, and you know about the Communist custodian of secret documents at Los

Alamos, Robert R. Davis. You know that a large number of Los Alamos scientists have threatened to quit if Davis is not cleared. And you know that the Atomic Energy Act was passed in the Senate by a voice vote without any provisions for personnel clearance.

Would you not be confused about how far to pursue a subject's "associations" and how seriously to take them? You may be sure the Atomic Energy Commission's personnel security clearance staff, and the Atomic Energy Commission itself, were confused.

A state of mind seriously and intentionally hostile to the public interest is hard to detect when it closely resembles a state of mind which has for any reason attained a foolish vogue among the public itself. If everyone comes to the masquerade disguised as Jimmy Valentine, it is no trick at all for the real Jimmy to mingle undetected with the guests, and the hostess should not be surprised the next day if some of her jewels are missing. From August 1945 to May 1949 one scarcely heard a speech or read an article on atomic energy—except in the Hearst and McCormick-Patterson papers—which did not show the influence of the anti-military, anti-secrecy, anti-security slogans of the organized scientists and the liberal press. Since these slogans were endorsed by the Communists, and obviously served the interest of the Soviet Union, a security officer of any degree of sophistication whatsoever could not encounter a zealous attempt to spread them without having his suspicions aroused; but, since the slogans were also repeated by thousands of voices charged with nothing more subversive than a kind of amiable fatuity, coexisting in many instances with intellectual faculties that were anything but fatuous on other subjects, the best informed security officer might very well be the most frustrated.

Today, the whole question of whether the Communists can divert to our destruction our own fissionable material hinges on whether there are many Communists in the project, and to that we have to answer we do not know for sure, because we have not set up any tests that a clever Communist (and there are a few) could not pass, but considering everything it would be quite surprising if there were not a fair number of Communists in the project.

Put it this way: we know they got in during the War, during the "gallant-ally-heroes-of-Stalingrad" era. We know it was almost impossible for three or four years after the War to distinguish them from "progressive" thinkers about atomic energy, including progressive capitalists and progressive military men. We have seen how it came to appear quite possible, during these post-War years, for their own attitudes toward American atomic production and military development to change in time with the moves of expansion and military preparedness on our part. Some of them can have it in the record now that they have helped the United States achieve its new atomic arsenal. The trouble is, we do not know on reflection what the practical consequences of the existence of that arsenal are going to be. One thing seems sure—there has never been a time when the atmosphere of the atomic energy project has not been one in which Communists could live, and there has never been a time when the intellectual fashions of the whole nation were not sufficiently fantastic to enable Communist thought to go unchallenged and inconspicuous.

*   *   *

With the Communists, an unchallenged thought is liable to mean an unchallengeable deed. That is their virtue. I do not know what the Communist thinking on atomic energy has come to be during the past ten years, but if I had been in their place I believe I should have developed (rather firmly by, say, 1948) a set of criteria somewhat as follows for the guidance of all apparatchiks strategically associated with the U.S. atomic energy project:

1. Maximize production, since the possibility of undetectable diversion of material is a positive function of total productive capacity.

2. Minimize internal security.

3. Establish and maintain a system of diversion of information and materials.

4. Establish and maintain some kind of veto power over the use of atomic weapons by the United States.

As corollaries of the preceding propositions:

5. Contribute to productive capacity and efficiency, and get the contribution recognized. With credit for this established you may attack internal security with impunity.

6. Establish diversion points as late in the production process as possible.

7. Concentrate material-accounting efforts as early in the production process as possible.

8. Elaborate, confuse, and generally weaken the official organization of the project, since this will allow maximum freedom of operation to the clandestine organization.

Except for 3 and 6, of course, all these points may be explained as admirable, innocent, or at worst stupid; and except in the cases of 3 and 6 we have no doubt they have all been acted upon.

The present danger is that 3 and 6 may also have been acted upon, and that in consequence Soviet agents may be in a position to assemble atomic bombs in the U.S.A., from components made in the U.S.A., for use against the U.S.A.

It is fleeting consolation to reflect that in any case the number of bombs in the Communist cover shops cannot be very great, for in the words of the *Scientific Information Transmitted to the United Nations Atomic Energy Commission:*

". . . the secret production of one bomb per year would create a definite danger, and the secret production of five or more per year would be disastrous." [139]

Part Two

PAST RECORD

Chapter VII ✑ Destination Tokyo—or Professor Blackett's Clue

The Soviet-Nazi pact emerged in the latter part of August 1939; the Soviets and Nazis quickly partitioned Poland; and World War II was under way. Earlier the same year the atomic energy project began.

In the general excitement of the scientific world over the implications of the recently discovered phenomenon of uranium fission, a few scientists—most notably, perhaps, Dr. Leo Szilard, émigré from Hungary to the United States via Great Britain—realized the potential political importance of the discovery in a world already committed to war, cold or hot. Dr. Szilard and his associate Dr. Eugene Wigner had two levers with which to budge the world of affairs. One was direct acquaintance with Dr. Albert Einstein, who by a trick of fate had achieved a unique reputation not only among scientists but also throughout an awe-stricken laity. The other was the possibility of contact with President Franklin D. Roosevelt through Dr. Alexander Sachs, economist, of New York City.[140]

About three weeks before the Nazi-Soviet pact was announced Dr. Einstein wrote a letter addressed to President Roosevelt, and about six weeks after the invasion of Poland Dr. Sachs, as courier for the letter and expounder of the implications of its contents, got his audience at the White House. From the date of that conference, October 11, 1939, the concern of the American Federal Government with atomic energy has been continuous. A succession of "high-level" committees was appointed to co-ordinate the activities of scientists in the work with uranium, and funds were allocated from time to time for the support of such work.

Dr. Szilard has said that from March 1939 to October 1939 the scientists had no official recognition, and that from October 1939 to the end of 1941 they had too much official recognition.[141] What he meant by this is not very clear. As we shall see below, Dr. Szilard may be that natural sort of human being who when he gets what he wants does not want it. In any case, he and his confrères wanted official recognition and they got it. Whether they got too much, or for whatever reason, the project seems to have languished for about two years.

"At the end of 1941," says Dr. Szilard, "there was an important change for the better. This change came in the wake of a visit which Dr. Oliphant of Birmingham, England, paid to this country around the middle of the war. Dr. Oliphant attended one of the meetings of the Uranium Committee as a guest and was not very much impressed by the organization and official guidance of our work. Disregarding international etiquette, he told anyone who was willing to listen what he thought of us. Considerations other than military secrecy prevent me from repeating the exact expressions he used. But he got results."[142]

Dr. Szilard, who has listed "brass-baiting" as one of his favorite hobbies, apparently amused as well as edified an after-dinner audience with this anecdote, told in a speech delivered December 3, 1945, at the Hotel Astor in New York, at the end of a three-day forum on "The Challenge of the Atomic Bomb," conducted by the "Nation Associates," celebrating the eightieth anniversary of the *Nation* (magazine, that is).

The "Dr. Oliphant of Birmingham" is Dr. M. L. Oliphant, Australian-born scientist and later adviser to Prime Minister Evatt. In August 1950 he was quoted by the *New York Times* as saying that he would consider the use of atomic weapons a moral crime,[143] but apparently he was less sensitive to such ethical considerations in 1941, and was merely outraged at the American lack of efficiency.

It is an accepted fact that there was a sharp acceleration of pace in the atomic energy project toward the end of 1941, but the Smyth report does not give Dr. Oliphant so much of the credit (or blame if he now prefers that). Neither will most Americans, who do not usually think of Pearl Harbor as being "around the middle of the war." There were undoubtedly a number of factors involved in the quick pickup: Dr. Oliphant's visit, the complementary visit to England of Dr. Pegram and Dr. Urey, Pearl Harbor, the political reunion of British and American Communists with their own countries following Hitler's invasion of Russia, and the inscrutable character of growth and development in general, whereby the graph of ascent is nearly always jagged.

From December 1941 to August 1945 the making of the atomic bomb is one of the most astonishing accomplishments in history. We shall not attempt to go into the details of it, but note that of the necessary phases—(1) research and development, (2) design and construction, (3) production, and (4) use—the first required scientists, the second and third engineers and workmen, and the fourth soldiers. The phases, though generally in chronological sequence, overlapped far more than usual because of the extraordinary sense of urgency.

Many things contributed to this, including the employment of rival processes, but all was dominated, of course, by the spirit of a drive toward victory, east and west. Research and development relating to the bomb mechanism itself continued to the very end. Indeed, at Hiroshima the first and last stages, i.e., development and use, seem to have coincided, for the Hiroshima bomb was apparently of a type that had never previously been tested, the Alamogordo and Nagasaki types being generally similar.[144]

But after making allowances for this overlapping, the scientists' schedule was still, for the most part, ahead of that of the other workers, and they were therefore able, as they were inclined, to speculate early on the future. This was particularly true at an installation like the Metallurgical Laboratory of the University of Chicago, where the whole program was developmental, and it seems to have been very particularly true of Dr. Szilard, a man of remarkable force and imagination, even if, as we hazarded the guess above, he delights more in the chase than the quarry. In this instance the hunt palled upon him before the kill, and he decided in March 1945 that the atomic bomb was a Bad Thing.

"During 1943 and part of 1944," he says, "our greatest worry was the possibility that Germany would perfect an atomic bomb before the invasion of Europe. . . . In 1945, when we ceased worrying about what the Germans might do to us, we began to worry about what the government of the United States might do to other countries." [145] This is shocking, and no doubt was meant to be. Dr. Szilard is a kind of Socratic gadfly.

There is nothing impishly provocative, however, about the following account of the initial formulation of Dr. Szilard's "worry about what the government of the United States might do to other countries," as given by Dr. Eugene Rabinowitch, editor of the *Bulletin of the Atomic Scientists,* in his book *Minutes to Midnight* (pp. 11–12):

In March 1945, Dr. Leo Szilard, one of the instigators of the Atomic Bomb project, directed a memorandum to President Roosevelt. . . . In this memorandum Dr. Szilard said that the role of the atomic bombs in the years following the war would become more important than their wartime use, and that they would adversely affect the position of the United States by their very existence. . . .

Dr. Szilard pointed out that at the end of her war with Germany, the Soviet Union would undoubtedly give a high priority to the work on uranium, but perhaps would not carry out this work on a large industrial scale unless we detonated at least one of our atomic bombs, and thus demonstrated the success of this development. He continued:

. . . "Keeping constantly ahead of the Russians in our production of these heavy elements [meaning uranium 235 and plutonium] will not restore us to a strong position," he said. "No quantity of these 'active' materials which we may accumulate will protect us from attack, and so far as retaliation is concerned, we might not be able to do more than destroy the large cities of Russia which are few in number and the economic importance of which is in no way equal to the economic importance of our own cities. Thus it would appear that we would not gain an overwhelmingly strong position in a war with Russia merely by accumulating an enormous quantity of these elements, or by increasing, as we might, the efficiency of our bombs.

"The strong position of the United States in the world in the past thirty years has been due to the fact that the U.S. could out-produce every other country in heavy armaments. THE EXISTENCE OF THE ATOMIC BOMB MEANS THE END OF THE STRONG POSITION OF THE UNITED STATES IN THIS RESPECT." [Capitals supplied.]

A certain number of Americans have found this, and still find it, an astonishing position for Dr. Szilard to take in March 1945. He is not the man to take a position without finding some sort of ground for his feet, but the speed of this about-face takes the onlooker's breath, if not Dr. Szilard's. Here is the man who promoted the atomic bomb—if it can be said that any one man did [146]—who successfully urged the United States to spend two billion dollars on the first atomic bomb, and just as it appears certain of success and nearly ready for use he says this kind of weapon is the sort of thing that from the point of view of the United States ought not to be allowed to exist at all, as it is peculiarly dangerous to this country even at a time when no other country is known to have it, and will be peculiarly dangerous to this country even if we should succeed in maintaining perpetually a lead in the quality and quantity of such weapons. The normal reaction to that opinion from that source is—Dr. Szilard, why didn't you think of that sooner?

Dr. Szilard is certainly a man who is usually very forehanded with his thoughts. He is by no means an ivory-tower dreamer. Two and a half years before Pearl Harbor he correctly anticipated the necessity for the United States to arm itself in the most progressive manner against Germany; and in March 1945, at a time when the Soviet Union was customarily referred to as our gallant ally, he was speculating on the nature of a war between the United States and the Soviet Union.

The fundamental characteristics of the respective power potentials of the U.S. and the U.S.S.R. have not changed appreciably over the past fifteen years, or if they have, it is a change in the direction of greater resemblance, not less. How then could such a prophetically astute observer as Dr. Szilard have urged upon the United States in 1939 so great a commitment to a weapon which in 1945 he was to state meant THE END OF THE STRONG POSITION OF THE UNITED STATES?

A similar question could be asked of sixty-odd colleagues of Dr. Szilard at the Metallurgical Laboratory. "On the afternoon of July 16, 1945," Dr. Robert M. Hutchins, the precocious former President of the University of Chicago and current grand vizier of the Ford Foundation, has told us, "a group of nuclear scientists met around a conference table in a small hushed room in the metallurgy building of the University of Chicago. They were meeting in an effort to save tens of thousands of civilian lives, if not, indeed, all humanity. At 5:30 that morning, on the desert in New Mexico, the first atomic bomb had been successfully detonated. THESE MEN WHO HAD HELPED CONSTRUCT THE BOMB HAD NOW DEDICATED THEMSELVES TO SUPPRESSING IT." [147]

The last sentence, which we have here capitalized for emphasis, and to show that we have not been careless in copying it, really says that the men who had helped construct the bomb had now dedicated themselves to suppressing it—on the day it was tested. The conversion of St. Paul on the Damascus road seems hardly more abrupt, but it might well be both irreverent and inaccurate to press the comparison further. Concerning these nuclear scientists, what, the ordinary American is bound to ask, was eating them?

"Their purpose," says Dr. Hutchins, "was not exclusively humanitarian." Their immediate practical purpose was to prevent, if possible, the use of the atomic bomb in the war against Japan. Why they wanted to do that, Heaven knows, and students of psychology may guess. But there was a very sufficient reason why anyone sympathetic to either the Soviet Union or international Communism would have been pleased with their action, as we shall see below when we examine the views of Dr. P. M. S. Blackett, the British apologist for Soviet policy. Meanwhile, let us return to the narrative of Dr. Hutchins, who does attempt to explain their motive. "They knew," he says, "that if an atomic bomb were dropped over Japan, all hope of preserving the atomic secret for the United States and other traditionally peace-loving nations would be lost forever.

"These men knew that once the bomb was dropped, once the world learned that fission chain reaction could be accomplished, atomic bombs could be produced by any reasonably advanced nation on earth, and that the end result could be annihilation of all life on this planet." If they knew this, which other equally eminent scientists did not know and do not know yet, we are still in the dark as to why they ever went to work for the Metallurgical Laboratory in the first place. If the knowledge that fission chain reaction can be accomplished involves the likelihood of annihilating all life on the planet, why had they striven so energetically for the accomplishment of fission chain reaction?

This opinion of Dr. Hutchins, that the Met Lab scientists were engaged in a kind of "retreat from reason" and because of a failure of nerve or some variety of anti-intellectualism were trying to put the djinn back in the jug, is at variance with the expressed judgment of the authors of the "Franck Report," prepared by a committee of seven distinguished scientists and transmitted to Secretary of War Stimson from the Metallurgical Laboratory June 11, 1945—five weeks earlier than the meeting Dr. Hutchins describes.[148]

The Franck committee and Hutchins' heroes were alike in that each group was supposed to represent the Met Lab and each had as its primary purpose "to warn against the use of the atomic bomb against Japan." [149] The quoted words are those of Dr. Rabinowitch, himself a member, as was Dr. Szilard, of the Franck committee. Dr. Rabinowitch concurs with Dr. Hutchins that the scientists were not actuated solely by idealism. "The moral and symbolical significance of the act of introducing atomic energy to mankind by wiping out the whole population of a city was not mentioned in the Franck Report, although it weighed heavily on the minds of its authors." [150] Why they were so bravely silent about this moral burden and when they began to feel it are not stated. What is stated makes clear that this group of distinguished men was NOT concerned with "preserving the atomic secret for the United States," or for anybody else.

"It would be foolish to hope to retain our leadership in nucleonics by secrecy," said the Franck Report, dispatched five weeks earlier than the meeting at which, according to Dr. Hutchins, the Chicago scientists were so much concerned to prevent the use of the atomic bomb against Japan in order to preserve the secret for the United States. And the Franck Report followed consistently its premise that an attempt at secrecy would be foolish.

". . . the military advantages and the saving of American lives achieved by the sudden use of atomic bombs against Japan may be outweighed by the loss of confidence and by a wave of horror and repulsion sweeping over the rest of the world, and perhaps even dividing public opinion at home," reads the Report.

"From this point of view, a demonstration of the new weapon might best be made, before the eyes of representatives of all the United Nations, on the desert or a barren island. The best possible atmosphere for the achievement of an international agreement could be achieved if America could say to the world: 'You see what sort of a weapon we had but did not use. We are ready to renounce its use in the future if other nations join us in this renunciation and agree to the establishment of an efficient international control.'"

Obviously, from such a "demonstration," even more surely than from use in battle, the world would have "learned that fission chain reaction could be accomplished." The "hope of preserving the atomic secret" would have been equally well lost, and in addition the time and nature of the Japanese surrender and the end of the war might well have been far otherwise than they came to be so soon. This is the hard core of the matter, as we shall see in a moment.

Insofar as Dr. Hutchins' account of the frantic gathering on July 16, 1945, is inconsistent with the statements of the

Franck Report we can be pretty sure the latter are more accurate. The articulate politically minded nuclear scientists of 1945 and all the subsequent years have never been interested in "keeping the secret." On the contrary they have never wearied of assuring the layman there is no secret to keep.

What these scientists were interested in, weeks and in some cases months before the end of the war, was international control. There is, of course, nothing unnatural or derogatory about this fact. A great many estimable people have been interested in international control. The inner circle of top scientists who started the atomic bomb project in the U.S.A. were international in origin.[151] They selected the U.S.A. for logical reasons as their dwelling place, their workshop, and a bastion against the dictatorships of the right from which the majority of them had fled. While during the years that have since elapsed they have probably developed for the land of their choice a devotion perhaps more intense than that of a native, and almost as unquenchable, they would naturally in their early years have escaped any chauvinistic prejudice in favor of the prosperous giant of the Western hemisphere.

There were good reasons why these men were interested in international control, and understandable reasons why they did not feel with the same force as the majority of their more silent colleagues at the University of Chicago's Met Lab the argument for the use of the bomb that it would be to the immediate military advantage of the United States and would save U.S. soldiers' lives. The last argument seems to have been the clincher with Dr. A. H. Compton, his brother Dr. Karl T. Compton, and other distinguished scientists whose advice finally prevailed. Perhaps the latter were less detached, perhaps their view was neither so long nor so broad as that of the Franck committee and the conference described by Dr. Hutchins. But the average American certainly agreed with the Comptons, et al., and even today is pretty much unmoved by what Dr. Hutchins seems to have considered a touching account:

"Before the hot dark closed down on Chicago that day [July 16, 1945], a solemn letter had been drafted to the President of the United States and signed by sixty-five members of the University's scientific staff. It petitioned the President to prevent the dropping of the bomb.

"Receipt of the letter was never acknowledged.

"Five days later, two members of the group were delegated to fly to Washington and appeal personally to James F. Byrnes, then Chairman of the President's Committee on atomic research. This appeal likewise was ineffectual. The bomb was dropped over Hiroshima on August 6, the next over Nagasaki.

"Then and there our opportunity to control atomic energy vanished." [152]

To the statement that the appeal not to use the bomb was ineffectual the average American will reply, Good; and to the statement that "Then and there our opportunity to control atomic energy vanished" he will reply, Nonsense, observing at the same time that Dr. Hutchins is now talking about "control," where previously he was talking about "preserving a secret."

Even so, the full and candid story of the whole episode has not yet been told, nor its consequences estimated. Pending a number of autobiographical revelations—and, of course, we do not know whose autobiography is going to be most revealing when it comes—the best we can do in attempting to understand this affair of Dr. Szilard's memorandum to President Roosevelt, the Franck Report to Secretary of War Stimson, the petition of the sixty-five scientists to President Truman, and the two-man mission to Mr. Byrnes, is to examine the known facts and try to fit them into a serious

pattern that makes some kind of sense. The reasons alleged
so far plainly do not cohere.

All hands have disclaimed moral idealism as the main
motive. It is hard to tell whether this disclaimer is due to a
genuine lack of moral conviction about the matter, or to
a belief that the persons whom they were trying to influence
would not be influenced by moral considerations. At any
rate, Dr. Szilard, Dr. Franck, and their colleagues undertook to argue not from moral principle, but from considerations of prudence, prudence exercised in the national interest of the United States. Their arguments centered largely
around the proposition that the United States is peculiarly
vulnerable to atomic attack, because of (1) its physical characteristics, notably its important concentrations of heavy
industry, and (2) its political and psychological characteristics, amounting to a constitutional inability to play the role
of aggressor, a role said to be peculiarly advantageous in an
atomic era. In view of this special weakness, particularly in
comparison with the Soviet Union, the argument ran, it was
extremely important that the United States should take the
lead in preventing the use of the atomic bomb in warfare,
even if this meant sacrificing a momentary advantage over
Japan.

"All of us," wrote the Franck committee, "familiar with
the present state of nucleonics, live with the vision before
our eyes of sudden destruction visited on our own country,
of a Pearl Harbor disaster magnified a thousandfold and
repeated in every one of our major cities." [153]

The inevitable question is, Why did this vision come before your eyes in 1945, when it was not there in 1942, 1943,
or 1944? When Dr. Oliphant rebuked you for not getting
ahead fast enough with the work on the bomb, and when the
Army by its security regulations allegedly interfered with
your progress in the rapid development of the bomb, where
was the vision then of a thousand Pearl Harbors?

The general characteristics of the United States, physical, political, and psychological, were the same in 1942 as in 1945. What caused these scientists to change their minds? It is not as if they had been drafted to do a job that they never really believed in anyhow, and at last saw an opportunity to make their opinions felt. These men—Dr. Szilard most conspicuously, but all of them collectively as well—sold this weapon to the United States, and criticized the United States for not buying it sooner. Then, on the eve of its practical utilization they initiated a vigorous campaign to persuade the leaders of the United States that the very existence of the weapon was dangerous to this country and that its use would imperil the eagle that used it more surely than the prey upon whom it was used. Who is to say that in the light of eternity this was not true? But who will aver that the nuclear scientists in this military-political imbroglio were viewing the thing in the light of eternity?

These men did not appear to seek the level of wisdom from which it is seen that they who take the sword shall perish by the sword; there was no doctrinaire pacifism in their counsel. They owed the United States war service, since they had not chosen the only honorable way out of such service, which is conscientious objection, on religious grounds, to all war. It is true that because of their extraordinary gifts of intellect, their service was not supposed to consist of blind obedience; but their deviation from that path was supposed to be away from the blindness rather than away from the obedience.

In a temporal frame of reference, it is simply not true that the United States is peculiarly vulnerable to atomic attack. It is true that we have important areas of industrial density, but the strategic distribution of these is certainly luckier than that of comparable areas in England, Germany, and Japan—or France and Italy, for that matter. To say that Russia's concentrations of heavy industry are less than ours is in part simply another way of saying she has less to lose; following that line, the geographic entity most secure against atomic attack is Antarctica. On balance, however, a sober estimate can be made that Russia has in this regard some physical advantage over us, for two reasons: (1) while the United States is a large country, the Soviet Union is larger, and (2) the Soviet industrial system is newer and may therefore be more consciously dispersed. Even this is no more than plausible conjecture, for (1) the nature of the Soviet dispersal is obscured by the extreme Russian addiction to that secrecy which some of our scientists never tire of telling us is such an impediment to material civilian and military progress, and (2) the consequences of dispersal are undoubtedly more complex than a mere reduction of the chances of any one installation's being hit under enemy attack, and all these consequences cannot be anticipated.

More important than the difference between the two great powers in physical vulnerability, which we will for the argument admit favors somewhat the Soviet Union,* is the difference in political organization and the public temper. The authors of the Franck Report contended that totalitarian governments have an advantage, but this is manifestly absurd. Even in the specific matter of "unlimited power over the movement of population and the location of industrial plants," which was mentioned as a qualifying advantage, it is to be doubted whether the Soviet Union has built many

---

* This concession is in error, if the following from the February 1953 *Fortune* is correct: "Grave military weaknesses [in the Soviet Union] remained [in 1950]. . . . Since air defenses remained immature and the bulk of production in many critical lines—steel, petroleum products, aluminum, tractors (tanks)— was concentrated in a handful of factories, the country and its industrial labor force, packed into the cities, *were acutely vulnerable to strategic bombing*." (Italics added.)

cities more rapidly than Oak Ridge was built, or whether there can be found in history any migrations of the scope and industrial efficacy of the American population shifts of World War II in general.

The extent to which we did or did not ourselves adopt totalitarian means to accomplish these shifts is at this point irrelevant, since we are for the moment arguing results; but we may note in passing that we had no concentration camps. Americans like to travel anyway. Management over here does not need "unlimited power over the movement of population and the location of industrial plants." Put up a plant in the Western desert or the Southern mountains, hang out a "Help Wanted" sign, and you will have applicants from every state in the Union, who want to see what you are doing and very shortly tell you how you really ought to be doing it. It is exasperating at times, but it gives the country a flexibility that the majority of Europeans and Asiatics do not understand.

Most of the psychological characteristics which give America an advantage in all-out war, atomic or otherwise, are of an amiable nature. This has led foreign observers to the conclusion that we are incapable of aggressive action, and such is the nature of our very considerable national vanity that we encourage them to believe, and we more or less sincerely tell ourselves, that Americans are a peace-loving lot who will take a great deal of shoving around before they strike back, and that Americans would never under any circumstances make the first move in war. How all this is supposed to square with the record of a nation that was born in revolution, that tested its powers of endurance in a civil war of greater magnitude than all the international wars of a century, that dealt far more summarily with the Indians than Rome ever dealt with the Gauls, and that has twice gone round the world to involve itself in the destruction of the most impressive armies of modern times—this is not explained by the Americans who boast of, or the foreign observers who seem to rely upon, the "peace-loving" nature of the American people. It is one thing to support official utterances that we seek only to maintain a just peace—such support is on the face of it our political duty, and so far as we can be sincere about it, it is our moral and religious duty as well; but we ought not to deceive ourselves about our natural characteristics.

The American tradition of political liberty and personal independence is of course of the greatest advantage in the final defense of the country against atomic attack, and it is the advantage which potential enemies are the most likely to miscalculate, since it is the one with which they have the least acquaintance. The Japanese people did not submit to the occupation by American forces merely because a great many Japanese had been killed at Hiroshima and Nagasaki; they submitted because the Emperor ordered them to do so. By contrast, there is no one in America with either the official or personal authority to command a surrender of the same kind. The degree of centralization of authority which gives dictatorships their vaunted ability to launch an all-out surprise attack more abruptly than is possible under a system of checks and balances simultaneously increases the vital dependence of the whole nation on its capital, and hence increases its vulnerability to a well aimed single attack.

Whatever the relative value and disposition of Russian and American industrial centers, there is little doubt that the destruction of Moscow would be a genuine decapitation of the Soviet organization, while it requires no cynicism to observe that the destruction of Washington would be primarily symbolic. The dispersal of authority, which we have accomplished through checks and balances, through states' rights, through private-enterprise economy, through separation of church and state (without either one's withering away), through the abolition of title and rank, and through a general spirit of intractability—popularly noticed most often in its Brooklyn and Texas manifestations, but actually pervading the whole country—this dispersal is more important than the physical dispersal of industrial centers.

The vulnerability of any country to atomic attack has a positive correlation with both its physical concentration and its organizational centralization. Japan was the ideal target. Japan's coefficient of vulnerability was on the order of the sum of Russia's and Great Britain's. The United States, of course, considering everything, is less vulnerable than any other major power, in spite of alarmist nonsense to the contrary. That is, less vulnerable to atomic attack by air. When the Franck Committee wrote that an aggressor "can place his 'infernal machines' in advance in all our major cities and explode them simultaneously, thus destroying a major part of our industry and a large part of our population, aggregated in densely populated metropolitan districts . . ." [154] they were indeed spotting Achilles' heel, as we have seen. But the situation in this regard was the same in 1939 and in 1945; hence this intrinsically important observation does not of itself account for the change in the attitude of these scientists.

The only reason for the change that stands up pretty well under analysis has been suggested by Dr. Szilard.

"IN 1945, WHEN WE CEASED WORRYING ABOUT WHAT THE GERMANS MIGHT DO TO US, WE BEGAN TO WORRY ABOUT WHAT THE GOVERNMENT OF THE UNITED STATES MIGHT DO TO OTHER COUNTRIES." [155]

The thinking of the most energetic of the original promoters of the atomic bomb project was dominated by fear of the Nazi threat, and when that threat faded all their thinking changed. When they argued that the United States was peculiarly vulnerable to atomic bombs, it is possible that they were seeing this for the first time because previously they had been obsessed with the image of Germany

—a country undoubtedly more vulnerable than the United States to atomic attack. The trouble is that neither the original emotion of fear of the Nazis nor the subsequent emotion of relief at the destruction of the Nazis can be reasonably supposed to have clarified their perception of the true relationship between the United States and the Soviet Union. Nor can it be supposed that such an international group would naturally be equally sensitive to the menaces of a blatant quasi-paranoid racism, such as Nazism, and of a theory of history and society, such as Communism, sponsored if not practiced by the Soviet Union, which had been one of the three great antagonists of Hitler.

In 1945 Dr. Szilard and Dr. Einstein could be coolly skeptical of the merits of military secrecy and other measures of internal security, but four or five years earlier, according to Dr. Alexander Sachs, the historic intermediary with President Roosevelt, "the scientists, Dr. Szilard, Dr. Wigner, and Dr. Einstein were all of the same view, that there had to be secrecy against leaks to the enemy." [156] Which time were they right? They were apparently more alert in 1941. A man cannot stay keyed up all the time. If their great crisis was past when General Eisenhower invaded the Continent, and ours was not, that simply means we should have turned more completely than we did to other advisers, to men who understood the menace of Communism as well as these particular atomic scientists had understood the menace of Nazism.

While this theory that a number of important scientists lost their momentum after the Nazi danger waned commends itself once we have seen it suggested by Dr. Szilard,[157] and while it is adequate to explain lack of enthusiasm for using the bomb against Japan, it seems of itself scarcely adequate to explain the fervor with which the opposition to such use was pressed. That fervor implies a political objective of some kind related somehow to the proposed American use of the atomic bomb against Japan.

It is not necessary to suppose that the authors of the Franck Report or the signers of the letter of July 16, 1945, knew what this objective was, but it is logical to suppose the existence of an objective—which was not abstract morality or Christian principle (as these were not invoked), was not quick American advantage (as this was to be sacrificed), was not demonstrable long-range American advantage (as the arguments here were in part self-contradictory and for the rest inconclusive), and was not mere relaxation after the defeat of the archenemy Germany (as the campaign against the use of the bomb was not relaxed at all, but vigorous).

A clue is given by Nobel-prize-winning British physicist P. M. S. Blackett, in *Fear, War, and the Bomb,* in his chapter "The Decision to Use the Bombs." The ordinary American, in whom the native hue of resolution is not sicklied o'er with the pale cast of thought, is surprised to learn that this decision was a matter of great controversy, his attitude being that expressed the day after Hiroshima by Mrs. T. O. Fitzgerald of Oak Ridge, Tennessee, who at the time had two brothers-in-law in the Pacific Area, and another, a Marine, who had been killed in action there.

"I think we all feel mighty proud to be a part of this place," said Mrs. Fitzgerald, as reported, along with the statements of a dozen other typical Oak Ridge workers, by the Knoxville *Journal* August 8, 1945. Simple pride, and gratitude for sight of the war's end were what they felt. Mrs. Fitzgerald and Professor Blackett seem to be pretty far apart. Actually, she undoubtedly understands him, by now, better than he does her, as he has been the one in the limelight.

According to Prof. Blackett, "The dropping of the atomic bombs was not so much the last military act of the Second World War, as the first major operation of the cold diplo-

matic war with Russia." [158] He considers quite inadequate
the official statement of President Truman on August 9,
1945, that "We have used it in order to shorten the agony of
war, in order to save the lives of thousands and thousands of
young Americans." [159] He is not impressed by the support
this statement received from Dr. Karl T. Compton, who
wrote in the *Atlantic Monthly* for December 1946, "I believe
with complete conviction that the use of the atomic bomb
saved hundreds of thousands—perhaps several millions—of
lives, both American and Japanese; that without its use the
war would have continued for many months." [160] Nor does
Secretary of War Stimson convince him by comparing the
results of the use of the bombs with what had been anticipated if they had not been used.

Writing in *Harper's Magazine* for February 1947, Mr.
Stimson had said, "We estimated that if we should be forced
to carry the plan [for the invasion of Japan] to its conclusion, the major fighting would not end until the latter part
of 1946 at the earliest. I was informed that such operations
might be expected to cost over a million casualties to American forces alone." [161]

Prof. Blackett is too clever to accept this reckoning of the
savings in human life as the real explanation of the American
decision to use the bombs as quickly as possible. When Mr.
Stimson writes, "We had no bombs to waste. It was vital
that a sufficient effect be quickly obtained with the few we
had," Prof. Blackett italicizes the last sentence as he quotes
it, and finds in it something sinister.

Noting that the invasion of Japan had originally been
scheduled to begin November 1, 1945, the Professor asks,
"Why this necessity for speed? . . . Since the next major
United States move was not to be until November 1, clearly
there was nothing in the Allied plan of campaign to make
urgent the dropping of the first bomb on August 6 rather
than at any time in the next two months. Mr. Stimson him-

self makes clear that, had the bombs not been dropped, the intervening period of eleven weeks between August 6 and the invasion planned for November 1 would have been used to make further fire raids with B29's on Japan. Under conditions of Japanese air defense at that time, these raids would certainly have led to very small losses of American air personnel." [162]

This penetrating analysis blandly ignores the fact that as it happened there was no "intervening period of eleven weeks between August 6 and the invasion planned for November 1" for the simple reason that the bombs employed on August 6 and August 9 made an invasion unnecessary. Also ignored are the facts that the actual atomic raids led to not "very small losses," but *no losses* at all of "American air personnel"; and that eleven weeks of fire raids in preparation for invasion has, from the humane point of view, nothing to recommend it as an alternative to two atomic bombs.

The fact that the outcome established Hiroshima somewhat above Agincourt and Hampton Roads in military history—the fact that the use of two revolutionary bombs was an unparalleled military success, producing surrender more quickly than even the most optimistic estimates had anticipated—this does not blind Prof. Blackett to the apparition of ulterior motives on the part of the United States. Staring steadily past the historic dates which mark the astonishing celerity of the Japanese downfall after Hiroshima, and past the simple statements of Truman, Compton, Stimson, and Mrs. Fitzgerald (sorry—he did not know about Mrs. Fitzgerald), the Professor observes, "A plausible solution of this puzzle of the overwhelming reasons for urgency in the dropping of the bomb is not, however, hard to find. It is, in fact, to be found in the omissions from both Dr. Compton's and Mr. Stimson's articles." [163] Every student of the debate over the decision to use the atomic bomb must be grateful to

Prof. Blackett for thus emphasizing the importance of what the witnesses do not say.

It is important to present Prof. Blackett's theory quite explicitly:

Let us consider the situation as it must have appeared in Washington at the end of July, 1945. After a brilliant, but bitterly-fought campaign, American forces were in occupation of a large number of Japanese islands. They had destroyed the Japanese Navy and Merchant Marine and largely destroyed their Air Force and many divisions of their Army, but they had still not come to grips with a large part of the Japanese land forces. Supposing the bombs had not been dropped, the planned Soviet offensive in Manchuria, so long demanded and, when it took place, so gladly welcomed (officially), would have achieved its objective according to plan. This must have been clearly foreseen by the Allied High Command, who knew well the great superiority of the Soviet forces in armor, artillery and aircraft, and who could draw on the experience of the European war to gauge the probable success of such a well-prepared offensive. If the bombs had not been dropped, America would have seen the Soviet armies engaging a major part of Japanese land forces in battle, overrunning Manchuria and taking half a million prisoners. And all this would have occurred while American land forces would have been no nearer Japan than Iwo Jima and Okinawa. One can sympathize with the chagrin with which such an outcome would have been regarded. Most poignantly, informed military opinion could in no way blame Russia for these expected events. Russia's policy of not entering the Japanese war till Germany was defeated was not only military common sense but part of the agreed Allied plan.

In this dilemma, the successful explosion of the first atomic bomb in New Mexico, on July 16, must have come as a welcome aid. One can imagine the hurry with which the two bombs—the only two existing—were whisked across the Pacific to be dropped on Hiroshima and Nagasaki just in time, but only just, to insure that the Japanese Government surrendered to American forces alone. The long-demanded Soviet offensive took its planned victorious course, almost unheralded in the world sensation caused by the dropping of the bombs.[164]

That is the way it looks to Prof. Blackett It may not tell us much about secret American diplomacy, but it tells us a good deal about the feelings of one who is able to look at things from the Soviet point of view. Mrs. Fitzgerald in Oak Ridge was thinking of her kin in the Pacific—one dead and two to be saved—but Prof. Blackett was thinking of the prestige and postwar position of the Soviet Union, and he assumes that the leaders of the United States were thinking in the same terms.

It ought to be surprising that he finds support for his view from prominent Americans, one of them subsequently Secretary of the Air Force of the United States. Prof. Blackett writes:

Strong support for the validity of this interpretation of these events is found in an account of the relation between the dropping of the bomb and the planned Soviet offensive, given in an article by two American writers, Norman Cousins and Thomas K. Finletter, originally published in the *Saturday Review of Literature*, June 15, 1946. They refer in detail to the report of the committee under James Franck. . . . After analyzing and approving in general the arguments in the report against an initial use of bombs against Japan, and in favor of a demonstration to be witnessed by the United Nations, they write as follows:

". . . any test would have been impossible if the purpose was to knock Japan out before Russia came in—or at least before Russia could make anything other than a token of participation prior to a Japanese collapse.

"It may be argued that this decision was justified; that it was a legitimate exercise of power politics in a rough-and-tumble world; that we avoided a struggle for authority in Japan similar to that we have experienced in Germany and Italy; that, unless we came out of the war with a decisive balance of power over Russia, we would be in no position to checkmate Russian expansion."

This interpretation by Cousins and Finletter substantially confirms our own analysis.[165]

Thus Prof. Blackett on and from Editor Cousins and Secretary Finletter. In one sense he certainly does them an injustice. Their analysis of the problem appeared more than two years ahead of his own, so that it is not really fair of him to say they support him—he should say he supports them. Also, they were more explicit than Professor Blackett's quotation reveals. "The atomic bombing of Hiroshima" was, they said, "the first error" and "the biggest error" of a policy which placed us in a "difficult and dangerous situation"— it was, indeed, "a mountainous blunder." [166] Their support of this statement largely takes the form, as Professor Blackett indicates, of enthusiastic references to the Franck Report.

It is one of the little ironies of history that the United States Air Force, the principal instrumentality for the use of the atomic weapons on which we were increasingly basing our hopes of national security, should have been so long administered in a day of officially designated national peril by a man who had been at some pains to disapprove the only occasions on which atomic weapons had ever demonstrably contributed to our national security. If ex-Secretary Finletter does not think the atomic bomb should have been used against Japan in August 1945, where and when does he think it ever should be used?

But we digress. Prof. Blackett sums up his case as follows: "The hurried dropping of the bombs on Hiroshima and Nagasaki was a brilliant success, in that all the political objectives were fully achieved. American control of Japan is complete [in 1948], and there is no struggle for authority there with Russia." [167]

The Blackett-Cousins-Finletter theory is inconclusive as an explanation of the U.S. decision to use the atomic bomb (a decision which from a national point of view was actually

obvious and inescapable), but it illuminates brilliantly and
for the first time the otherwise incomprehensible campaign
within the atomic energy project to prevent the use of the
bomb. Whether the Americans saw it or not, the Communists
saw that the use of the bomb would mean that the United
States would control Japan, while abstention from use of
the bomb would leave the way open for possible control of
Japan by the Soviet Union.

It may be doubted whether either Dr. Szilard or Dr. A. H.
Compton, the leaders of the divergent groups at the Met
Lab in the summer of 1945, knew that the debate in which
they were engaged was in effect a struggle for the control of
Japan, but in the light of Prof. Blackett's clever exposition
of the whole affair, that is the way it looks now. The fact
that the Compton group won is ground for hope in the current campaign of the secret war. And Dr. Szilard—perhaps
he is glad he lost that round. As Brunhilde disobeyed Wotan's
second command to carry out his first, so America disre-
garded the advice given by Dr. Leo Szilard in 1945 in order
to fulfill with achievement the prophetic counsel he gave
in 1939.

Epilogue for the Franck Report

"The advent of the atomic bomb," Secretary of War Henry
Stimson wrote in September 1945, "has stimulated great
military and probably even greater political interest throughout the civilized world. . . . In many quarters it has been
interpreted as a substantial offset to the growth of Russian
influence on the continent." [168] Can anyone doubt this? And,
consequently, can anyone doubt that astute Communists
would have been fully sympathetic to the efforts of Dr.
Szilard and the Franck committee to prevent that "advent
of the atomic bomb" which was to be such "a substantial
offset to the growth of Russian influence on the continent"?
Let alone the more immediately and sharply decisive effects

in the Far East observed by Professor Blackett and Messrs. Cousins and Finletter.

The *New York Times* for October 8, 1945, carried a radio dispatch by C. L. Sulzberger from London, dated October 7:

"Relations between the great Allied powers, the Soviet Union on the one hand and the United Kingdom and the United States on the other, are unquestionably cooler at this juncture than at any period since the Yalta conference. . . . Soviet irritation against Britain and the United States arises from various differences of opinion. . . .

". . . Stalin . . . Molotov and the Presidium of the Supreme Soviet are said to be especially angry at the United States because of American insistence that, American armed forces having played by far the largest and longest role in defeating Japan (if one excepts China in the calendar sense), an American general should be the supreme executive officer in occupied Japan.

"The Soviet propaganda machine has carefully spread the idea, not only in the U.S.S.R., but also in bordering lands, that the Japanese surrender was principally caused by the entry of the Red Army into the war. The importance and the effects of the atomic bomb have been minimized in this publicity.

". . . it is particularly humiliating to Moscow that . . . orders in the occupied zone should be given by General MacArthur. . . ."

Chapter VIII ⟶ The
Silhouette of Secret War

The air of mystery surrounding the Japanese campaign of the secret war has by no means been entirely dispelled. The whole extraordinary episode took place within the confidential circles of persons involved directly in the atomic bomb project, or in its supervision from the higher levels of administration. There is, however, enough published material to indicate with a minimum of ambiguity that the debate over the use of the bomb was in effect a struggle for the control of Japan. The outcome of that struggle was a disappointment to Communists.

One campaign does not make a war—especially with the Communists, whose special skill is to get somebody else to do their fighting for them. In this instance their forces—conscious and unconscious—though repulsed were intact, and were quickly regrouped, reinforced, and reanimated. Where the campaign not to use the bomb had been a disguised movement within an open war, the new campaigns of the secret war would have to be adjusted to the conditions of a cessation of open hostilities. Not soon again would there be a termination so dramatic as the use of the bomb over Hiroshima, and the almost immediately succeeding American occupation of Japan. But more clearly at stake than ever was world hegemony.

The annulment of Soviet power and the affront to Soviet prestige represented by possible American monopoly of the atomic bomb were not to be endured. It was essential that Russia be provided with atomic information and materials. To this goal there were three main avenues:

(1) Independent research and industry by the Russians,
(2) Espionage and theft by Soviet agents in the American project, and
(3) Acquisition of partnership status in the American project.

The first two of these were, of course, to be used in any event. The third, however, was by far the shortest and easiest, if only the barriers of American "security" could be removed. For espionage and theft the barriers had only to be, and were, penetrated; for the acquisition of partnership status they had to be legally taken down. These barriers, supported by a nationalistic attitude on the part of certain Americans, consisted of military control of the atomic energy project and the systematic employment of official secrecy in regard to atomic science and technology.

Fortunately for the Communists, there were a great many Americans who shared, though for different reasons, their strong aversion to this kind of "security." An impatience with discipline and a recklessly optimistic, open manner characterize the nation generally. Imputations of rigidity and arrogance to the "military mind" are quickly credited, and those who shiver with delight at cloak-and-dagger fiction accept with alacrity the assurance that *only* in fiction are espionage and counter-espionage matters of life and death. Among the influential academic minority these propensities are aggravated by the imperfectly understood international tradition of science, and by admiration for a vaguely defined cosmopolitanism. Thus Americans could readily be found who were glad to do for the Communists, most energetically, what the latter could not do for themselves—discredit the good faith and competence of the armed services of the United States, and attack with ridicule or righteousness the follies and dangers of secrecy.

Among the majority of the population these tendencies were somewhat more than offset by distrust of foreign ideas in general, and Communism in particular; by natural pride of accomplishment in the production of the atomic bomb; and by frank satisfaction in the possession of what was at once assumed to be a decisive national advantage. It was this attitude of the average American which the Communists wished to destroy.

Innocently but effectively enlisted in the attack were many of the better elements of the population, those with zeal for improving their fellows in one way or another—ministers, schoolteachers, members of women's clubs, etc. Far and away the most important were the organizations of "scientists" at the various atomic installations, most notably Chicago, followed in fairly close order by Oak Ridge and Los Alamos. The use of quotation marks around the word "scientists" is appropriate, for some of the genuine scientists at Chicago, Oak Ridge, and Los Alamos did not belong to these organizations, while among those who did belong were a number that could be called "scientists" only by a most unusual extension of the term. The present writer, whose graduate work was done in language and literature and whose later experience has consisted of teaching the "humanities" and of administrative work in the atomic energy project, was urged to sign up as a scientist, and before finally declining was induced to attend two "inner-circle" meetings, and very instructive they were, too. More typical was the case of, say, a chemist or engineer with a pretty good job, not caring to argue with the nagging little group, mostly physicists, whom he privately regarded as somewhat neurotic, but whose hostility might be uncomfortable, considering that they were obviously, for the moment, riding the crest of some kind of wave.

Members of the little group, for their part, were often men with considerable latent ability to organize and promote, eager to leave their impress upon a world which in their own opinion had previously all but ignored them. Capable men, they illustrate anew the difficulty in reconciling the claims of science and ambition. It is not to be blinked, however, that these organizations of "scientists" did include, or were sponsored by, some of the keenest scientific minds in the country.

The task in which these brilliant minds, and others, were so savagely exploited involved the formulation and establishment of (1) a system of national control of atomic energy which would prevent the military development and use of atomic energy in the United States, and (2) a system of international control that would facilitate the general development and use of atomic energy in the Soviet Union.

While it was easy to enlist pacifistically inclined persons in the preliminary work necessary for these massive labors—and thus plans like those of the original McMahon Bill and the Acheson-Lilienthal Report could attract widespread (or seemingly widespread) support and arouse much optimism among the Communists—it was altogether another matter to lay finally in place the capstone of success. As a matter of fact, this was never to be done, and the entire Communist strategy had later to be altered, but hopes were high at the outset.

Accordingly, as preparation for the twin campaigns for anti-military national control and pro-Russian international control, there was set in motion a fantastically energetic propaganda drive with the objective of convincing the American people:

(1) That their magnificent accomplishment in producing an atomic bomb was essentially trivial,

(2) That the atomic coup de grace administered to the aggressive forces responsible for Pearl Harbor was in reality a shameful action,

(3) That the sense of power naturally arising from this successful invention and exploitation of a revolutionary weapon was a dangerous illusion,

(4) That the American monopoly of the new technology and the new weapon was so precarious as to constitute somehow a material liability as well as a moral embarrassment,

(5) That the underlying reason why this new development appeared so much in the guise of a Frankenstein-monster was not the technical development itself, but the sovereign national power of the United States, which had made the very expensive technology possible and in so doing had acquired, alas, full legal authority over it.

These propositions are in themselves so absurd, and so alien to the normal habits of thought of the American people, that their relatively successful propagation in the United States is one of the paradoxes of history. It could not have happened if a number of important scientists had not lent the weight of their justly acquired reputations to organizations including scientific and political charlatans, and encouraged by Communists if not controlled by Communism.

If one looks at the behavior of the United States as a whole in the twelve-month interval beginning August 6, 1945, one seems to see a wavering giant, uneasy with his own imperfectly co-ordinated strength, not quite the dupe of cunningly parasitic advisers, but not quite free either from the quasi-hypnotic spell of their audaciously repeated counsel of self-destruction.

Any detailed expression of the suicidal concepts was, of course, unsuitable for frequent verbatim, or nearly verbatim, repetition; for that purpose were developed the slogans:

(1) There is no secret.
(2) There is no defense.
(3) International control is essential to survival.

Of these, the first was the most important. The second was extensively played upon in a kind of psychological warfare, which was later seen to be of dubious value to the Communists, or anybody else. The third was so complex as to create schisms even among the zealous. One school wanted world government; another, an international agency. But on the first, the no-secret slogan, there was great and enthusiastic agreement.

It cut so many ways. It offended American national pride and undermined American national confidence, both of which had been stimulated by the extraordinary security accomplishment of keeping the atomic bomb secret (successfully against Germany) as well as by the technical and military success. It suggested that anyone else could have done the same thing, technically, if he had wanted to; that our "security" was ineffective and ridiculous; and that morally we were no better than we should be. Finally, it laid a groundwork for amnesty for those who had already violated security. Above all, of course, it suggested partnership status in the atomic energy project for the Russians.

Patient exploration of some of the documents through which these notions were propagated is a perhaps necessary preliminary to understanding today's world conflict of power and principle—a conflict in which the Korean affair may prove to have been a tragic diversion, while the decision beyond appeal was being fought out in the United States in our own atomic energy project.

Look:

(1) The world conflict is not over.

(2) The American atomic energy project is both a major factor in determining the course of that conflict, and potentially a major prize for the victor.

(3) The project is well understood by a relatively small number of persons, mostly scientists, who are internationally, though unevenly, distributed.

(4) The political attitudes of these persons are of great practical importance today.

(5) These political attitudes were most freely expressed and the arguments by which these key personnel were influenced or with which they influenced others were mostly vigorously pursued during the years 1945–49, the pattern having been largely set by June 1946.

Conclusion: The politico-scientistic writings of the period following V-J Day and extending to the beginning of the Korean action are worth careful study.

An immediate analysis, however imperfect, may yet approximate accuracy sufficiently to enable us to take the action necessary to avert a disaster that has been in the making ten years, but has not yet occurred. It may occur any time. The clues to its nature are in the atomic literature. The atomic literature was frankest in 1945 and 1946. Like Edgar Allan Poe's purloined letter, the intent to put the American military program in stand-by and to construct for the Russians the most important atomic-weapons facilities was openly displayed, and—perhaps *therefore*—ignored by the American public. The present writer has shown to several well informed persons the paragraph of the Acheson-Lilienthal Report in which it is proposed that plants like Oak Ridge, Hanford, and Los Alamos be constructed in Russia, and without exception each of these persons said, "I didn't know that was in there." One can only suppose that such persons had never imagined the existence of the degree of daring required to make such a proposal, and thus were incapacitated from recognizing what was frankly delineated before their unobstructed eyes. But more of this later.

But for all this open audacity there is yet much that is veiled and much that is confused. We speak here of campaigns of a secret war, and we hardly know whether we are using a figure of speech or not. To the extent that words are not guns, and to the extent that the speakers and writers of words often had in mind innocent purposes—far other than the only purposes which in fact their words could in a world at war possibly serve, we are speaking figuratively. But to the extent that words in the pattern of the no-secret, no-defense slogans were ceaselessly stimulated toward the end that the balance of physical power in the world might be drastically shifted from favoring the United States to favoring the Soviet Union we are not speaking figuratively at all.

Our "campaigns," which for convenience we label the McMahon campaign and the Acheson-Lilienthal campaign, without assuming that these men were anything but well meaning, are campaigns from the point of view of whatever anonymous agents cherished the purposes rationally attributable to the actions taken. Perhaps in fact no one had any rational purpose. Perhaps the whole monstrous configuration assumes a sinister coherence only as a cloud is backed like a camel, or the rock of the mountain is weathered to a great stone face. It is not possible for us to state with certainty that anyone knew what he was doing. But just to make the thing easier to talk about we may talk *as if* someone knew what he was doing.

Chapter IX ~ Scientific Attitude

To the present writer the conduct of the organized scientists in 1945 appears pathological, but a lucid and sympathetic account of it has been given by Prof. E. A. Shils, social scientist and member of the Board of the *Bulletin of the Atomic Scientists*.

"The detonation of the first atomic bomb against the Japanese in August 1945," writes Professor Shils,[169] "was greeted with great enthusiasm by most journalists and by the populace at large. Only a small proportion of the population saw the catastrophic possibilities, and these people were mainly scientists who had been at work on the bomb over the preceding seven years.

"A group of scientists, numbering about a thousand, formed the nucleus of a great effort to modify American opinion. Of these only a few hundred were really very active. This action taken by American physical scientists was unprecedented. For the first time scientists on a grand scale showed awareness of the effects of their work and a sense of responsibility to prevent its misuse. Their fervor came partly from their deep and guilty insight into what the bomb could do, partly from their startling discovery of their political potency,

and partly from their long-rankling dissatisfaction and un-
easiness over the military's regimentation of their scientific
skills for the purposes of destruction."

It is hard to say whether this passage is more remarkable
for what it reveals or for what it conceals. It reveals, or purports to reveal, a group of chronologically mature men becoming suddenly aware, *for the first time,* of the consequences of their own actions. It reveals, or purports to reveal,
these men with a sudden access of feelings of *guilt,* a state
of consciousness which, if the exclusively rational approach
were proper, would be neurotic, and, if the rational approach
alone were inadequate, would argue the inadequacy of science. It reveals that in spite of these feelings of guilt these
men are eager to exploit a newly discovered advantage over
their fellows in politics, and it reveals a state of envy.

But what it conceals (unwittingly, without doubt) is perhaps of more importance to the rest of us. For the motives
adduced—(1) a guilty conscience, (2) a sense of power, and
(3) a dislike of the Army—do not suffice by themselves to
account for an effect so momentous as the no-secret, no-
defense propaganda drive. It takes more than spontaneous
fervor, it takes planning and organization to make possible
a drive of the scope and intensity of that which supplanted
the May-Johnson Bill with the McMahon Bill for domestic
control, and committed the United States to some kind of
variation on the Acheson-Lilienthal plan for international
control of atomic energy. No doubt the kind of fervor to
which Professor Shils refers gave a well timed boost to the
efforts of those who saw the necessity of redressing a balance
of power which the atomic bomb had shifted against the
Soviet Union, but the co-ordination of effort and the systematic propagation of fervor imply somewhere the attention of organizers whose understanding of the nature of
power and whose hostility to any military forces rivaling

the Red Army did not begin with a sudden moral revulsion against the bombing of Hiroshima.

The guilty conscience motive, which on account of its "subjectivity" must not be permitted to detain us long, is nevertheless a fascinating topic for speculation. Dr. Oppenheimer said that the scientists had by their work on the atomic bomb "known sin." One infers that previously they had not, which suggests a singular degree of either purity or vanity. Professor Shils' version suggests that it was all, in any case, due to "the military's regimentation of their scientific skills for the purposes of destruction." This attempt to evade moral responsibility overlooks the fact that the atomic laboratories were not concentration camps. The only scientific personnel in the atomic bomb project on anything but a voluntary basis were some of the members of the "Special Engineer Detachment," and a few other uniformed personnel, who were indeed regarded as unfortunate compared to some of their colleagues in civilian clothes, drawing larger pay checks for similar work; but who were, on the other hand, for the most part very well satisfied with their positions when they thought of the alternatives in the South Pacific, North Africa, etc. As for the older and more eminent scientists, it was a group of these, headed by Dr. Szilard, who, as we have observed, got the military into the atomic bomb business—not vice versa.

Dr. Oppenheimer indicated that the moral onus is not to be readily transferred. Waldemar Kaempffert in the *New York Times* of October 7, 1945, published a letter from a "young physicist on the staff of the Los Alamos Laboratory" to his family, relating how Dr. Oppenheimer "specifically stated that he would not say one word to alleviate the fears of those of us who might feel we had done a terrible thing, and indicated that this should remain a problem to be solved by our own consciences."

After this bit of severity, Dr. Oppenheimer softened somewhat. "He felt, though," wrote the young physicist, "that we owed a great deal to the people of this country, and that, at the least in the short-term view of things, we had to some extent paid our debt."

There are two disquieting matters here: (1) the coolly objective, let's-try-to-be-fair attitude toward "the people of this country"—who are these people at Los Alamos? of what country are they?—and (2) the apparent feeling that the debt is just about square. In a country where church and state are separate it would appear to be sound doctrine that the individual does not owe his country what is contrary to his religion (thus we make provision for conscientious objectors), but that within the limits of his duty to God he owes his country his life, his fortune, and the allegiance of his sacred honor. Nor is it easy to find a place in this doctrine for differences between the "short-term view of things" and the long-term view. But Dr. Oppenheimer's remarks were evidently well received. "Immediately after the speech, which was greeted with general applause, we saw the photographs of the test you must have read about."

Alternation of qualms and pride was a real or affected fashion of the day among various kinds of sophisticates. Professor Blackett has spoken of the weapon America "was so proud to have developed and so ashamed to have used." [170] If his acquaintance had not been confined largely to an academic minority, Professor Blackett could not in all good faith have applied his statement to "America," as we shall see in a moment, but it is apt enough as a characterization of the more indefatigably articulate of the scientists and the more "advanced" representatives of journalism, the clergy, and the law.

The pride of the scientists was spontaneous—we are told that in the first lurid glare at Alamogordo "Dr. Kistiakowsky threw his arms around Dr. Oppenheimer and embraced him with shouts of glee." [171] The shame was more reflective. "The pattern of the use of atomic weapons," said Dr. Oppenheimer eloquently, "was set at Hiroshima. They are the weapons of aggression, of surprise, and of terror. If they are ever used again, it may well be by thousands or by tens of thousands. . . . But it is a weapon for aggressors and the elements of surprise and terror are as intrinsic to it as are the fissionable nuclei." [172]

W. R. Higinbotham, one time President of the Federation of American Scientists, has told us how the scientists were "weighed down by moral responsibility." [173] This general moral awakening, as Professor Shils has suggested, appears to have been a new thing. The more fashionable attitude previously seems to have been that of Professor Kinsey, who has explained with lofty patience that as a scientist he has no concern with morality. But such an attitude, while it may be all very well for relaxing the force of legislation controlling sexual energy, will never do as a means of establishing legislation for the control of atomic energy.

Dorothy Thompson reported a meeting in Chicago in September 1945, attended by seventeen scientists who worked on the atomic bomb, "who expressed in no uncertain terms their indignation at the 'tragic use' made of the discovery." [174] There is nothing like the scientific attitude—absolutely nothing.

In the original view of the "populace at large," as Professor Shils has observed, the use of the bomb was anything but tragic. The natural American attitude seems to have been rather accurately expressed in a feature story published by the Knoxville *Journal* August 8, 1945, quoting opinions concerning the Hiroshima bomb of various employees at Oak Ridge. We have previously noted the feelings expressed there by Mrs. T. O. Fitzgerald. Other citizens quoted in the same article were M. P. Shelley, Fred Blackwell, James R. Whitcomb, Fred Kibler, James Kirk, Mrs. M. L. Piker, Mrs. J. A. Elkins, Mrs. Helen Cole, T. F. McVeigh, the Rev. Robert Lundy, Mrs. Eliza Hofferbert, James Welch, Mrs. Roberta Phillips, and A. A. Oldfield.

These people, most of whom are known to the present writer, are in many ways a good cross section of America. They came to Oak Ridge from the North, South, East, and West. They did have above the average general education, and they had at the time, of course, well above the average immediate knowledge of the atomic bomb project. They were not, however, scientists, though one of the ladies was the wife of a chemist who had an important position in the electromagnetic isotope-separation plant. Most important, they were interviewed before the propaganda drive had got beyond the most select laboratory circles and the staffs of the more liberal newspapers and periodicals.

We shall not quote them all, but note that Mrs. Phillips, of Charlottesville, Virginia, whose husband, Lt. A. E. Phillips, and brother, Lt. Cmdr. S. C. Stoneham, were then on duty with the Navy in the Pacific, said: "The news was really more thrilling to me than the V-E Day broadcast. Now I know they'll both be home sooner than I had dared hope."

Mr. Oldfield, veteran of World War I, and Commander of the Oak Ridge American Legion Post, said: "To me it was a real thrill. I think it was a notice to Japan that President Truman's warning of several days ago was no idle statement. I believe it means Japan will quit suddenly now that she has had a taste of it. The news has done wonders for the morale of the workers here. I can't remember when I have seen so much enthusiasm."

It was this spirit which the newly organized "scientists" were quickly exploited to blight. It was to be blighted and baffled, depressed and humiliated, wherever and whenever it appeared, but of course primary attention was given to its frustration in the Houses of Congress, where unless it was checked it might lead to action taken from the point of view of the United States.

"From a state of uncritical jubilation," reports Professor Shils, "the majority of both Houses of Congress were gradually moved to a sober awareness of the political implications of the bomb. The increased sobriety was produced by repeated stress on the certain loss of the monopoly of atomic bombs after a decade, even though the strictest security and national control were maintained." There has certainly been nothing like it since the uncritical jubilation of Othello was destroyed by Iago.

The way sane legislators felt before the atomic experts went to work on them, the "American opinion" which there was such a "great effort to modify," appears in a statement by the Members of the House Appropriations Subcommittee for the War Department, reported by the *New York Times* October 2, 1945: "This subcommittee handled the appropriation of funds and maintained the secret of the atomic bomb project. We recommend the immediate creation of a commission representing the scientists who directed the project, the Joint Chiefs of Staff, the State Department, and the Congress to study all phases of atomic power. Pending such study and its findings, we recommend against the release of the atomic bomb secrets."

Here the Subcommittee went to the heart of the matter. What the Communists could not tolerate, and their naive associates would not, was the maintenance of American scientific and technological secrecy. Ignoring the fact, as reported by Professor Enrico Fermi,[175] and abundantly corroborated by others, that the original nuclear scientists had "set up a voluntary censorship and treated the matter as confidential long before its importance was recognized by the government and secrecy became mandatory," the organized scientists of the postwar era developed with increasing intensity of feeling the suggestion of the Franck Report that "it would be foolish to hope to retain our leadership in nucleonics by secrecy."

In the days of the Nazi threat it had not seemed foolish to these men even to attain leadership with the aid of secrecy. In 1939, according to the Smyth Report, "American-born nuclear physicists were so unaccustomed to the idea of using their science for military purposes that they hardly realized *what needed to be done.* Consequently the early efforts both at *restricting publication* and at getting government support were stimulated largely by a small group of foreign-born physicists centering on L. Szilard and including E. Wigner, E. Teller, V. F. Weisskopf, and E. Fermi." [176] (Italics supplied.) Dr. Alexander Sachs has told us how "the scientists, Dr. Szilard, Dr. Wigner, and Dr. Einstein, were all of the same view, that there had to be secrecy against leaks to the enemy." [177] Dr. Harold C. Urey, in testifying before the McMahon Committee expressed his opinion that "our capacity to produce atomic bombs and the number stockpiled should be known by the people of the United States." When Senator Hickenlooper questioned this, Dr. Urey replied, "If we are at peace my argument applies. If we are essentially at war I would agree with you." [178]

Obviously, under the menace of Hitler the scientists agreed there should be scientific and technical secrecy. Once Hitler was gone most of them did not believe we were "essentially at war." It was most convenient for the Communists that so few scientists, and so few hyperliterate Americans in general, could see that Communism was a menace to anything which they consciously cherished. In consequence many sincere, vibrant voices were raised to chant with the Communists, "There is no secret (or if there is there ought not to be)."

Dr. Frederic Joliot-Curie, whose frankness in espousing Communism should not lead us to forget his eminence in science, his extraordinary talents in organization, and his apparently very considerable personal influence, told a group of nuclear scientists in London: "What is serious is that it should henceforth be admitted by certain people that it is possible to keep secret results obtained by scientific research in the field of Nuclear Science. . . . We count on the Union of Scientists in every country to militate against the maintenance of secrets and to obtain a wide divulgation of the discoveries." [179] How fascinatingly scientific that we should agree *henceforth* not to *admit* that secrecy is *possible!*

Secrecy was at the heart of the issue. Power and prestige were both affected. From the Russian point of view the acquisition of the secrets of American atomic technology was an objective of first-rank importance. C. L. Sulzberger reported from London in the *New York Times* October 8, 1945: "One wise statesman who participated in the recent Foreign Ministers' council meetings believes there are two keys to better relations with Russia on a free and parity basis. These are, he thinks, the administration of the atom secret and the matter of American credits to Moscow."

The issue was vital and enduring. Two years later Prof. N. F. Mott, Chairman of the British Atomic Scientists' Association, was, as reported by Dr. Rabinowitch of the *Bulletin of the Atomic Scientists,* to call "for a compromise [of the American-Soviet clash over international control] on the basis of the Soviet inspection proposals. . . . Professor Mott thinks that the degree of security which can be achieved by such inspection is high enough for America to pay for it with the dismantling of her bombs, relaxation of secrecy in nuclear science, and even large reconstruction loans to the U.S.S.R." [180]

But it was, of course, in the Soviet interest to pretend that secrecy was not important. The attitude to be taken was one familiar to all practitioners of the third degree—"I know anyhow, so you might as well tell me." There is always some difficulty in maintaining this position with dignity, but one relies on one's official station, as policeman or academic, to remedy this defect. After all, the person addressed is a suspected criminal in one case—in the other, a layman.

Neither the Communists nor the scientific zealots could ever quite make up their minds whether they should say loudest: (1) There is in the nature of things no secret, (2) There is a secret and that is bad because it will hurt science, or (3) There was a secret but the stupid military (and, later, a few eccentric spies) have let it out (or betrayed it). Actually, they said all these things, mutually exclusive as they are, repeatedly and with the fullest assortment of the flowers of rhetoric. The duller ones did not know they were being illogical, and the brighter ones did not care, as they were (1) contemptuous of the analytical powers of their audiences, and (2) in no position to expose the real logic of their position, which was, quite simply, to redress the balance of power in favor of the U.S.S.R. through the most systematic dissemination possible of scientific and technical information relating to atomic energy. This was an objective of many who were not Communists, but who had somehow led themselves to believe that it would not be good for the United States to have a preponderance of military power.

There were three classes of people in those days—(1) an unscrupulous Communist minority that was never confused but always confusing, (2) the populace at large, who, according to the plan, were to be always confused and never confusing, and (3) the joiners of atomic scientists' associations and other uplift societies, who were both thoroughly confused themselves and aggressively confusing to others.

We return to the succinct narrative of Professor Shils: "With the aid of newspaper and wireless commentators, and a few public-spirited university people, the atomic scientists established themselves in Washington, where they began a strenuous campaign to instruct the members of the House of Representatives and the Senate in the meaning of the atomic bomb." It is regrettable that the members of Congress were then so docile as to encourage the utmost presumption on the part of the scientists and the "newspaper and wireless commentators." The restraints of an older era were discarded, and the opinions of a university president were indistinguishable in form or content from the captions under the photographs of mushroom clouds which picture magazines interspersed between the bathing beauties.

It is to the credit of the Congressmen that they seemed to be serious, even if mistaken. A group of Senators undertook to study nuclear physics. It is difficult to say which was the more improbable: (1) that they would actually learn any nuclear physics, or (2) that it would help them in drafting appropriate legislation if they did learn it. It was as if a judge in traffic court should become apprentice to an automobile mechanic—interesting stuff, and related, but not particularly helpful for the business in hand.

The scientists and journalists were apparently less confused about the genuine relevance of scientific and technical matters in a political struggle. The truth or falsity of a statement seemed to be intrinsically immaterial. What counted was who made the statement and which side he was on. Waldemar Kaempffert, Science Editor of the *New York Times*, published an article in the *Times* August 16, 1945, purporting to give a digest of the Smyth Report. After a blunder-infested account in which he said plutonium is "otherwise known as U-239. . . . After bombardment U-235 becomes neptunium . . . and plutonium breaks down into U-235" (none of which is correct), Mr. Kaempffert pronounced, "ALL THIS MUST BE BORNE IN MIND TO UNDERSTAND PROFESSOR SMYTH'S REPORT."

Think of all of us literate ignoramuses gravely weighing that in the *New York Times* in August 1945, conscious of our responsibility toward those too frivolous to read the *New York Times*, studiously bearing in mind this solemnly propounded mess of misinformation, in order "to understand

Professor Smyth's report," and so be in a position to exercise civic virtue by writing our Senator to be sure and vote in favor of science. Of course if Mr. Kaempffert had happened to have the information straight, it would not have helped us any more to come to any sensible conclusion about pending legislation. It does not really matter whether you have the right answer or not when you are on the wrong problem.

Mr. Kaempffert probably had Dr. Johnson's excuse of "Ignorance, Madam, pure ignorance," but what about the scientists? If they refrained from correcting his answer on the ground that he had the wrong problem, why did they not make clear to the public that the political issue was quite independent of whether plutonium is "known as U-239," or, as it is, as Pu.

There seem to be two scientific opinions that account for the scientific apathy regarding boners of this type: (1) The irrelevance of the technical subject matter should not be exposed, as an assumption of its relevance strengthens the political position of the scientists, and (2) It does not matter whether technical information given to laymen is accurate, as they do not understand it anyhow. Nor is it desirable that they should understand it, as the purpose is not to enlighten them, but to confuse them, convince them of the superiority of scientists, and insure their docility under the political tutelage of the scientists. Cicero spoke Greek to the Romans; charlatans for a thousand years have spoken hocus-pocus Latin to the vulgar; it is only natural that the sharper promoters since August 1945 should make noises like a scientist.

Dr. Rabinowitch has told us that "The founding of the *Bulletin of the Atomic Scientists* was a part of the conspiracy to preserve our civilization by scaring men into rationality." [181] Read that one again—"conspiracy to preserve our civilization by scaring men into rationality." Naturally, if this is your approach, you are not going to give anybody a clear explanation of anything—that would spoil the effect.

Scare men into rationality. There is no secret. There is no defense. *Why don't you give up?* Any suggestion, then, that the atomic bomb might be used to enhance or protect the relative power or prestige of the United States was mercilessly attacked. There is no secret! There is no defense! But there was no clear unanimity on the wording of the conclusion to be drawn. What was wanted was a punchy variant on "National sovereignty must be modified at least through international control of atomic energy," but no one had the courage to say flatly, "The United States must go."

It was not so much that they did not think this—though many of them would have flinched at such logic even in their own minds—as that they felt a statement of this sort would not be well received. No proposition was judged for content; all were judged for effect. When you said, "There is no secret," you were not even thinking about whether there was or was not a secret; you were only thinking about how acceptance of your statement might influence the listener.

A dissertation has been written on the effect of atomic propaganda on the public attitude, and the scientists from time to time have concluded that what they said should not have been said, *because it did not have the result they had expected.* But it is difficult to find any re-examination of the early slogans which asks the simple question: Were they true? Even when a writer in the *Bulletin of the Atomic Scientists* in June 1951 [182] observes sadly, "Lack of interest in civil defense stems largely from a fatalistic attitude resulting from the well known statement: 'There is no defense against the atomic bomb,'" he still leaves the reader wondering whether the original "well known statement" was false, and from this falsity has proceeded a mistaken apathy; or whether the statement was true, and hence civil defense really is much ado about nothing.

The present writer would be glad to see evidence that he is mistaken in thinking the propaganda of 1945–46 was less than candid. But he cannot forget hearing a particularly well-informed and brilliantly persuasive scientist at Oak Ridge in the winter of 1946 say to a group of younger intellectuals: "We will say the opposite of what General Groves says, *no matter what it is.*"

If it is true that power corrupts, then it is not surprising that the scientists have become cynical and arrogant. Mr. Roland Sawyer of the *Christian Science Monitor* has said, "The point is not whether the nuclear scientists are right. Rather, it is that the nuclear scientists are constantly striving to make their influence felt upon the course of political events at a high level at home (as they did in the passage of the United States Atomic Energy Act of 1946), and to speak to their counterparts, as well as to all men, abroad." [183]

What narcotic do you take to get into the kind of trance where "the point is not whether the nuclear scientists are right"? If a diagnostician prescribes major surgery, is it not a point whether he is right? Does one say, The point is not whether he is right, it is just that he is trying to make his influence felt? If the swimming coach tells you to dive from the tower, that the water is ten feet deep, is there a point in whether he is right, or is there not? Maybe it is only ten inches. But that is not the point; the point is rather that he is trying to tell you what to do. Don't you see?

Mr. William L. Laurence, of the *New York Times*, has shown the same neutrality as Mr. Sawyer as to whether the judgment of scientists is correct or not. In writing about the dispute between General Groves and Senator McMahon as to whether General Groves did or did not have prior to July 16, 1945, a "ninety-nine per cent certainty" that the atomic bomb would work, Mr. Laurence observes that "While General Groves turned out to be right, it was by no means the opinion of the top scientists who designed the bomb." The fact that you were right, General, is of no consequence—it is not the point. The point is that you are not a scientist, and you would be well advised not to try to make your influence felt.

A powerful tendency exists for any profession to be debased when an unrepudiated organized group within its ranks flouts the basic principles of the profession. The politically organized atomic scientists of 1945 staked their own reputations and the welfare of their country on the slogan, There is no secret of the atomic bomb. Practically, this proposition is demonstrably either an error, a lie, or an equivocation. Scientifically, it just does not mean anything. All scientists know this, but so few have spoken out in clarification of the facts that the whole fraternity is blanketed in a smog of suspicion—not so much concerning their patriotic loyalty as concerning their candor, detachment, and courage, qualities without which it is impossible to conceive of a scientific fraternity as continuing to exist.

Chapter X ⟿ Darkling Plain

Historians and columnists write as if they knew what they were talking about. The style of authority is often convenient, and endless apologies—*alleged's, it seems to me's,* etc., are tedious. But no historian or columnist really knows what he is talking about all the time. The best ones have a few facts and a more or less reasonable theory to give the facts significance. But it is very difficult to be sure of a fact if you were not there, and it is difficult to see the larger significance if you were there. The testimony of others can be checked for internal consistency, and a good reputation can be credited while it lasts, but you are always guessing to some extent. The present work is of course no exception.

The main point of the present work is not historical at all, but prognostic—that the American atomic stockpile will not do the United States any good unless the United States gets better control of it. That prediction is subject to verification or confutation in the regular course of events, and the writer hopes the prediction is wrong.

Right or wrong, it involves a view of the history of the atomic energy project, which ramifies into the broader history of World War II and postwar national and international politics. Obviously, complete systematic treatment is out of the question here. We do the best we can with glimpses and conjectures of the main stream, and hope the near future is less rocky than it looks.

So many important persons are dead—Stimson, Patterson, Forrestal, Stettinius, Vandenberg, McMahon. In several cases the deceased have left papers which have been edited and published. Illustrative of the difficulties in getting a straight story are the following episodes of conflicting implication from two of those departed—Forrestal and Vandenberg—regarding a third, McMahon. Also involved is Mr. James F. Byrnes.

In the *Forrestal Diaries* as edited by Mr. Walter Millis is the following (bracketed language is that of Mr. Millis):

"[. . . Senator Brien McMahon of Connecticut, chairman of the special Committee on Atomic Energy, had appeared with a list of questions concerning the number of atomic bombs in existence, costs of the atomic projects, and so on, for which the Congress wanted answers.]

"4 December 1945　　　　　　　　*Atomic Energy*

". . . The President said that it is impossible for him to approve release of this information to the Senate Committee because among the thirteen members it was almost a certainty that one would consciously or otherwise let some of this information become public. . . .

"He said if the Senate Committee insisted upon the information it would of course have to be given, but he wanted to make clear what he considered to be the risks involved. Judge Patterson [then Secretary of War] spoke very strongly against giving the information and I supported him. . . ." [184]

President Truman is said to have told Forrestal on another occasion, "he was aware that Senator McMahon was out to get publicity for himself," [185] and in 1949 he rebuked Senator McMahon for even bringing up the subject of publishing stockpile information. [186]

(Stockpile information, which the Joint Committee has voted to deprive itself of, seems to have almost obsessed

Senator McMahon from the start. In 1947 he participated in the following colloquy during the hearings on the confirmation of Mr. Lilienthal:

"Senator McMahon. If I want to know how many bombs there are I want to be told.

Senator Vandenberg. I am not clear that I want you to be told.

Senator McMahon. I am just as clear on my right to know." [187])

In contrast with this picture of Senator McMahon as a determined seeker after information which Senator Vandenberg thought he ought not to have, and which President Truman and top Cabinet members thought he ought not to have, consider the following from *The Private Papers of Senator Vandenberg*, as edited by Arthur H. Vandenberg, Jr. and Joe Alex Morris:

December 10, 1945.—Secretary of State Byrnes this afternoon called in the special Committee of Foreign Relations—also three members of the Atom Bomb Committee—and talked with us about his Moscow trip. He said he proposed to suggest an exchange of atom scientists and scientific information with Russia as his first step; then that Russia join us in setting up an Atomic Commission under the United Nations Organization to carry on. His plan was a great shock to the entire committee. Everyone spoke earnestly. . . .

December 11, 1945.—The President received our full committee this morning. We stated our case and disclosed our fears. The President said he agreed with us, but that he was sure we had misunderstood the Secretary. . . . We pointed . . . out to the President . . . that . . . it would be possible for the Secretary to prematurely give away, while in Moscow, at least half of all our "trading stock" when we seek essential controls. . . . For some inscrutable reason, the President seemed to fail to grasp our point. . . .

In any event we have made the record—and we shall hold the

Executive Department responsible. It is our unanimous opinion that the Byrnes formula must be *stopped*.[188]

If data of this sort are confusing to the historian, the original situation was probably more confusing to the actors in the drama. The Senators were trying to keep the Executive from giving away the secrets; the Executive was trying to prevent the secrets' leaking through the Senators' Committee. The scientists, of course, were saying, There is no secret. And all the while the Russians were getting secrets in clandestine fashion and agitating to get many more in the open fashion provided by the McMahon Bill, which originally established, in its own words, "A program for the free dissemination of basic scientific information and for maximum liberality in dissemination of related technical information."

Inasmuch as Senator Vandenberg says the Senate Committee's opinion was unanimous that "the Byrnes formula must be *stopped*," it appears that Senator McMahon was deeply concerned lest Secretary Byrnes give away atomic secrets. But Secretary Byrnes is reported in the *Forrestal Diaries* (see p. 179 below) as being "most strongly opposed to imparting any of this information to the Russians," and as feeling "that undue emphasis was being given to the views of the scientists," those same scientists, of course, who, as Professor Shils has told us, aided in the drafting of the McMahon Bill. In other words, McMahon was worried lest Byrnes' activities give away the secrets, and Byrnes was worried lest McMahon's activities give away the secrets.

Confusion is not resolved when Dr. Rabinowitch, writing of the Moscow Resolution, tells us, "*To placate certain sections of public opinion at home,* Secretary Byrnes said that 'neither we nor any other government would be expected to share our armament secrets until it was certain that effective safeguards had been developed.'"[189] Do the words here italicized mean Secretary Byrnes was insincere, or simply that in Dr. Rabinowitch's opinion this was a lot of foolishness?

One is reminded of Dr. Oppenheimer's testimony before the Joint Committee in 1949 that the international distribution of isotopes "is one of the few areas in which we are free to act the way we would like to act, generously, imaginatively, and decently; in the things that involve security we are inhibited from doing that, and our friends abroad understand that." [190] Beset by the security restrictions of stingy, stupid, gross American nationalists, it is consoling to generous, imaginative, decent scientists to remember the sagacious tolerance of the comrades across the sea.

THE BRAINWASHING OF HENRY STIMSON

Secretary of War Henry Stimson's first reactions to the atomic energy problem seem to have been normal. As the Cabinet officer with immediate responsibility for the development of the atomic bomb, and as one who spanned the break in Administration occasioned by the death of President Roosevelt, he held a position of enormous importance.

In April 1945 "it was already apparent," he has said, "that the critical questions in American policy toward atomic energy would be connected with Soviet Russia. . . . There was no assurance that the Russians would hasten to agree on controls, nor could any agreement including Russia be regarded with any great confidence unless it contained such far-reaching rights of inspection as to counter-balance (and perhaps, in Russian eyes, to undermine) the protective and fearsome secrecy of a police state." [191] It is tragic that Mr. Stimson ever lost this clarity of vision.

During the Potsdam Conference he wrote a memorandum to President Truman, in which he said, "I am of the belief that no world organization containing as one of its dominant members a nation whose people are not possessed of free speech, but whose government action is controlled by the autocratic machinery of a secret political police, can give effective control of this new agency [atomic energy] with its devastating possibilities.

"I therefore believe that before we share our new discovery with Russia we should consider carefully whether we can do so safely under any system of control until Russia puts into effective action her constitution [which on paper gave in Russia the civil liberties that Communists consider so important in America]. If this is a necessary condition, we must go slowly in any disclosures or agreeing to any Russian participation whatsoever and constantly explore the question how our headstart in X [atomic energy] and the Russian desire to participate can be used to bring us nearer to the removal of the basic difficulties which I have emphasized." [192]

This makes sense. But after a talk with Ambassador Averell Harriman, Secretary Stimson changed his advice. In September 1945 he wrote to the President, "I am not unmindful of the fact that when in Potsdam I talked with you about the question of whether we could be safe in sharing the atomic bomb with Russia while she was still a police state. I have come to the conclusion that it would not be possible to use our possession of the atomic bomb as a direct lever to produce the change. I have become convinced that any demand by us for an internal change in Russia as a condition of sharing in the atomic weapon would be so resented that it would make the objective we have in view less probable." [193] Somehow he has been worked around to the point of view where we must share "the atomic weapon" (not, observe, just atomic energy), and with no strings attached.

"Unless the Soviets are voluntarily invited into the partnership upon a basis of cooperation and trust," continued Secretary Stimson, "we are going to maintain the Anglo-

Saxon bloc over against the Soviet in the possession of this weapon. Such a condition will almost certainly stimulate feverish activity on the part of the Soviet toward the development of this bomb in what will, in effect, be a secret armament race of a rather desperate character. There is evidence to indicate that such activity may have already commenced. . . .

"Whether Russia gets control of the necessary secrets of production in a minimum of say four years [if we accept President Truman's announcement of September 23, 1949, this is an astonishingly close prediction] or a maximum of twenty years is not nearly as important to the world and civilization as to make sure that when they do get it they are willing cooperative partners among the peace-loving nations of the world. It is true if we approach them now, as I would propose, we may be gambling on their good faith and risk their getting into production of bombs a little sooner than they would otherwise.

"To put the matter concisely, I consider the problem of our satisfactory relations with Russia as not merely connected with but as virtually dominated by the problem of the atomic bomb." [194]

This record of Secretary Stimson's thinking in September 1945 is required reading for an informed citizen, but it is assuredly depressing. Here is the Cabinet officer with primary responsibility for our defenses asserting in obvious good faith and with a straight face that we must approach the Soviet Union with the atomic bomb in our open hands, "upon a basis of cooperation and trust . . . gambling on their good faith." Mr. Truman is recorded as having said of "Mr. X," widely identified as Henry Wallace, that "X is a pacifist 100 per cent. He wants us to disband our armed forces, give Russia our atomic secrets and trust a bunch of adventurers in the Kremlin Politbureau. I do not understand a 'dreamer' like that." [195] Mr. Wallace has been attacked quite generally—and not without reason—for his myopia with regard to Russia, but there is no just reason to make him the solitary scapegoat for the atomic folly of 1945. The contagion of perverse brilliance radiating from the atomic laboratories was very powerful, infecting Secretary Stimson, as we see, so quickly as to reduce him in a month from a position where he would bargain rationally to fatuous abjection before the Soviet. (It is a sad fact that when perverse brilliance is radiated, the perverseness continues to be propagated long after the brilliance has completely faded.)

The Secretary of War of the United States, within a month of the most dramatic stroke of victory since the Armada, finds his nerves so shot that he is in great fear lest our "relations may be perhaps irretrievably embittered by the way in which we approach the solution of the bomb with Russia. For if we fail to approach them now and merely continue to negotiate with them, having this weapon rather ostentatiously on our hip, their suspicions and their distrust of our purposes and motives will increase." [196]

This appearance of neurotic timidity is complicated by what looks like a naive kind of arrogance, for the Secretary seems to think that we and the Russians not only live under different political and economic systems, but are in some more fundamental way different kinds of human beings.

"The chief lesson I have learned in a long life is that the only way you can make a man trustworthy is to trust him; and the surest way to make him untrustworthy is to distrust him and show your distrust." [197] Mr. Stimson was greatly concerned over the possibility that the Russians might be made untrustworthy by our not trusting them, but showed no sign of fearing that we might be made untrustworthy by their showing their distrust of us. What are we—superhuman? It would not be at all surprising if certain Russians detested above all other Americans some of those who are supposed to be "pro-Russian," and who continually recommend approaching the Russians as if they were merely the spoiled children of eccentric neighbors.

The strategy of pacifying the petulant Muscovites with our atomic technology lest in their exasperation they develop one of their own was not endorsed with absolute unanimity in the United States. Mr. James F. Byrnes, though he has since been accused of having had some responsibility for a "get soft with Russia" policy, appears to have sided with the late James Forrestal in wanting to play the cards close to the vest as far as atomic energy was concerned.

Mr. Bernard Baruch seems to have been always of the opinion he expressed in 1947. At the hearings on the confirmation of Mr. Lilienthal as AEC Chairman, Senator Hickenlooper said to Mr. Baruch: "At least one group of scientific opinion believes that if you free all of this knowledge [of atomic energy science and technology], then the act of freeing the knowledge and giving it to other countries will act as a pacifier to those countries and they then in gratitude will not use that knowledge against us. That is one view that is taken by a certain group, is it not, on the question of freedom of science?"

"That is so nauseating to me," responded Mr. Baruch, "that I never understood it, Senator." [198]

It is very nearly certain that the great majority of Americans silently agreed with Mr. Baruch, but the circumstances of the time and the audacity of their opponents kept them largely silent. The voices that were heard were almost entirely the voices of those who were arguing with each other over *how* we were going to share the bomb with the Russians.

WHO INFLUENCED WHOM?

It is impossible to trace lines of influence with complete precision and assurance of the direction of flow. The *Daily Worker* and the *New York Times* on the same day, August 8, 1945, more than a month before Secretary Stimson's memorandum, presented similar editorial views, which does not, of course, necessarily indicate similar motives. The chief difference between the *Daily Worker's* analysis and that by Secretary Stimson is that the *Worker* had a big plug for the United Nations, whereas the Secretary thought it would be a great mistake to get involved in a discussion to which a lot of small nations were admitted, and wanted to confine the serious talk to the United States, Great Britain, and Russia (astonishingly, he does not even include Canada; he indicates France and China may be brought in later). The procedure actually followed by the United States was closer to the line recommended by the *Daily Worker* than it was to the suggestion of the Secretary of War, whereupon the fellow-traveling press, as reliably represented by the periodical *Soviet Russia Today,* blasted U.S. policy and said we should base everything on an agreement between the Big Three, which is what Secretary Stimson had proposed.

The main point with the Communists and their hypnotized subjects of the day seems to have been not to reach an agreement on any one plan in a hurry, but to attempt a series of approximations, each one closer than the last to yielding "all power to the Soviets." When any reversal was met, then, and only then, an earlier plan might be referred to with favor.

Thus the original McMahon Bill and the original Acheson-Lilienthal Plan, both of which were favorable to the Soviet Union, received no praise from the Communist press until *after* the introduction of modifications by Senator Vandenberg and Mr. Baruch, respectively, in the interests of the United States. *Then* the *Daily Worker* and *Soviet Russia Today* rushed to the defense of the McMahon Bill and the Acheson-Lilienthal Plan. In military parlance, even your most advanced salient does not represent a position of great intrinsic worth till it is threatened by a counteroffensive.

The following excerpts from the *Worker,* the *Times,* Secretary Stimson's memorandum, and *Soviet Russia Today* are offered both as substantiating evidence of the preceding assertions, and as matters not without intrinsic interest of their own:

New York *Daily Worker,* August 8, 1945, Editorial (in part): "Many nations are capable of the same scientific development as we are. . . . The alternatives, therefore, are: competition in the use of this new weapon, or cooperation.

". . . We believe that this is the time to fight even more strongly for a fundamental cooperation of the great powers —especially our own country and the Soviet Union. . . .

"The scientific potentials of which we are capable are in revolt against the political straitjacket of our social relations. . . .

"The immediate answer is to strengthen the democracy in our country, and to fortify the United Nations, that great bulwark against fascism."

The *New York Times,* August 8, 1945, Editorial (in part):

"There has never been a more striking example of international cooperation in science than that presented by the development of the bomb. Is this to be the end? Are we to lapse into the old more or less nationalistic pursuit of science when great issues are at stake? . . . Apart from the overwhelming social potentialities of utilizing atomic energy we shall have learned little socially if we do not apply the system of organization, planning, and direction that gave us the bomb to solve the scientific and technological problems of peace."

The common theme, expressed not without verbal similarities, that a national outlook is inadequate, that atomic energy requires social changes, and that great potentialities wait upon international co-operation, published in both papers before the dust had settled in Hiroshima or been stirred up in Nagasaki, of course does not mean that the

Times had been influenced by the people that controlled the *Worker*. But the national policy course thus anticipated eventually hastened the flow of technical knowledge and material from the United States to Russia, while as far as the record shows, it has never resulted in any flow of anything useful from Russia to the United States.

From Secretary Stimson's memorandum of September 11, 1945:

"If the atomic bomb were merely another though more devastating military weapon to be assimilated into our pattern of international relations, it would be one thing. We could then follow the old custom of secrecy and nationalistic military superiority relying on international caution to proscribe the future use of the weapon as we did with gas. But I think the bomb instead constitutes merely a first step in a new control by man over the forces of nature too revolutionary and dangerous to fit into the old concepts." [199]

This is almost straight Marxism—the notion that the means of production are logically and effectually anterior to our moral, philosophical, political, and religious "concepts"— but so successful has Marx been in the past hundred years that there is almost no chance the Secretary realized he was parroting the export philosophy of the Kremlin.

"I emphasize . . . the importance of taking this action with Russia as a proposal of the United States—backed by Great Britain. . . . Action of any international group of nations, including many small nations who have not demonstrated their potential power or responsibility in this war would not, in my opinion, be taken seriously by the Soviets," said Stimson. [200]

This prediction seems to have been pretty close to the mark. Next January (1946), *Soviet Russia Today* said, ". . . it should be clear to all . . . that there can be no peace and security in the world unless Britain, the Soviet

Union, and the United States can see eye-to-eye on the major problems of the world. . . .

"The Soviet Union . . . was entitled to participate in the Washington discussions. . . . [*i.e.*, in November 1945.]

"It was a fundamental mistake to have called that meeting without inviting the Soviet Union to participate, regardless of the fact that Britain, Canada and the United States were the three nations possessing the technological know-how of the atomic bomb [at this point the Party line blurs a bit]. Failure to invite the Soviet Union was tantamount to public declaration that as far as Britain and the United States were concerned, the entire principle of Big Three unity was to be discarded [remember Secretary Stimson's "Anglo-Saxon bloc over against the Soviet"]. . . .

"Of course it is correct that some international authority must be constituted to control atomic energy. . . . But that international authority must be based upon the same fundaments on which the entire United Nations Organization rests—the Big Three."

In a later issue *Soviet Russia Today* spoke of then Senator Claude Pepper, who "summarized this situation well in the following words, 'It is senseless to think that there can be a stable and secure world as long as only a part of the major powers have the atomic bomb.'"

Someone may very well ask, even at this time, what was so bad about proposals of the general nature of those advanced by Secretary Stimson and *Soviet Russia Today*, or about attitudes like those of the *Daily Worker* and the *New York Times*. The answer is, in part, that these proposals and attitudes were very poor preparation for what was to become within two years, and then to remain, the declared policy of the nation—atomic superiority. Everybody now is in favor of atomic superiority, or says he is; but these proposals and attitudes of 1945, and the far more melodramatic expressions of most of the self-styled atomic scientists, as-

sumed that atomic superiority not only provided no security,
but might actually be a positive danger.

In its issue for September 8, 1945, the *Nation* included an
editorial paragraph written obviously under the same astro-
logical configuration as Secretary Stimson's memorandum:
"We welcome the hint from Stettinius in London that the
United States and Great Britain may be prepared to share
the secret of the atomic bomb with our allies and to place
its development under the control of the new United Nations Organization. We agree with the Russian publication,
New Times, that since the fundamental principles are known,
'it is simply a question of time before any country will be
able to produce atomic bombs.' Under such conditions war
would be suicidal, and the *reductio ad absurdum* of the nationalistic attitude is the New York *Daily News* editorial suggesting 'two atomic bombs for one.' . . . Altogether too
little thinking is being done about the implications of the
atomic bomb for warfare and for the future of society. . . ."

Perhaps so. At any rate "two atomic bombs for one" is
now the national policy, urged and supported by most of
those who in the autumn of 1945 agreed with the *Nation*
about the suicidal absurdity of the nationalistic attitude of
the New York *Daily News.*

Probably among them are some who came gradually to
the realization (during 1947 and 1948 mostly) that instead
of trying to convince America she would be better off to
quit making atomic bombs because Russia did not have
any, it would be much more convenient to encourage America to make enough atomic bombs for both herself and
Russia. But that is quite a sophisticated approach, and even
the Communists took a few years to work it out.

It is difficult to choose the best sample of atomic in-
cunabula (which we define as anything published on the
subject prior to Dr. Szilard's first reading the May-Johnson
Bill during a visit to Washington, D. C., in October 1945),

but judicious collectors will not neglect the following, by Freda Kirchwey in the *Nation* for August 18, 1945:

"The atomic bomb represents a revolution in science—the greatest revolution ever accomplished. It calls for a comparable revolution in men's thinking and in their capacity for political and social readjustment. . . .

"First, if anything is sure about the atomic bomb it is that no physical protection against it will ever be possible. . . .

"Other nations are now working on atomic explosives. . . . The secret was guarded long enough to enable us to smash Japan. It will not last much longer. . . .

"A new conference of the nations must be assembled to set up a World Government, to which every state must surrender an important part of its sovereignty. In this World Government must be vested the final control over atomic energy. And within each nation the people must establish public ownership and social development of the revolutionary force war has thrust into their hands. This program will sound drastic only to people who have not yet grasped the meaning of the new discovery. It is not drastic. We face a choice between one world or none."

The essential ideas are there. The number of times they were to be repeated is almost inconceivable. And the difficulty of speaking against them cannot be exaggerated. Even Mr. Baruch had practically to mutter, or take refuge in humor, as when he would cut off his hearing-aid to preclude further reception of the accepted clichés of the day. Mr. Byrnes was out-maneuvered and kept on the defensive. Mr. Forrestal was reduced to caged impotence.

At a historic Cabinet meeting September 21, 1945, Forrestal, Mr. Walter Millis tells us, "made the point that the bomb and the knowledge that produced it were 'the property of the American people,' which the administration could not give away until they were very sure that it was the sense of the people that they should do so." [201] Of the Russians, Forrestal, differing with Stimson and Henry Wallace, said: "It seems doubtful that we should endeavor to buy their understanding and sympathy." [202]

"Mr. Byrnes," wrote Forrestal, "indicated that he was most strongly opposed to imparting any of this information to the Russians. He stated that he felt that undue emphasis was being given to the views of the scientists on this subject. He said that while it was all very well for the scientists to say as they did that science has no boundaries, that certainly did not apply to either Mr. Molotov or Mr. Stalin; that in his view it is idle to expect that we would be allowed any access for purposes of inspection of Russian factories producing atomic bombs. . . ." [203]

It is eight years now, and that view of Mr. Byrnes looks pretty good. But at the time it did not have a chance. If Forrestal thought he could cope with *The Nation*, or Byrnes thought his opinion mattered in comparison with that of the scientists, those gentlemen had a lot to learn.

Chapter XI ✒ Law of the Lemmings

We must not pretend to know more than we do. There is much that is still secret about the maneuvers relating to the May-Johnson Bill. It was an Administration Bill. On October 3, 1945, the President delivered a message to Congress, urging the creation of an atomic energy commission, and containing philosophic observations quite in line with the "liberal" propaganda of the scientists.

"Scientific opinion appears to be practically unanimous," said the message, "that the essential theoretical knowledge upon which the discovery is based is already widely known. There is also substantial agreement that foreign research can come abreast of our present theoretical knowledge in time." [204]

The same day Representative May and Senator Johnson introduced in their respective houses bills which they said were intended to carry out the President's proposals. [205] "Representative May said his measure was introduced at the request of Secretary of War Patterson, who authorized the explanation that it had been drafted by a committee approved by President Truman and after several months work and consultation with leading scientists," the *New*

York Times reported. Actually, the Bill seems to have been drafted by Kenneth C. Royall and William L. Marbury, with the policy guidance of the same Interim Committee that recommended the use of the bomb against Japan.[206] Its members included, it will be recalled, Dr. Vannevar Bush, Dr. Karl T. Compton, and Dr. James B. Conant. Representative May also reported that Dr. J. Robert Oppenheimer, Dr. Enrico Fermi, and Dr. E. O. Lawrence sent Secretary Patterson a telegram endorsing the Bill and warning against delay.[207]

It seems, however, that none of this had been cleared with Dr. Szilard. "Early in October," he has told us, "in a visit to Washington, I happened to pick up a copy of the May-Johnson Bill and brought it back with me to Chicago." [208] Apparently he was horrified, though it does not appear to this day exactly why. In the ensuing battle of words it was to be alleged that the May-Johnson Bill (1) was a "War Department" measure, (2) did not represent the scientists, and (3) was being railroaded through. The fact is, as we have seen, that it was drafted under the supervision of scientists, and three of the most eminent atomic scientists warned against delay in passing it. The Bill was questioned at first only by a few conservative Democrats and a few Republicans. In the House, for instance, it was Mrs. Clare Booth Luce whose maneuver blocked speedy completion of work on the Bill.[209] Like Senator Vandenberg, who with Senator Connally created a parliamentary roadblock in the Senate,[210] she presumably did not intend that the delaying tactics should result, as they finally did, in giving the play to Senator McMahon, who was then a rather obscure freshman in the upper house.

No one imagined on October 3, 1945, that it would later be possible for Professor Blackett, for example, to speak in the following terms: "At the time of the appearance of the Lilienthal Plan a bitter political fight was being waged over the question whether atomic energy in the United States should be controlled primarily by the military or by civilians. Supporting military control (the May-Johnson Bill) were lined up, by and large, the main conservative and isolationist groups [like Truman, Barkley, Conant, and Oppenheimer], while supporting civilian control (the McMahon Bill) were the ex-New Dealers and other liberal groups." [211]

Our bracketed identification of some of the "isolationists" who were "supporting military control" is, it must be confessed, not entirely fair to Professor Blackett, since the Administration and the scientists did later support the McMahon Bill, the introduction of which was made possible by conservative, isolationist objections to the May-Johnson Bill (or simply out-party objections), and the conservatives and isolationists being thus scourged with the scorpions of Rehoboam McMahon had no choice but to plead for the chastisement with whips of Solomon May-Johnson.

Why did the scientists change their minds? Did Szilard alone have so much more influence than Conant, Bush, K. Compton, Oppenheimer, Fermi, and Lawrence combined? *

---

* James S. Allen (*i.e.*, Sol Auerbach; see p. 38 above, and Note 48), in *Atomic Imperialism* (International Publishers, 1952), has a chapter called "The Science Hierarchy" (Chapter 11, pp. 143–55). "The upper scientific hierarchy," he writes, "is well typified by Vannevar Bush, Karl T. Compton, and James B. Conant," and he speaks of "the division between the hierarchs and the majority of scientists, which began during the wartime atom bomb project, and was intensified in the inner controversy over the use of the bomb against Japan. . . . Within a month after the end of the war, the scientists engaged in work on the atomic weapon formed associations in four research centers—Columbia University, University of Chicago, Los Alamos, and Oak Ridge." Relating how these groups quickly developed into the Federation of American Scientists, Allen says, "For the first time in the United States, a national organization of scientists frankly pro-

And how did it happen that one who is normally so far ahead of the game as Dr. Szilard did not know what was in the May-Johnson Bill till it was formally introduced? Professor Shils has said that the McMahon Bill was "drafted with the aid of some of the atomic scientists who had played the most active role in the political campaign." [212] But atomic scientists had given aid in the drafting of the May-Johnson Bill also. Why the tremendous difference in the political success of the two? Was it a schism within the scientific fraternity—the members of the Franck Committee versus the Interim Committee, the former smarting under their defeat on the Japanese issue, striking back smartly in a surprise return engagement? That is a natural question, in view of Dr. Szilard's role, and in view of a key role played later by Dr. T. R. Hogness, another member of the Franck Committee, in getting the Vandenberg amendment tacked on to the McMahon Bill.[213] But we shall not know the answers to these questions—or even whether we have asked the right questions—unless some of the original actors in that confused drama decide to speak out more freely than they have done so far.

It is assuredly worth noting that Dr. Szilard read the May-Johnson Bill at about the same time Secretary Byrnes was announcing the stalemate conclusion of the Foreign Minis-

---

claimed social and political aims. . . . This was a challenge to the hierarchy of militarized science . . . the Federation led an energetic legislative fight against the May-Johnson Bill . . . and sought to check an avalanche of such restrictions upon the freedom of science as security clearances, loyalty tests, and F.B.I. dossiers." At the time of its fight against the May-Johnson Bill the Federation was "at its height," according to Allen. Later, it "fell far short of the aims originally proclaimed . . . for at best it remained confused about the general aims of American foreign policy."

ters' Conference in London.[214] At this conference the Russians may have hoped to get partnership status, and been bitterly disappointed. A United Press dispatch from London September 10 read, "British sources said the Anglo-Americans firmly opposed discussion of future control of the atomic bomb at the conferences. Britain's official spokesman expressed surprise at a London Star report that Russia, France and China would be given atomic bomb secrets by the council, reportedly at the request of Russia." [215]

The attitude of many scientists and of much of the American liberal press may very well have encouraged the greatest optimism in Moscow.[216] If so, then Russian disappointment over the stalemate in London may have been keener than our own. In March 1945 Dr. Szilard had written, "As to our chances of persuading the Russians to accept mutual control, much may depend on the proper timing of our approach to Russia. It would appear that such an approach would have to be made immediately after we demonstrated the potency of atomic bombs." [217]

In the field of international diplomacy "immediately" is an elastic word. U.S. officialdom was given time through the London Conference to get the Big Three atomic partnership set up. When the Conference ended with nothing of the sort accomplished, it was time to revolutionize officialdom's approach.

Dr. Szilard's entry in *Current Biography* (1947) reads: ". . . through September, erroneously believing that negotiations concerning the bomb were in progress among the Big Three, the scientists expressed no opinions on its political implications. Early in October, however, on a visit to Washington Szilard secured a copy of the May-Johnson Bill for the drastic control of atomic energy, and this together with newspaper reports that the bill had received only one hearing in committee, spurred them into action."

President Truman's message of October 3, 1945, had been carefully tailored to the no-secret, no-defense model. "The hope of civilization," he had said, "lies in international arrangements looking, if possible, to the renunciation of the use and development of the atomic bomb, and directing and encouraging the use of atomic energy and all future scientific information toward peaceful and humanitarian ends. The difficulties in working out such arrangements are great. The alternative to overcoming these difficulties, however, may be a desperate armament race which might well end in disaster." This is reminiscent of Secretary Stimson's "armament race of a rather desperate character." [218]

But—

On October 8, according to the *New York Times* of the next day, President Truman, in a press conference at Union City, Tennessee, "declared . . . that the United States would not give away its engineering 'know how' which produced the atomic bomb to any nation. He said that the information would be useless to any other country anyway, since only the United States had the combination of industrial capacity and resources necessary to produce the bomb. . . . Of the knowledge which came out of the $2,000,000,000 wartime experiment, Mr. Truman said in answer to questions at a press conference that that was our business and others would just have to catch up with us. Asked whether Russia might not eventually be able to acquire the engineering skill as well as develop the resources and industrial capacity needed for processing the atomic bomb, the President said the questioner's guess was as good as his."

In order to estimate the effect of this on many of those most interested in the subject, it must be remembered that an attempt was evidently in process to eliminate from President Truman's behavior, as previously from Secretary Stimson's, the normal consequences of national spirit, common sense, and steadiness of nerve.* The President's formal message introducing the May-Johnson Bill sounded as though he were under control. Now, only five days later, he was talking as if the atomic bomb were something that gave the United States an advantage over other nations—Russia, in particular—and, worst of all, he did not sound scared! Clearly, he was not reliable. Something had to be done to show him who, in atomic matters, was boss. At least he had to be shown that he was not the boss. And he was shown that.

October 9, "President Truman puzzled today," says the *Times*,[219] "over the excitement created by his announcement yesterday that this country would not share the 'know how' secret of the atomic bomb with other nations. The President thought he had made it perfectly clear in his recent message to Congress that the know-how behind the bomb's perfection would not be disclosed."

October 10, the *New York Herald Tribune* editorialized, "There was an ineptness in President Truman's almost casual declaration that the secret of the atomic bomb will be given to no one which awakens a sudden doubt as to whether the President himself has really grasped the transcendent importance—although he has repeatedly emphasized it—of this frightful and revolutionary weapon."

And the Chicago *Sun:* "The statement was a major setback for the United Nations and Allied unity. It calls for prompt

---

* That the elimination was temporary in the case of Mr. Stimson is attested by an entry in the *Forrestal Diaries* at the end of 1946, a year after the Moscow Resolution. Secretary Byrnes told President Truman that Stimson "had said to him that in view of the conduct and general attitude of the Russians since the cessation of hostilities he saw no reason to be in any particular hurry to give them any information about atomic energy or the atomic bomb."

reversal. American opinion should demand, and the President should lead, for the earliest possible transformation of the United Nations to world government with adequate power for control of atomic energy."

And what had the man said? He had simply said we would not give away our engineering "know how." Doesn't everyone say that? What did we execute the Rosenbergs for?

October 11, from Chicago (Special to the *New York Times*): "Atomic scientists at the University of Chicago were reported in a state of near revolt today against continued surveillance by Army security police who were accused of instituting a 'rule of fear' to halt the scientists in their efforts to warn the public about the future perils from the atomic bomb."

October 12, Representative Helen Gahagan Douglas urged the House Military Affairs Committee to reopen its hearings on the May-Johnson Bill, "asserting," the *Times* relates, "that 'ninety per cent of the atomic scientists working at Chicago University and ninety per cent of the scientists who worked at the Clinton Laboratories [in Oak Ridge]' had demanded that they receive an opportunity to be heard. These scientists, she asserted, had been 'forbidden to speak,' although they alone 'can tell us fully what is in store.' "

October 13, at Los Alamos, reports the *Times,* "Foreseeing atomic bombs 'thousands of times more powerful' than those dropped on Japan, 400 scientists who helped develop the weapon at the Government's laboratory asserted in a statement today that to try to keep it from the rest of the world 'will lead to an unending war, more savage than the last.' "

October 14, Philip Murray, President of the CIO, in a telegram to Speaker Rayburn of the House of Representatives declared (according to the *Times*), "that an effort was being made to railroad through a control commission which would 'hand over to a little group the power to censor all scientific research on atomic energy and to blacklist any scientists who do not submit to such censorship.' He stated he was appealing to President Truman 'to call together at once the Democratic leadership in Congress to arrange adequate public hearings.'"

October 17, Dr. J. Robert Oppenheimer, testifying before the Kilgore Committee on the National Science Foundation, edged over a bit from his previous position of endorsing the May-Johnson Bill, for he said the powers of the proposed Commission, "if . . . exercised unwisely, could stop science in its tracks."

October 19, Dr. Urey in the *New York Times:* "The May-Johnson Bill would create a potential dictatorship of science and would have the effect of serving notice to the world we were opening an armaments race."

October 20, editorial in the *Nation:* "The May-Johnson Bill sidesteps all the larger issues. There is no question of sharing secrets with others, of creating an international body to control the bomb, of consolidating a world organization to prevent a third world war, in which the bomb would be put to the fatal test. It discusses the issue of atomic power in such narrow terms of national security we have a strong suspicion the bill came straight from the War Department to the desks of Senator Johnson and Representative May. For the War Department is apt to think in strategic categories that fail utterly to comprehend the world problem with which the achievement of nuclear fission has confronted us. The Bill now being crowded through Congress with hysterical urgency provides a frail shield of national defense. If the autocratic powers of the Administration are used as they well may be used, the free scientists of America are going to refuse to function within the straitjacket into which they have been strapped."

October 29, editorial in the *New Republic:* "The May-Johnson Bill is a War Department Bill. Under its provisions the Commission could be dominated entirely by the Army.

. . . We need an atomic energy bill. This is an atomic bomb bill. As it stands now, with no world program behind it, it may well sound the shot that will start an atomic armament race, ending inevitably in war."

What made all these people talk like this? They are surely not all Communists, nor, as we mortals go, are any of them really stupid. Notice how the intensity mounts. On October 20 the *Nation* has a "strong suspicion"; by October 29 the *New Republic* states flatly, "The May-Johnson Bill is a War Department Bill." Equivocation. It was a War Department Bill in a sense. The War Department was responsible for the atomic bomb project. The Secretary of War was Chairman of the Interim Committee. But Secretary of War Stimson had been the first important official to recommend the maximum sharing of information with Russia, and his successor, Secretary Patterson, had made no break with this line. Conant, Bush, and K. Compton were on the Committee. Are they brass hats? * There is every reason to believe, as President Truman obviously believed, that on October 3, 1945, the May-Johnson Bill was acceptable to liberal groups, to scientists. But for some reason, by the end of the same month, the same Bill was drawing from the liberals and from the scientists—most of whom had probably not seen a copy of the Bill—language just short of vituperation. Why? Why do the lemmings go down to the sea? They do it.

Meanwhile, in Washington, October 12, "The Senate Interstate Commerce Commission," says the *Times*, "approved today a resolution by Senator Brien McMahon, Democrat of Connecticut, for the creation of a Special Committee of nine to have charge of all bills dealing with the control of atomic energy. Senator McMahon himself characterized this as 'the end of the procedural fight.' Senator Alben W. Barkley of Kentucky, the majority leader, indicated he would accept the

---

* In effect, yes, according to James S. Allen. See p. 182 above.

McMahon resolution and thus clear the way for the Senate to go forward with consideration of the Administration's bill [May-Johnson!] for establishing a Federal commission to control and nationalize atomic energy."

It seems likely that then Senator Barkley did not know what he was doing to the Administration's bill, but it does not matter. Everything was now set to show the Administration, and the opposition as well, that no one, including the President, was going to be permitted to speak of any "secret" of the atomic bomb without rebuff.

Chapter XII ~ S. 1717

"Wide Divulgation of the Discoveries"

The Communists wittingly and many of the atomic scientists wittingly or unwittingly worked in 1945–46 toward legal partnership status for the Soviet Union in the atomic energy project. Such status could not be complete without an international arrangement, but an extremely important step toward it could be taken in setting up a U.S. national commission. The main points were, first, exclusion of the armed services, because, as the *Nation* observed, they are "apt to think in strategic categories that fail utterly to comprehend the world problem with which the achievement of nuclear fission has confronted us" [220]—they are, in fact, apt to think in "narrow terms of national security;" [221] and second, the elimination of technical secrecy—in Joliot-Curie's phrase, "wide divulgation of the discoveries."

The original McMahon Bill (S. 1717, introduced December 20, 1945) provided very simply for no participation at all in the atomic energy project by the armed services of the United States.

Not quite so simply, it provided also for practically no secrecy. In order to see how effectively secrecy would have been eliminated, we may compare certain provisions of S. 1717, as originally introduced by Senator McMahon, with the Atomic Energy Act of 1946 as it looked after a "reactionary" House of Representatives got through with it, and as it became law August 1, 1946.

The McMahon Bill provided that "basic scientific information" in nuclear fields might "be freely disseminated," and it defined "basic scientific information" to include, "in addition to theoretical knowledge of nuclear and other physics, chemistry, biology, and therapy, *all results capable of accomplishment*, as distinguished from the processes or techniques of accomplishing them." (Italics added.)

The special care to include "results capable of accomplishment" explicitly under the heading "basic scientific information" is significant. The distinction between "basic scientific information" and "related technical information" was made of cardinal importance in the original Bill, which put few restrictions on the dissemination of the latter, but none at all on the former.

Now scientists and other students of the problem have repeatedly testified that positive knowledge concerning possibility of accomplishment is a vital "secret"—the most vital secret, some of them say—connected with any scientific or technological project.[222] They have also, on other occasions, classified this kind of information as technology rather than science. That question, debated in a vacuum, is scholastic, but in a legal context where "science" is to be freely disseminated while "technology" may be restricted, the question whether "results capable of accomplishment" shall be classified as science or technology may very well be practical enough to affect the balance of national military power and world hegemony.

Mr. Lilienthal told the Joint Committee that the Smyth Report was "the principal breach of security since the beginning of the atomic energy enterprise," and said, "I call your attention, for example, to the fact that in that report four different ways of separating [isotopes] were generally described, *and then the statement was made that all of them had succeeded.*" [223]

Senator McMahon added, on that occasion, "It has been estimated that that has brought other countries from one and a half to two years closer to the achievement of our own knowledge of atomic secrets."

The *Bulletin of the Atomic Scientists* (February 1947) composed variations on Mr. Lilienthal's theme, saying, "Revelation that plutonium can be and was fabricated in large plants, that it can be and was used for filling bombs, was in no way urgent, and an invitation to engineers abroad to try to duplicate processes which they know can be successful." This in a paragraph beginning scornfully, "Unfortunately neither the Congress nor public opinion has a clear understanding of the distinction between science and technology."

"It is ironical," the *Bulletin* continues, "that scientists are accused of a desire to reveal 'atomic secrets' . . . while the only important . . . revelations concerning the military and industrial aspects of atomic energy have come from the professed 'guardians of atomic security.'" That would be ironic, but it is a fact that S. 1717, which the *Bulletin of the Atomic Scientists* vigorously supported—to put the connection no closer—classified "all results capable of accomplishment" as "basic scientific information" and provided that they "may be freely disseminated."

The McMahon Bill further provided for "the dissemination of related technical information with the utmost liberality as freely as may be consistent with the foreign and domestic policies established by the President." It authorized the Commission to "designate by regulation the types of related technical information the dissemination of which will effectuate the foregoing policy," and provided that "Such designation shall constitute an administrative determination that such information is not of value to the national defense and that any person is entitled to receive such information within the meaning of the Espionage Act."

Note that *types* of information were to be declared by this agency from which the armed services were excluded as "not of value to the national defense," and once the determination had been made no one could be prosecuted under the Espionage Act (the only law that was allowed to govern at all) for publishing or otherwise doing as he pleased with any information included in the types. The definition of the types would always be a matter of controversy, and the burden of proof would always be on the prosecution.

Even if information could by no stretch of the imagination be classified under a "type" which had been approved for release, you could never have convicted anyone for releasing anything, for if the Commission had not designated a type as free from the Espionage Act, it was provided that "Failure to make any such designation shall not . . . be deemed a determination that such undesignated information is subject to the provisions of said [Espionage] Act."

Senator McMahon once said to Michael Amrine, then Managing Editor of the *Bulletin of Atomic Scientists,* "I have noted reference in Mr. Forrestal's *Diaries* about the scientists who were eager to take all secrets out of the country to Moscow," and Mr. Amrine replied, "We used to have that from two ends—it used to come out of the Pentagon or Manhattan District, and it used to come out of the Communist party circles at the other end. [It would be interesting for Mr. Amrine to document this—not that it is not quite plausible on its face, since both the Pentagon and the Communist Party are capable of telling the truth on occasion, sometimes even the same occasion—but in order to enlarge our knowledge of Communist Party channels of communication.] They were both interested in seeing that the scientists were pictured as wanting to give atomic energy secrets to the Soviet Union. These two kinds of people were feeding this idea into the channels of public opinion, while the Federation of American Scientists tried to keep the record straight." [224]

Now let's do keep the record straight. Whatever the scientists meant, and whatever Senator McMahon thought they meant, or meant himself, it is obviously true that S. 1717, which was the scientists' Bill with Senator McMahon's name on it, had it been put into effect, would have given all the atomic secrets to Russia, and to the rest of the world as well.

The Commission would have had no concern to control basic scientific information at all, except for a general duty to disseminate it, and it would have been responsible for providing for "the dissemination of related technical information with the utmost liberality as freely as may be consistent with the foreign and domestic policies established by the President." An abundance of expert scientific testimony could have been summoned, or would have been eagerly volunteered, to the effect that full publication of any and everything was the quickest path to "Security by Achievement." Experts with a generally contrary view would have been hard put to it to defend the concealment of any particular item when so much had been published (even the Smyth Report according to Mr. Lilienthal, made it "very difficult . . . to say, 'No, you can't,'" to "people who have done a piece of scientific or technical work . . . of which they are very proud").[225] Consequently, it would have been altogether impracticable to set any limit on the publication of technical information.

". . . Love for Russia . . ."

The first attempt to alter S. 1717 in any significant manner provoked wild outcries. Early in March 1946 Senator Arthur Vandenberg proposed the creation of a "Military Liaison Committee" to keep the armed services posted on what the Atomic Energy Commission was doing. This was reported by the *Daily Worker* (for March 13, 1946) in the following manner:

"Washington, March 12.—The Senate Atomic Energy Committee today, by a 6 to 1 vote, approved a proposal by Senator Arthur Vandenberg (R., Mich.) which would give a military board virtual dictatorial powers over atomic development. [The characterization is, of course, false.]

"The committee overrode its own chairman, Senator Brien McMahon (D., Conn.), who voted against the proposal, and President Truman. The action also ignored the scientists who had warned of the dangers of military control. . . .

"McMahon said it would empower the military board to pass on 'anything from the hiring of janitors at atomic energy establishments to the construction of atomic bomb plants.' He said it also would give the board power to 'check every telephone call, every memorandum written and the hiring of personnel.' . . .

"Vandenberg said world conditions made it imperative to give the military dominant control. . . .'"

Naturally, Senator Vandenberg did not say this, nor would his amendment as first offered have done it, nor did the amendment as passed do it. No one of any consequence in those days would have dared suggest giving the military dominant control, though it might have been a good idea. In an editorial the next day the *Worker* said the Vandenberg amendment gave "the army exclusive control." These boys work themselves up as time goes by.

The *Worker's* report of Senator McMahon's comments is apparently more accurate. The *New York Times* (March 17, 1946) says McMahon "made some ironical comments . . . about the Vandenberg amendment," and Arthur H. Vandenberg, Jr. and Joe Alex Morris write,[226] "McMahon claimed the Vandenberg amendment would enable the military to 'look into every single telephone call, every single file, every single action' the commission would take. It might be civilian control, the Connecticut senator argued, but it would be such control only with the military looking over the civilian's shoulders and ever able to take over."

Vandenberg, Jr. and Morris also relate how "many American scientists, still raw-nerved from their experiences with General Groves's war-time program, arose in loud protest. The bitterest critic of all . . . was Henry A. Wallace, then Secretary of Commerce. . . . The scientists in newly formed organizations descended on Washington; a large portion of the press, usually in Vandenberg's corner, came out swinging; and an alarming cross-cut of the public joined in the growing opposition." [227]

The *New York Times*, on March 17, reported "protest against the Vandenberg amendment continued to flow into the Capitol. Stephen H. Fritchman of the *Christian Register*, Boston, left at the White House a letter signed by himself and seven other ministers deploring the failure to share the atomic secret and urging Mr. Truman to resist military control of atomic energy. The committee itself [i.e., the Senate committee] received a protest signed by eighteen organizations." (Incidental moralizing: the influence of a few busy-bodies with a pen can be terrific. The Senators apparently really thought there was a kind of swell of public opinion, when the average American never heard of the Vandenberg amendment, but would certainly have been in favor of it if he had.)

According to his editors, Senator Vandenberg wrote in his diary as follows:

March 14, 1946.—[A] little tempest in a teapot . . . has blown up during the last forty-eight hours regarding atomic energy. There is a perfectly legitimate demand in the country (especially among scientists and educators) that final peace-time control of atomic energy should rest in civilian hands. In other words, the peacetime emphasis in respect to atomic energy should be transferred from military to civilian uses. I totally agree. But! I do not agree that in the present state of world affairs the Army and the Navy should be totally excluded from consultation when they deem the national security to be involved. . . .

The trouble with those who have been most violently urging civilian control is that they all but ignore the national security factor. Of course, they are supported in this viewpoint by every Communist and every fellow-traveler and every parlor pink in the country, because these latter groups would like to make our national security as insecure as possible.[228]

This lonely man worrying about the security of his country here classifies the energetic promoters of S. 1717 as (1) "scientists and educators" who wanted "emphasis . . . transferred from military to civilian uses," and (2) Communists, fellow-travelers, and parlor pinks, who "would like to make our national security as insecure as possible." In 1953, with the atomic energy project undergoing a gigantic expansion program based on military requirements, it is worth while taking a backward glance to see which of the two groups— the scientists and educators, or the Communists and fellow travelers—knew better what they were doing when they joined forces to emasculate the American armed services by enactment of the original McMahon Bill.

The *Daily Worker* had an editorial on March 14, 1946, entitled " 'Atomic' Fascism," in which the case against the Vandenberg amendment was presented in the fair and square manner we associate with the *Worker:*

Senator Vandenberg has just stampeded the Senate Committee for the control of atomic energy into a 6 to 1 vote giving the army exclusive control of all atomic energy production and research in the United States.

Under the Vandenberg scheme the most destructive force mankind has ever known will be taken out of the hands of the nation and the civil government.

It will go into the hands of professional militarists who will clamp down an "iron curtain" of secrecy on every aspect of this mightiest of human achievements. . . .

No wonder Secretary Wallace has warned that the Vandenberg plan means "military fascism." . . .

If the army can clamp a reign of terror on all American science, it can extend this "thought control" to all walks of American life. . . .

Vandenberg is pushing his plan because the administration's policy of expansion and bullying rests on the exclusive control of a secret weapon. . . .

Where is the labor movement in this crisis? It, and the entire nation, must awaken to the situation. It must demand of President Truman and of Congress *that atomic secrecy must end,* that it must be used for a better world, not as a weapon for the wrecking of the United Nations.

The *Christian Science Monitor* in another connection once referred to "every shade of American opinion . . . opinions ranging from those of Henry A. Wallace and the Federation of American Scientists to conservative columnists and members of Congress." [229] In this matter of the Vandenberg amendment—the first attempt to give the armed services any voice in or current knowledge of what was soon to be their principal reliance for the country's defense—the broad category of Henry A. Wallace and the Federation of American Scientists also included Senator Brien McMahon and the New York *Daily Worker.*

Senator McMahon, of course, was on the legislative firing line, as the other opponents of Senator Vandenberg were not. Some kind of compromise had to be reached. Considering that the Committee voted twice—6 to 1, and 10 to 1 when more members were present—against Senator McMahon and for Senator Vandenberg (the *one* was McMahon himself in each case), the question might be raised as to how McMahon had the strength to get even a compromise out of the situation; but to raise such a question would indicate naive unawareness of the political power of the scientists.

"Vandenberg," his editors tell us, "could convince neither the scientists, the press, nor McMahon. . . . Something had to be done, and Vandenberg did it. He called on Dr. Thorfin R. Hogness, a University of Chicago chemist who had been intimately a part of the atomic project and in whom he had confidence. He told Hogness that he was willing that the scientists 'write [their] own ticket' as long as it fell four-square within the purpose of assuring proper liaison between the military and the ultimate civilian authority, and that the military phases of atomic energy were not to be neglected in an aura of wishful thinking about a brave, new postwar world. Hogness worked as middleman between Eisenhower for the military, the scientists, and Vandenberg. The distilled result was a new version of the now famous military clause . . . [in which] the Military Committee's authority was narrowed down to 'military applications' of atomic energy alone, not to the far broader field of 'common defense and security.' The military group, also, was placed directly under the control of the War and Navy Secretaries, reporting only through them and with their concurrence to the President.

"Vandenberg happily announced that the new version met the 'common objective' of all concerned. The Senate Committee unanimously approved the redraft; the military and the scientists were well pleased, and the fight was over." [230]

Things were probably not so Pollyannafied as Messrs. Morris and Vandenberg, Jr., here indicate, nor is it clear from their account why everyone should have been so glad. Perhaps the fact that in the original proposal of Senator Vandenberg the Military Liaison Committee would have had "authority to make written recommendations to the Commission from time to time as it may deem appropriate," whereas in the final compromise this authority was omitted, made the difference. More likely, the "scientists and educators" and almost certainly the Communists and fellow-travelers never really feared the Military Liaison Committee half so much as they valued the opportunity of being able to attack it, and were consequently quite content to leave some kind of practically impotent military attachment to the organizational machinery. It must be allowed that the Military Liaison Committee has done little to justify the alleged fears of its early opponents, whatever it may have done to fulfill the hopes of its original advocates.

The obstreperous objections to the Vandenberg amendment were about the last public demonstration of the atomic Zouaves in the field of domestic legislation. The Acheson-Lilienthal Plan for international control was published shortly after, and the troops were deployed in readiness for whatever might come of that. As it turned out, unexpected forces came into play, and all the strategy was altered. It is probably not too much to say that the failure of the comrades on this side of the water to push the Acheson-Lilienthal Plan to its logical conclusion resulted, in June 1946, in the assumption by Moscow of international managerial responsibilities which during the preceding twelve or fifteen months had been exercised in New York, Washington, Chicago, etc. That would explain why the amendments to the McMahon Bill made by the House of Representatives in July 1946 attracted comparatively little attention, though they were actually far more drastic in frustration of the original intent of S. 1717 than was the Vandenberg amendment. By July 1946 it was too late to matter very much. Whoever the "boys in the back room" were, they were about ready to abandon exploitation of what we might call the Szilard-Stimson One-World approach in favor of the Blackett-Gromyko national-integrity approach.

Be that as it may, March 1946 saw the high tide of public interest in legislation for a U.S. Atomic Energy Commission.

Mr. Hanson W. Baldwin, in the *New York Times* of March 17, 1946, wrote the following summary of the situation:

Most of those who opposed the May-Johnson Bill, including Secretary of Commerce Henry Wallace, have supported the so-called McMahon Bill, sponsored by Senator Brien McMahon of Connecticut, Chairman of the Senate's Atomic Energy Committee. This bill, in a long series of hearings now ended, has won the endorsement of the great majority of the scientists who testified, and President Truman has twice expressed himself as in favor of the McMahon Bill, though with amendments.

But the original McMahon Bill, military and some other observers charged, has swung the legislative pendulum to the opposite extreme of the May-Johnson measure, and if passed as originally phrased, would virtually exclude the War and Navy Departments from any control over the development of atomic energy, even for military purposes.

The military also feel that the security measures proposed by the McMahon Bill leave something to be desired. It was to meet these objections that the McMahon Committee last week three times outvoted its chairman to pass amendments to the bill designed to insure the participation of the military.

The issue of atomic energy control thus becomes another "battle of Washington." It is a battle that could be relatively easily resolved if the administrative framework of the Atomic Energy Commission was in reality the only issue; the most obvious and logical compromise would be to amend the McMahon Bill to provide specifically for minority military representation.

But behind this issue of the type of desirable legislation lie undefined and shadowy but nevertheless viable differences—nationalism versus internationalism; fear of Russia versus love for Russia; the United States or the United Nations Organization.

Seldom has the issue been presented so well.

Chapter XIII ~ Valley (of the Shadow) Authority

BLUEPRINT FOR SOVIET LOS ALAMOS

The Acheson-Lilienthal Plan was a preliminary design for the international control of atomic energy. It was admirably suited to Communist purposes, being a complement to the original McMahon Bill. The latter would have disarmed the United States atomically and published all the scientific and technical information; the Acheson-Lilienthal Plan would have given the Soviet Union physical command of fission-able-materials plants and an atomic-bomb laboratory constructed in Soviet territory, theoretically for an international "Atomic Development Authority."

The Plan provided for the construction and operation of atomic bomb laboratories all round the world in accordance with a principle of "strategic balance" designed to reduce the existing American advantage and bring other nations to a position equal to that of the United States. This approach was developed by Americans employed as consultants by the State Department of the United States. It seems to be without historical parallel. The key passage follows:

In strengthening security, one of the primary considerations will relate to the geographical location of the operations of the

Authority and its property. For it can never be forgotten that it is a primary purpose of the Atomic Development Authority to guard against the danger that our hopes for peace may fail, and that adventures of aggression may again be attempted. [These men are not impractical dreamers.] It will probably be necessary to write into the charter itself a systematic plan governing the location of the operations and property of the Authority so that a strategic balance may be maintained among nations. In this way, protection will be afforded against such eventualities as the complete or partial collapse of the United Nations or the Atomic Development Authority, protection will be afforded against the eventuality of sudden seizure by any one nation of the stock piles, reduction, refining, and separation plants, and reactors of all types belonging to the Authority.[231]

It was claimed later by Chester I. Barnard, as by others, that the Plan was not to go into effect until adequate safeguards had been established.[232] Yet here it is plainly stated in the Acheson-Lilienthal Plan that the principle of "strategic balance" is introduced because it is recognized that other safeguards may break down. This principle of strategic balance could operate only in the interest of countries previously on the unfavorable side of an imbalance, which at the time the Plan was devised meant any and all countries other than the United States.

The report continues:

. . . At present with Hanford, Oak Ridge, and Los Alamos [N.B., this one is *not* omitted.] situated in the United States, other nations can find no security against atomic warfare except the security that resides in our own peaceful purposes or the attempt at security that is seen in developing secret atomic enterprises of their own. Other nations which, according to their own outlook, may fear us, can develop a greater sense of security only as the Atomic Development Authority locates similar dangerous operations within their borders. Once such operations and facilities have been established by the Atomic Development Authority and are being operated by that agency within other nations as well as within our own, a balance will have been established. It is not thought that the Atomic Development Authority could protect its plants by military force from the overwhelming power of the nation in which they are situated. Some United Nations military guard may be desirable. But at most, it could be little more than a token. The real protection will lie in the fact that if any nation seizes the plants or the stock piles that are situated in its territory, other nations will have similar facilities and materials situated within their own borders so that the act of seizure need not place them at a disadvantage.[233]

As an illustration of the principle in that last sentence: Once the "strategic balance" had been achieved, and atomic plants constructed in the Soviet Union, then if the Soviet Union seized the plants—which, it was granted, she could readily do—we would not have been "at a disadvantage" because we could have seized the plants that were situated in our territory. But we had those plants already, and the Soviet Union had none. So American "thinkers" at a time when the United States had atomic plants and the Soviet Union had none were *alarmed* and devised as a *hope for security* a situation where the U.S. plants would be surrendered to an international Authority, the Authority would construct plants in the Soviet Union, and if the Soviet Union seized them, the United States could "seize" back her own.

This seems less pacific than provocative.

The theoretical essential feature of the Acheson-Lilienthal Plan was that it established a partial world government. The international Atomic Development Authority would have superseded national sovereignty in the making of final legitimate decisions in the field of atomic energy. This is the very feature which conservative Americans instinctively distrust, the feature which seems to them "communistic" in nature. But so great was the wave of humanitarian idealism in the United States in 1946 that most conservative Americans of influence convinced themselves they had better overcome their natural reluctance to such a concept as world-govern-ment-ownership in order to save the human race from the dire consequences predicted by the pious and learned if complete national sovereignty anachronistically lingered long in the atomic age.

The reward of this amiable stupidity was the rejection of the Plan by the Soviets on the ground that it interfered with national sovereignty. When this happened many Americans felt silly and ashamed, like a Puritan getting slapped by a demimondaine.

PUT JELLY ON IT

Why did the Soviets reject the Plan? In general, apparently, because of boundless rapacity. Always reject the first offer, no matter what it is; you may get more later.

They could well have been encouraged to hold out for still greater concessions by the statements of certain Americans. We have referred to an essay by Norman Cousins and Thomas K. Finletter which appeared in the *Saturday Review of Literature* June 15, 1946, just at the time Mr. Baruch was presenting to the United Nations Atomic Energy Commission the American proposals which were, essentially, the Acheson-Lilienthal Plan, with one notable addition made by Mr. Baruch. The Cousins-Finletter article was in the form of a review of the Acheson-Lilienthal Report, which had been issued as a trade book by Doubleday & Co. Following are some significant passages from the review, which was entitled, oddly enough, "A Beginning for Sanity":

"There seems to be no perceptible resistance to the idea of relying upon an atomic armaments race for security, or to the dangers that are inherent in such a race. . . . A bigger stock pile of bombs offers little or no security to a nation which is hit first, particularly since the first blow may be the conclusive blow . . . a superior stock pile of atomic bombs may actually represent an added margin of danger rather than of defense in that it increases the chances of that nation being hit first in order to get it out of the way. . . ."

It is the right of any citizen to hold these views, but did we have to make him Secretary of the Air Force? If he thought "a superior stock pile of atomic bombs" represented "an added margin of danger rather than of defense," why did he accept the Cabinet post involving most immediate responsibility for using what we officially hope is our superior stock pile of atomic bombs?

The question grows more acute as we read of the "dangerous plausibility . . . of competitive systems of security rather than of workable world organization."

If our late Secretary of the Air Force did not believe in competitive systems of security, no wonder we have seemed to be losing the competition.

The main conclusion of the Cousins-Finletter review of the Acheson-Lilienthal Plan was that the latter offered "real encouragement in an otherwise discouraging picture. . . . In its statement of the problem, in its definition of the issues, in its suggestion for a *starting point* in attacking the problem, it offers solid ground for high-level public and government discussion. . . ."

But Cousins and Finletter saw that Acheson and Lilienthal had not, alas, had a free hand, that their treatment of the atomic energy problem was "further complicated by several conditions. . . . One such condition was that the State Department was anxious to assure Congress that any plan of international control, should it fail, would still enable the United States to retain its 'relatively secure position, compared to any other nation.' Another such condition . . . was that the United States would still be allowed to manufacture its atomic bombs after a plan of international control was put into operation, although 'at some stage' such discontinuance would probably be required."

"Now THESE," say Norman Cousins and Thomas K. Finletter, "ARE OF COURSE IMPOSSIBLE CONDITIONS." The conditions they are talking about are (1) that if the plan of international control should fail the United States should retain its "relatively secure position, compared to any other nation," and (2) that the United States should retain the right to manufacture bombs for any period of time following inauguration of the international-control scheme, including, say, any "try-out" period.

To say that (2) was an impossible condition was plainly to give Mr. Gromyko an invitation, if he needed any, to insist, as he did, on the immediate outlawing of atomic weapons, and the destruction within three months of existing stock piles, as the first step toward international control.

To say that (1) was impossible is more astonishing. If the man who was later to be Secretary of the Air Force could say at the time the Baruch proposals were being put forward that any attempt to guarantee the United States a relatively secure position was an impossible condition, what could the Soviets not hope for in the way of future concessions, provided they stood firm at the outset? In this atmosphere, the offer to construct atomic-materials plants and an atomic-bomb laboratory within the physical borders of the Soviet Union must have seemed to the resolute Muscovite not a rare opportunity to be quickly seized, but a token of weakness, of Western combat fatigue, a gesture of appeasement which only whetted the appetite it might have been supposed to assuage.

FOXY GRANDPA

From a normal American point of view the Acheson-Lilienthal Plan was an invitation to disaster, a proposal enormously favorable to the Soviet Union, and we could not in advance depend upon Communist greed to overmaster Communist judgment. Unamended, the Acheson-Lilienthal Plan might well have been accepted by the Kremlin, which might have agreed with Cousins and Finletter that "Despite all flaws, despite conditions of unilateralism favoring the United States which the Committee had to take into account, we believe it of the utmost importance that the Report be used as the basis for immediate discussion and action. . . ."

Professor Blackett, writing in 1948 after the impasse over international control had developed between the U.S. and the U.S.S.R., and expressing the Communist line very persuasively (his book was used by Andrei Vishinsky at Lake Success to make points for the Soviet), said, ". . . the Lilienthal Plan did represent at the time a constructive effort to solve the problem of atomic energy on an international basis, and so stood in marked contrast with the drive for a purely national control and development by America alone, which was sponsored by the opposing groups. And, at the time of its appearance, less than a year after the death of President Roosevelt and the end of World War II, it did not seem impossible that modifications might have been put forward to make it more acceptable to the Soviet Union. . . ." [234]

Fortunately for the United States, its Representative to the United Nations Atomic Energy Commission, Mr. Bernard Baruch, had other ideas. Clearly he did not agree with Cousins and Finletter that the flaws of the Acheson-Lilienthal Plan were "conditions of unilateralism favoring the United States," nor with Professor Blackett that what was needed were "modifications . . . to make it more acceptable to the Soviet Union." The one significant modification made by Mr. Baruch—the proviso of "no veto" with reference to atomic violations—was to make the plan more acceptable to the United States. It turned out that this made the whole thing quite unacceptable to the Soviet Union.

No one has ever been able to prove that Mr. Baruch produced this result deliberately, but no one has been presumptuous enough, either, to think that he merely blundered into it.

Senator Taft, to whom the Acheson-Lilienthal Plan seemed "to be the limit of all asininity on our part," [235] and Professor Blackett, in whose view the Lilienthal Report was a "brilliantly written document" characterized by "verbal felicity," a "logical method of analysis," and a successful appeal to "deeply felt internationalist longings" [236]—Senator Taft and Professor Blackett alike spoke of Mr. Baruch as of a very foxy Grandpa, to the obvious gratification of the Senator and the evident chagrin of the Professor.

In opposing the confirmation of Mr. Lilienthal as Chairman of the U.S. Atomic Energy Commission, Senator Taft said, "I think we should work out some plan of international control. But I believe that is impossible at present. . . . This report discusses the question of other nations seizing plants . . . it says that if we build a plant and it is seized, that is a danger signal. Then we will know that the enemy are going to war. Of course we will know it. We will know that they are going to war with the bombs which we let them build and for which we built the plants. . . . Let me say that I . . . shall be glad to have negotiations continued, but I would not begin by putting atom-bomb plants in Russia. That would seem to be the limit of all asininity on our part. . . ." [237]

Senator Lucas then put a natural question to Senator Taft: "The Senator says the report is naive, is simple, and indicates we are giving everything away to Russia under this plan. Can the Senator tell me, if that be true, why Russia does not accept this plan in a hurry?" [238]

Senator Taft replied, "I think it is because Mr. Baruch came in with a veto power [i.e., with a provision to eliminate the veto power], and they thought the left-wingers in the United States, like Mr. Lilienthal and others, were going to get this thing through without the [elimination of the] veto power. They did get Mr. Baruch out of the picture. In that much they were successful." [239]

Mr. Baruch, at the time Senator Taft spoke, had rather recently been replaced by Mr. Warren Austin. Relevant to the allegation that "Mr. Lilienthal and others were going to get this thing through without [elimination of] the veto power" is the following from *Minutes to Midnight*, by Dr. Eugene Rabinowitch: "Chester Barnard . . . recalled later that he and Mr. Lilienthal 'implored' Mr. Baruch not to introduce the proposal for a change in the veto rule. . . ." [240]

Senator Taft continued his response to Senator Lucas: "The Senator wants to know why they did not take it. I think it was because they thought they could get the Lilienthal report in its original form, the way Henry Wallace wants it, the way all the left-wingers in the United States want it." [241]

The Senator's view that Mr. Baruch's "no veto" addition to the Plan was the cause of its rejection by the Soviet Union, together with a possible implication that Mr. Baruch may not have failed altogether to calculate this result, gets inferential support from certain remarks by Mr. Baruch, and direct support by Professor Blackett.

Mr. Baruch told the Senate Committee on Atomic Energy: ". . . you see, when their report was first made, I had not been appointed. But after I was appointed, there seemed to be some difference of opinion in this respect: They seemed to want to go just so far on control and inspection and reporting. I wanted to go further, with no violator being able to escape punishment by veto or otherwise."

Senator Johnson: "You are speaking now of the Acheson-Lilienthal report?"

Mr. Baruch: "Yes, sir. Then Mr. Lilienthal came to me.

At first there seemed to be some difference of opinion between them and myself as to how far we ought to go. Later on, in about a month, Mr. Lilienthal came to see me and most generously offered his cooperation—and not only offered it but gave it." [242]

A bit later in the same session (this was during the Hearings on the Lilienthal confirmation), Mr. Baruch said: "That Acheson-Lilienthal report was a very remarkable report, Senator [McKellar]. I wish they had held it up until I was made American representative, because I would like to have toned it down a little, but I—"

Senator McKellar: "You cannot have things your own way, you know. Those things will happen." [243]

It appears, however, that Mr. Baruch did see to it that other people did not have things their own way either.

Possibly even more revealing of Mr. Baruch's attitude was his first reaction when the Acheson-Lilienthal report was new, as reported in the *New York Times* March 27, 1946, by Anthony Leviero.

"After his 45 minute conference in the White House," reads the *Times*, "Mr. Baruch was asked whether he had read the draft of a policy for the international control of atomic energy that Dean Acheson, Under Secretary of State, secretly presented to the Senate Atomic Energy Committee yesterday.

" 'Frankly, I did,' said Mr. Baruch, who had no hand in writing the policy. . . .

"Mr. Baruch was asked what he thought of it. He laughed, said, 'I can't hear you,' and walked away."

CHAGRIN OF PROFESSOR BLACKETT

The final word here on the fate of the Acheson-Lilienthal Plan is deserved by Professor Blackett, who on this subject, as on the decision to use the bomb against Japan, ascribes to the framers of American policy an astuteness that ought to be pleasing to us in about the same degree it is deplorable to Professor Blackett:

> Paralleling the objective dilemma facing Britain and America in search of a foreign policy, is the personal dilemma facing the atomic scientists themselves. . . . we have already outlined some aspects of the mental conflict arising from the use of the bombs on Japan, and have referred to the gradual discovery that the weapons that they had developed had been used by their Government not so much to end the second World War, as to inaugurate a third cold one. Their warnings as expressed in the *Franck Report* had gone unheeded and the evils prophesied, before even the experimental bomb had exploded, had duly come to pass. The appointment by the President of the Board of Consultants under David Lilienthal gave them another opportunity to retrieve the situation. This was brilliantly taken. This "bold and inspiring" document was essentially the atomic scientists' attempt to wipe away the stain of Hiroshima and Nagasaki and to turn the atomic bomb into a boon rather than a curse for mankind.[244]

"The stain of Hiroshima and Nagasaki" is probably not pacifism. Professor Blackett has explained elsewhere how Hiroshima and Nagasaki were brilliant successes from the point of view of American diplomacy. But that means they were "a stain" from the Communist point of view. And from that point of view also, the Acheson-Lilienthal report was indeed "bold and inspiring," no matter how intended. Professor Blackett credits it not to Mr. Lilienthal, as Senator Taft did, but to "the atomic scientists."

Triumphantly successful at first—or so it appeared from the universal acclaim with which it was received in the Western world—the clearer-sighted among them gradually perceived their idealistic plan metamorphosed before their eyes into its opposite. The Lilienthal Plan, the creation of the atomic scientists themselves, became the chief ingredient of the Baruch Plan and so of the Atomic Energy Commission [UN] proposals. What was intended by the atomic scientists to bring cooperation with Russia became an instrument in the hands of the American Government to coerce her. It is doubtful if the American Government would have succeeded so well in convincing the world of the purity of its heart in all matters relating to atomic energy and of the blackness of that of the Russians, if they had not had ready at hand the fine phrases and genuine idealism of the Lilienthal Plan, with which to clothe with specious generosity the hard-bitten *Realpolitik* of the Baruch Plan. In short, the atomic scientists were outmanoeuvered—for a second time.[245]

It is impossible to dismiss Professor Blackett. He presents with lucid expository artistry the same essential explanation as that toward which Senator Taft moved swiftly and intuitively in his impromptu exchange with Senator Lucas. The Acheson-Lilienthal Plan was an attempt by the atomic scientists "to bring cooperation with Russia," and it was frustrated by Mr. Baruch, who insisted on maintaining an attitude of "hard-bitten *Realpolitik*" with an American bias. "On balance," says Professor Blackett again, "the Baruch Plan, in spite of its rejection by the U.S.S.R., must be considered historically as an astute move and a very considerable victory for American diplomacy," [246] and all we disagree with there is "in spite," which ought to read "because."

It was a close call. If President Truman had appointed anyone but Mr. Baruch—If Mr. Acheson had been Secretary instead of Under Secretary—The whole thing could easily have gone otherwise. Not that we ought to exaggerate the extent of our deliverance. We are probably sustaining now a vigorous crop of Soviet agents as parasites in our own atomic plants and laboratories, and the Russians have an undetermined number of atomic bombs manufactured with an undetermined amount of aid from us. But at least we have escaped, thanks to Mr. Baruch, the foolish ignominy of establishing a legal international agency for the specific purpose of insuring the creation and maintenance of a "strategic balance" between ourselves and the Soviet Union in regard to potential atomic armament, a precarious balance, subject to instant destruction by whichever of the two powers should prove more lawless. (If we were lawless we had no reason to propose the bargain in the first place.)

HISTORIC ROLE OF HERBERT MARKS

We are far from knowing enough to give the whole story of the Acheson-Lilienthal report. If we did we should be able to be far more explicit about the entire secret war, for like Tennyson's flower in the crannied wall its full explanation would involve the explanation of much else besides. We note a bit of expert testimony about its genesis.

Secretary Acheson (then Under Secretary) appeared before the Senate Committee during the hearings on Mr. Lilienthal in order, primarily, to attest the patriotic loyalty of Mr. Herbert S. Marks, then General Counsel of the Atomic Energy Commission, formerly general assistant to Under Secretary Acheson, and formerly an attorney with the Tennessee Valley Authority. Mr. Marks had been associated with Communist activities in the TVA, according to the testimony of persons cited or called before the Committee by Senator McKellar,[247] notably two attorneys of Knoxville, L. B. Bolt, Jr. and Jack Comer. The latter characterized himself as "just a plain East Tennessee hillbilly, and that is all there is to it," [248] while the former confessed, "Being an east Tennesseean, I am not inclined to draw fine distinctions between a fellow traveler and a sympathizer or what have you." [249] Neither man would state flatly that Mr. Marks was a Communist, whereas Secretary Acheson had no hesitation in saying, ". . . I should stake my life and my reputation on the fact that all of those allegations are untrue." [250]

Mr. Lilienthal thought so highly of Mr. Marks that he risked the displeasure of Senator Hickenlooper (the Chairman of the Senate Committee) by appointing Mr. Marks

General Counsel at a salary of $14,000 at the very time when the confirmation of Mr. Lilienthal's own appointment by the President was being debated by the Committee.[251] Mr. Baruch had stated his opinion that the position of General Counsel was one of the two most important in the AEC, outside the five-man Commission itself, the other being that of General Manager,[252] held at the time by Carroll L. Wilson.

Secretary Acheson's testimony is worth quoting rather fully:

Mr. Acheson: . . . In August 1945, Mr. Byrnes asked me to become Under Secretary of State, and I became Under Secretary at the end of August 1945. At that time, I asked Mr. Marks to come over into the new office with me and be my new general assistant.

There he was called on to go into practically all of the affairs of the Department of State. . . .

In October of 1945, the Department of course became very active in connection with the control of atomic energy. . . . Much of such work as it fell my lot to do was carried out by and under the direction of Mr. Marks. . . .

In the opening days of January 1946, Mr. Byrnes was preparing to go to London for the meeting of the Foreign Ministers. . . . The meeting of the three heads of State had recommended, or had agreed upon, a statement, which was later taken to Moscow, and there in Moscow got Russian adherence, and in January 1946 was laid before the General Assembly of the United Nations and finally became their resolution of January 16, 1946, setting up the [United Nations] Atomic Energy Commission.

The Secretary of State foresaw that it would be necessary, when that atomic energy commission met, to have a program; and therefore preliminary work had to be done. To that end, he set up a committee. He asked me to be the chairman of the committee. The committee met in the early days of January and went to work on the problem.

I asked Mr. Marks to be the secretary of the committee. He acted in that capacity throughout.

. . . finally it was decided to have a panel of consultants, or a board of consultants.

That board was set up by the unanimous approval of our committee, and Mr. Carroll Wilson acted as its secretary. . . .

It may be of interest, as showing the views of members of that board of consultants, for me to read to you a letter which I received from one of the board . . . Mr. Chester I. Barnard.

He wrote to me on April 10, 1946, as follows:

"Dear Mr. Acheson: In conversation by telephone with Mr. Winne—"

Mr. Winne was another member of the board of consultants and is a vice president of the General Electric Co.

"In conversation with Mr. Winne this afternoon about another subject, we fell into a discussion of something that has disturbed us both. This is the fact that so little public recognition of the great contribution of Mr. Marks to the report of the International Control of Atomic Energy has been possible. In our foreword, reference is made to the help of Mr. Marks and Mr. Wilson, but the fact is that both these men worked along with us in practical effect as members of the committee. Particularly in the case of Mr. Marks, it seemed to me that his broad understanding of the objective and his persistence toward it indicated that he must have contributed greatly to your decision to establish the Board of Consultants. If so, he contributed not only as a working member of the Board, but also as among the initiators of a project which I must confess at first seemed to me to have some elements of the grotesque. . . . In writing to you of my appreciation of his service, I am attempting to relieve myself of the discomfort which I think is shared by all of us in being publicized as the authors while Mr. Marks is left out.

"Very truly yours,

CHESTER I. BARNARD."

To that I wrote Mr. Barnard on April 23, 1946:

"Dear Mr. Barnard: Thank you very much indeed for your letter of April 10. I am happy that you and Mr. Winne, and I know the other members of the Board as well, have received so clear an impression of the quality and ability of Herbert Marks.

He has a depth of understanding, a persistence of purpose, and a complete absence of confusing ego, which is unhappily all too rare in this work. You are quite right that he contributed greatly to the decision to establish the Board of Consultants, and *I have leaned upon and learned from him in all my thinking about this subject.* [Italics added.] I should be very glad indeed if there were some effective method of giving, as you suggest, public and historical recognition to Herbert Marks' contribution. I know that this does not concern him in the least. His interest is in making the contribution and not in having it recognized. For the present, I cannot think of a way but I know that he would agree with me that the soundest course is to go forward with the development of the ideas contained in the report and let the matter of recognition take care of itself.

"With kindest regards,

"Most sincerely yours,

DEAN ACHESON." [253]

Had we gone forward with the development of the ideas contained in the report (we did not because of the intransigence of Mr. Gromyko, as provoked, perhaps, by the craft of Mr. Baruch), it may be doubted whether even a man so self-effacing as Mr. Acheson depicts Mr. Marks as being would have been content with the kind of recognition he or any other American would have received. As things have turned out so far, there seems to be no quicker way to begin giving Mr. Marks some public and historical recognition than by reproducing here the testimony and letter of Secretary Acheson, together with the letter to Secretary Acheson from Mr. Barnard, and speculating on the importance of Mr. Marks' great contribution to the decision to establish the Lilienthal Board and thus initiate a project which even to Mr. Barnard at first seemed to "have some elements of the grotesque."

Quite possibly Mr. Marks is the most important non-scientist in the postwar history of the atomic energy project, though his passion for anonymity (Mr. John Lord O'Brian said Mr. Marks "has a rather shy personal character")[254] has contributed to the concealment of the fact, if it is a fact. Certainly he was a vital link between Secretary Acheson and Mr. Lilienthal. Mr. Barnard's indication that in the work of the Board of Consultants Mr. Marks was even more important than Mr. Carroll Wilson (though the latter was the Board's own secretary, whereas the former was there for liaison with the Secretary of State's Committee) is consistent with an impression common among the staff of the Atomic Energy Commission in 1947 that the General Counsel carried more weight than did the General Manager. The General Manager, however, seemed to have more staying power, for Mr. Marks resigned as General Counsel as of the effective date of an appropriation bill "rider" prohibiting the use of AEC funds to pay nonscientific and nontechnical personnel in excess of the rates provided by the Classification Act.[255] (At that time this meant a ceiling of $10,000; Mr. Marks was getting $14,000.) The rider, it was carefully explained in Congress, was intended to apply to "attorneys and clerks."

Following Mr. Marks' departure from AEC the post of General Counsel was held for a time by Adrian Fisher, who had just left the Department of Commerce, where he was a member of a loyalty review board that cleared Dr. Edward U. Condon. After a relatively short tenure Mr. Fisher left AEC to become Legal Adviser to the State Department. Mr. Joseph Volpe, Jr., succeeded Mr. Fisher as General Counsel. Mr. Volpe, a man of extraordinarily broad and intimate knowledge of the atomic energy project, while in uniform had been an important aide to General Groves in the Manhattan Project.* He reached a peak of administrative influ-

---

* The Lilienthal Board of Consultants, after thanking "General Groves and his associates in the Manhattan District," added "and

ence in the AEC during the summer of 1949, when he commanded a task force charged with the defense of Mr. Lilienthal against Senator Hickenlooper's accusation of incredible mismanagement. During the following year, however, Mr. Volpe had occasion to make an interpretation of the Atomic Energy Act which directly conflicted with an interpretation made and rather substantially supported by the then new Commissioner Gordon Dean, himself a lawyer.

After Mr. Dean was made Chairman in the summer of 1950, Mr. Carroll Wilson, it will be recalled, resigned with a blast against Mr. Dean. The next winter Mr. Volpe resigned, without fanfare, to enter private law practice. He is reportedly retained, in association with Mr. Herbert Marks, by Dr. J. Robert Oppenheimer.

It appears to be worth noting that Mr. Barnard by inference credited Mr. Marks, whose persistence he noted, with the not at all obvious inspiration to establish the Board of Consultants and launch it upon its somewhat "grotesque" career, and that Secretary Acheson, repeating the word *persistence*, specifically and fully confirmed the initiating role of Mr. Marks—"I have leaned upon and learned from him in all my thinking about this subject." [256] When the Secretary of State leans upon and learns from a man in all his thinking about atomic energy, then that man, if history is to be fair, should not remain obscure.

OPERATION JACOB

Why was the Lilienthal Board of Consultants appointed? Secretary Byrnes had named a Committee, with Under Sec-

Captain Joseph Volpe, Jr., for his liaison services." See *Report on the International Control of Atomic Energy* (Department of State Publication 2498, Second Reprint), p. [VIII], where the Board also expresses "our great indebtedness to . . . Mr. Herbert S. Marks . . . and to . . . Mr. Carroll L. Wilson."

retary Acheson as Chairman, and with other members: Dr. Vannevar Bush, Dr. James B. Conant, General Leslie R. Groves, and Mr. John J. McCloy. There is reason to believe these were bona fide Byrnes appointments.* There is also reason to believe that they would never themselves have drafted anything very closely resembling the Acheson-Lilienthal report.

After that report had come out, "It was a remarkable sign of the times," said Dr. Eugene Rabinowitch, "to see the signatures of General Groves, chief of the Manhattan Engineer District, J. J. McCloy, Assistant Secretary of the Army, and Vannevar Bush, head of the wartime Office of Scientific Research and Development, affixed to a letter transmitting to the Secretary of State an atomic energy control plan which, in its radical internationalism, went far beyond any proposals previously made in public discussion." [257] It was remarkable, all right. Dr. Rabinowitch goes on to speak of "the misgivings these men must have felt in endorsing proposals which called for America's assistance in the liquidation of her monopoly of atomic energy," [258] and of safety devices which they tried to introduce (thus serving as forerunners to Mr. Baruch, who introduced the big safety device of making sure the Russians would reject the whole thing).

Even so, the maneuvering which resulted in these signatures was masterly, and the whole thing was essentially due, it appears, to Mr. Marks. For we cannot doubt Mr. Barnard and Secretary Acheson when they credit Mr. Marks with the decision to establish the Board which actually did the work that Secretary Byrnes appointed the Committee to do. The value of this from the Marks-Lilienthal-Acheson point of view

---

* Two of them—Bush and Conant—were, of course, in what James S. Allen calls "the upper scientific hierarchy." See p. 182 above.

was that they were thus able in effect to supplant a Committee appointed by the Secretary of State with a committee appointed by the Under Secretary of State—and those on whom he leaned and from whom he learned. One might call it Operation Jacob.

Secretary Acheson said that "all the members of the committee were either very busy Government officials or presidents of universities, et cetera," and that "they themselves could not give full time to the study of this question." [259] That seems very reasonable if you do not think about it too long. Then you consider that the Board of Consultants, appointed to do the work which these men were too busy to do, consisted of:

Mr. David E. Lilienthal, Chairman of the Tennessee Valley Authority, who acted as Chairman,

Mr. Chester I. Barnard, President of the New Jersey Bell Telephone Company,

Dr. J. Robert Oppenheimer, of the California Institute of Technology and the University of California,

Dr. Charles Allen Thomas, Vice President and Technical Director, Monsanto Chemical Company, and

Mr. Harry A. Winne, Vice-President in Charge of Engineering Policy, General Electric Company.

And you start to wonder. Of course Under Secretary Acheson was a busy man; of course Dr. Bush and Dr. Conant were busy men; it is not too clear why General Groves and Mr. McCloy were so busy at that particular time; but let it go that a majority of the Committee were busy men. Was not the Chairman of TVA a busy man? Was not the President of the New Jersey Bell Telephone Company a busy man? Was not Dr. Oppenheimer, as a member of two distinguished faculties, a busy man? Was not the Vice President and Technical Director of Monsanto Chemical Company a busy man? Was not the Vice-President in Charge of Engineering Policy for the General Electric Company a busy man? How busy can you get?

THE DENATURING HOAX AND THE VETO

Secretary Byrnes rather pointedly refrained from giving his approval to the Acheson-Lilienthal Plan. As a Foreword to the officially published report, Mr. Byrnes wrote:

"The intensive work which this document reflects and the high qualifications of the men who were concerned with it make it a paper of unusual importance and a suitable starting point for the informed public discussion which is one of the essential factors in developing sound policy. The document is being made public not as a statement of policy but solely as a basis for such discussion."

Morris V. Rosenbloom has observed, "The evidence appears to indicate that Byrnes accepted [the Acheson-Lilienthal report] unenthusiastically. Certainly the foreword . . . tended to damn it with faint praise." [260]

Quoting Mr. Byrnes' account of how he recommended Mr. Baruch in the first place " 'for the task of translating the various proposals stimulated by the Acheson-Lilienthal report into a workable plan,' " Mr. Rosenbloom says, "Note the word 'workable.' " [261]

The main reason for ever doubting the workability of the Acheson-Lilienthal Plan—if one assumes Soviet consent to participate in it—related to the veto problem. At the time of Mr. Lilienthal's confirmation hearings this problem seemed to disturb Senator Knowland, and he persistently interrogated Under Secretary Acheson on the subject:

Senator Knowland: "Mr. Acheson, in connection with the Acheson-Lilienthal report, which I have read several times, I should like to bring to your attention the fact that I can find no mention in it of the problem of the veto. . . . Did not the veto come up?"

Mr. Acheson: "Well, Senator, may I tell you a little bit

about what this report is or was? . . . The problem of what you do with a violator who . . . is embarked on something which must mean aggressive war, is a matter for statesmen who are organizing international forces to repress that sort of illegal action, and not for people who are examining the basic problem of how you set about the control of atomic energy." [262]

Most people thought the reason for international control was to prevent aggressive war, and thought Dean Acheson and his associates were statesmen trying to organize (or prepare a plan for organizing) international forces to repress that sort of illegal action. In fact, to the average citizen that would seem like a definition of international control of atomic energy.

Acheson, however, persisted that the problem of international control was technical:

"The committee and the Board of Consultants undertook to limit what they were doing. . . . We undertook to deal with the basic physical problems." [263]

At this point Senator Vandenberg came to his support.

"I quite agree with Senator Knowland," said Vandenberg, "that in the final show-down the veto becomes perhaps Exhibit A. . . . But I think I would have to testify from my own association with the development of the enterprise that the problem presented [to the Committee and the Board of Consultants] was purely an answer to the question: Can you physically, factually, mechanically, actually, control atomic energy?" [264]

The reason why Senator Vandenberg fell for the twaddle that the Acheson-Lilienthal report was technical appeared later in the hearings, when he asked Mr. Acheson:

"Was not the chief original contribution to the national thinking on this subject, which was made by the Lilienthal report, the disclosure of the new fact that it is possible to denature fissionable material so that it cannot be used for destructive purposes unless it is renatured, which is a very difficult process? Is that not a fact?" [265]

"That was a very important contribution," said the Under Secretary, adding guardedly, "I don't think it was the most important, Senator, but it is a very important one."

"From my point of view," insisted Vandenberg, "it was the most important one. . . ."

It would have been more important if it had been entirely on the level.

This is not the place to expound fully why it was, as Senator Johnson called it,[266] "a cruel hoax" to speak of denaturing fissionable material, but it may be stated that the so-called denaturing was found on inquiry to consist of physically mixing nonfissionable isotopes with fissionable isotopes. The separation of such isotopes is indeed, in Senator Vandenberg's words, "a very difficult process." It is, in fact, the same process by which one kind of fissionable material, U-235, is accumulated in the first place. Natural uranium is "denatured" uranium. If you have a plant which will enrich natural uranium enough to call it fissionable material, you have an isotope separation plant. But an isotope separation plant is what "renatures" "denatured" U-235. The proposed international agency, under the Acheson-Lilienthal Plan, was going to have isotope separation plants,[267] and in accordance with the principle of strategic balance it was going to have them all round the world. In other words, the denaturing business *depended on* the enforcement power of the agency and *did not contribute to* that power.

Apart from the *ignis fatuus* of denaturing, the separation of the technical and the political problems in the control of atomic energy is impossible, and the Board of Consultants clearly did not attempt any such separation.

"It may be helpful," says the Acheson-Lilienthal report, "to summarize the characteristics that are essential to an effective system of safeguards.

"*a*) Such a plan must reduce to manageable proportions the problem of enforcement of an international policy against atomic warfare. . . ."

Secretary Acheson said to Senator Knowland, "We undertook to deal with the basic physical problems. . . . We did not undertake to go into the questions of international law . . . finance . . . armaments to repress aggression. . . ." How can you take it as your first criterion in devising a system to "reduce to manageable proportions the problem of enforcement of an international policy," and then not talk about international law or international armaments? The reason why the suggestion of "denaturing" itself was seized upon with such eagerness was not that it was a technical rather than a political process, but that it was, allegedly, a technical process which would solve a political problem.

Enrico Fermi has said, "There is no denying the fact that the possible use of plutonium for aggressive warfare constitutes a difficulty for the industrial uses of atomic energy that is much greater than any technical difficulty that we can foresee. The problem of preventing this use is essentially political and not technical." [268]

The whole point of the Acheson-Lilienthal report was that the nature of atomic technology was such as to require for its effective control more than inspection, was such as to require *management* by an international authority, of certain fundamental activities denominated as "dangerous." These activities were, of course, intimately related to the military applications of atomic energy, and were therefore of the essence of what was considered the commanding violence of the world. To suggest international management in this field is to suggest modification of national sovereignty. As the world is organized today, the right of veto in the Security Council of the United Nations is the hallmark of national sovereignty, first class. You can no more suggest international management of atomic energy without deciding what you are going to do about the veto than you can suggest martial law without deciding what you are going to do about habeas corpus.

It seems plain enough that the authors of the Acheson-Lilienthal report, Mr. Marks and the others, did not, as Secretary Acheson says they did not, overlook the question of the veto. They settled the question. The Acheson-Lilienthal report considers what happens in the case of serious violations, and proposes "strategic balance" as at once a preventive of and response to such violations.

It will probably be necessary to write into the charter a plan governing the location of the operations and property of the Authority so that a strategic balance may be maintained among nations. In this way, protection will be afforded against such eventualities as the complete or partial collapse of the United Nations or the Atomic Development Authority, sudden seizure by any one nation of the stock piles, [et cetera] . . . belonging to the Authority.

[Here follows the shocking suggestion about building Los Alamos, etc., abroad.] . . . The real protection will lie in the fact that if any nation seizes the plants or the stock piles that are situated in its territory, other nations will have similar facilities and materials situated within their own borders so that the act of seizure need not place them at a disadvantage.

In other words, in case of a serious violation there is a reversion, legally, to the status quo ante, which is to say the right of veto is not affected.

Thus the Lilienthal Board and the Acheson Committee made the decision not to ask for abolition of the veto in matters relating to atomic energy. Mr. Baruch, whose authority superseded theirs, made a contrary decision.

❊   ❊   ❊

Every once in a while during the past seven years the Atomic Energy Commission has had to debate the proper location of a new plant or laboratory. Should it be in Texas or Idaho? Should it be in Ohio or South Carolina? If Mr.

Baruch had not overruled the authors of the Acheson-Lilienthal Plan on the veto matter, those debates might well have been even more vexing, posing such questions as: Should the next gaseous diffusion plant be situated in India or Czechoslovakia? Should the new plutonium reactor be placed in the Ukraine or in China? [269]

The weapons laboratory in the Urals should have been coming up with some interesting developments by now. No new installations in the United States, of course, as we should hardly yet have achieved "strategic balance."

*   *   *

Since the above chapter was written, confirmation of much of it has appeared. On June 25, 1953, J. Anthony Panuch, former Deputy Assistant Secretary of State, testified before the Jenner Committee: ". . . shortly after I came into [the State] Department, there was a so-called Acheson-Lilienthal Plan for the international control of atomic energy. . . . Mr. Herbert Marks had charge of it for Mr. Acheson. . . . [Mr. Panuch and certain associates] opposed it for the simple reason that we believed [the U.S.] had an edge in atomic energy and atomic weapons and we should keep that to ourselves and not dish it out to people who might be our mortal enemies."

Senator Welker: "Then your team . . . sought out and received the aid of Bernard Baruch?"

Mr. Panuch: "Yes, sir. Through Secretary Byrnes and President Truman."

In response to another question by Senator Welker, Mr. Panuch said: "I would definitely say that Mr. Acheson and Mr. Hiss at the time that I was in the Department were sympathetic to the Soviet policy." (From official stenographic transcript, Alderson Reporting Co., 306 West 9th St., N.W., Washington, D. C.)

Chapter XIV ⏤ Sit-down Strike

Has any real harm been done? Granted an effort to nullify the American A-bomb in a post-Hitler world, the effort has not succeeded:

(1) We did use the bomb against Japan.

(2) The *revised* McMahon Bill did include military representation and provisions for secrecy.

(3) The Acheson-Lilienthal Plan was modified by Baruchian sagacity and rejected by Soviet stupidity.

Why worry?

I hope you're right.

In fact, however, our "Achievement" is not what it might have been, having been negatively sabotaged by unidentified scientists on at least three occasions.

STRIKE ONE

The *New York Times* for February 16, 1946, carried the following letter:

To the Editor of the *New York Times*:

. . . we would like to suggest a declaration of policy of the following nature by the President of the United States . . . :

1. The United States will at once stop the production of bombs from material currently produced. . . .

2. For one year . . . we will stop accumulating purified pluto-nium and uranium-235. . . . As produced, these will be elimi-nated by appropriate means, such as dumping them into the ocean or returning them to their original mixtures.

3. We are prepared to have the disposition of our present stockpile of bombs considered as one of the items in an agree-ment to be entered into by us and the other Governments.

> L. C. DUNN, IRWIN EDMAN, A. P. EVANS, SELIG HECHT, P. C. JESSUP, R. M. MAC-IVER, EDGAR MILLER, F. C. MILLS, GEORGE B. PEGRAM, I. I. RABI, JAN SCHILT, C. S. SHOUP.

New York, February 13, 1946.

The signers of the foregoing letter are, respectively, professors of zoology, philosophy, history, biophysics, public law, sociology, biochemistry, economics, graduate faculties (dean), physics, astronomy, and economics.

This letter is important because during the twelve months following its publication *no bombs were manufactured*. Offi-cially, the policy recommended by these Columbia professors was not adopted. In practice it governed.

November 28, 1945, General Groves told the McMahon Committee, "We have to keep operating everything from the standpoint of having a sufficient supply of bombs on hand until somebody makes up his mind as to what is to be the future of this work." [270]

The next day Dr. Urey told the Committee, "We are mak-ing bombs and storing them and are thus a threat to other countries. . . ." [271]

Again, on the same day, Dr. Urey said, ". . . we now have a supply of bombs." [272]

And again, "I believe our international situations are being poisoned day after day because we are accumulating a sup-ply of bombs. . . ." [273]

Here, at the end of 1945, is testimony from the General in command of the project that official policy was to have a supply of bombs, and testimony from a Nobel-prize-winning atomic scientist that we did have such a supply and were daily augmenting it.

Two and a half months later three other atomic scientists —Professor Hecht, Dean Pegram, and Professor Rabi—together with several learned colleagues, including Ambassador Jessup, recommended the cessation of atomic bomb production.

The actual situation a year later, early 1947, was set forth in the Majority Report of the Joint Committee on Atomic Energy following its investigation of Senator Hickenlooper's charges of "incredible mismanagement":

Uncontradicted testimony shows that in 1947 when responsibility was formally transferred from the Manhattan Engineer District to the Commission, our weapons position verged upon the tragic. The United States then possessed so few bombs, according to Mr. Lilienthal, that we might have tempted fate if public statements even mentioned the importance of numbers in building an atomic deterrent to aggression. Dr. Robert F. Bacher, an original member of the Commission, and now Chairman of the California Institute of Technology Physics Department, told the Joint Committee that he personally made an inventory of our stock pile early in 1947 and that he was both surprised and "very deeply shocked" by the meager findings.[274]

Dr. Bacher was head of the bomb physics division at Los Alamos when the war-time bombs were made. He was the. first scientist chosen to serve on the Atomic Energy Commission. He is a real expert.

After a year's absence he was "both surprised and 'very deeply shocked'" when he "personally made an inventory" of U.S. atomic bombs! Why? What had been going on at Los Alamos in that year Dr. Bacher had been gone? If a layman had made the inventory, if a Senator had made the inventory, even if General Groves had made the inventory, it might be credible that he should have been both surprised and very deeply shocked. But this man had been head of the bomb physics division, and he had been gone only a year! Is it any reasonable lag, any ordinary bottleneck in production that can cause such an expert examiner to be "both surprised and 'very deeply shocked' "?

The Joint Committee Majority apparently took this to mean that Manhattan District had fallen down on the job in 1946, and that Mr. Lilienthal and the rest of the first AEC had come in and saved us from a typical Army SNAFU. That is nonsense. The Army did not understand what the scientists at Los Alamos were doing, and neither did Mr. Lilienthal. If a scientist wants to soldier, a soldier cannot prove it on him. Neither can a lawyer. If Dr. Bacher, a scientist, was surprised and shocked at the lack of accomplishment by his fellow scientists during the course of a year, the explanation lies with the scientists, and nowhere else. This hiatus in production which was so shocking to Dr. Bacher occurred at the very time when Ambassador Jessup and associates suggested a hiatus in production.

STRIKE TWO

Had an incident, say in connection with the Berlin airlift, precipitated war in 1948, we could not have used the atomic bomb, though at the time the atomic bomb was, in the judgment of Forrestal's editor, Walter Millis, "the real core of American strength . . . indeed, about the only form of military strength which remained after the evisceration of the April 'balanced' program." [275]

In the spring of 1948, shortly before the Berlin blockade began, a civilian official from Washington, D. C., made a trip to Los Alamos. This was a year and a half after Dr. Bacher's inventory.

The official traveler, whom I shall call Ordway because that is not his name, had a check-list of atomic bomb components, and was authorized to look and see whether they were there and what shape they were in.

One of the components of the 1948 model of the bomb was a perishable commodity. Like yeast, its age made a lot of difference, and the way it was stored made a lot of difference.

Other components were more stable. The essential fissionable components were and are more stable. This was not the main component, but in the 1948 model you had to have it, just as you have to have yeast in a bakery. Like yeast, it could be graded according to its health and vigor.

Ordway found that at Los Alamos they had no grade-A yeastcakes. He got the impression that the Los Alamos scientists were not much interested in these components.

This means the United States had no sure-fire A-bombs in 1948.

The "real core of American military strength" was rotten.

Strike Three?

In October 1952 Stewart Alsop and Dr. Ralph Lapp gave "The Inside Story of Our First Hydrogen Bomb" in the *Saturday Evening Post*.[276] Alsop and Lapp cite Dr. Hans Bethe as authority for the statement, "the Soviet Union may explode the hydrogen bomb before this country."

That prediction now seems to have been wrong, but apparently it was the Soviet Union's own fault, as we stalled around long enough to give them more than a sporting chance.

"Between July, 1945, and January, 1950," say Alsop and Lapp, "there was *no serious or concerted American effort to make the hydrogen bomb*." (Italics in the original.)

The theory of the H-bomb was far advanced in July 1945. John J. McCloy, in a speech at the Life Underwriters' convention in December 1946, said, "I have been told by scientists who are not mere theorists but who actually planned and made the bomb which was exploded in New Mexico that, given the same intensive effort which was employed during the war toward the production of that bomb, we were within two years time at the close of the war of producing a bomb of the hydrogen-helium type, i.e., a bomb of approximately one thousand times the power of the present bombs." [277]

In other words, we might have had the hydrogen bomb in 1947.

Work was not started until 1950, and would not have been started then except for Edward Teller and Lewis L. Strauss.

Teller as a scientist and Strauss as an AEC Commissioner saw and took the position required by our national interest and held it against all comers until Truman, just one week after Fuchs' initial confession to W. J. Skardon in England, gave the Presidential directive to proceed with developmental work on the hydrogen bomb.

Fantastically, vision and courage of the high order possessed by Teller and Strauss were required to make possible this obvious step. It was opposed by Bacher, Oppenheimer, and Lilienthal—formidable opposition.

Alsop and Lapp say, "The causes of the lag . . . have nothing whatsoever to do with treachery." But Alsop and Lapp are here speaking from ignorance.

It is clear enough that the United States could have had the hydrogen bomb about four years sooner if the scientists as a group had wanted the United States to have it.

*   *   *

Now there is a plausible objection to classifying this as a sit-down strike against the United States. That objection does not consist of elaborate rationalizations concerning the expense and relative inefficiency of the hydrogen bomb, but simply of the observation that, according to the main principle purportedly revealed in this book, hypothetically unpatriotic scientists might be supposed to have been willing enough to go along with the H-bomb development as part of the specious doctrine of Security by Achievement, feeding to the Soviets all the time the resulting information and materials. If this hypothesis is reasonable, how could they also have been supposed to have obstructed American progress?

Unfortunately, it is not a sufficient defense against a circumstantially supported charge of criminal neglect to allege inconsistency in the accusation because of previously introduced evidence of positive viciousness.

The drunken father cannot argue that of course he would not carelessly have starved the child, since, as the neighbors will testify, he went to all the trouble only last Tuesday to beat the kid half to death.

Either charge may be false. Either charge may be true. Both may be false. Both may be true. The charges must be judged on the evidence as to the facts in each case, and not on whether all the charges together suggest a consistent pattern of original conduct. People are often inconsistent. And certainly this book will have missed the mark very widely if it leaves the impression that our adversaries in the secret war always know what they are doing and always do it well.

Still, we look for patterns. And there is consistency in the A-bomb and H-bomb stories on at least two counts:

(1) The instigators of each project were obviously at the time more zealous than sophisticated.

(2) Reaction amounting to sabotage was in each case the policy of those who through passage of time or other circumstance lost or lacked the instigator's zeal.

In each case the instigation was in accord with the prima facie national interest of the United States, and in each case the reaction was in accord with the prima facie interest of the Soviet Union. We are aware that subtle analyses might present the interests in a different light, and we do not judge motives of individuals. It remains probable that a majority of those who promoted first the A-bomb and second the H-bomb intended to serve the interest of the United States, and that a significant minority of those who opposed first the use of the A-bomb and second the development of the H-bomb intended to serve the interest of the Soviet Union.

In the case of the A-bomb I think the impracticability of continued negative sabotage forced the Communist underground in this country to develop a highly sophisticated scheme of diversion of information and materials. The H-bomb development would not be the kind of "Achievement" that would make that operation either easier or more effective.

On the other hand, U.S. prestige would be enhanced by a demonstrably successful development of the H-bomb, and the Soviets would not like that. The old line of terrifying Americans with psychological warfare based on the destructive capacities of their own bombs could be—and has been —tried again. But it never worked with the A-bomb, and there was and is no good reason to suppose it would work with the H-bomb.

For these and other reasons I find no essential inconsistency in the hypothetical use by Communists in the American atomic energy project of both the stratagem of co-operation in building bigger and better fissionable-material plants and the stratagem of blocking development of the hydrogen bomb.

Chapter XV ⟋ Truth and Consequences

I have been at once eager and reluctant to write this book. Eager because Communist exploitation of the atomic energy project is a relatively unexplored subject (as far as critical analysis is concerned), reluctant because to explore this subject is to disturb established reputations.

The praise and blame of individuals has not been my purpose. I am not qualified to judge the persons involved in this secret war, nor do I wish to judge them. In the "confused alarms of struggle and flight, Where ignorant armies clash by night," it is not always possible even to identify friend and foe, and it is seldom possible to be sure that either friend or foe is intelligently true to his own cause.

Our friends, moreover, may provoke us with what seems to be their folly, and our foes may excite our admiration with what seem to be their skill and daring. But we are not thereby deterred from the pursuit of a just victory.

If without names I could with verity and verisimilitude have sketched the outline of the conflict, it would doubtless have been decent to do so. But I think that what I have said will be credited only with great difficulty in any case. Without specific instances to illustrate general allegations, it would never be credited at all. Specific instances, to be verifiable, must include places, dates, and names.

There are two reasons why I am sorry the names of certain persons had to be included: first, the inclusion may harm those persons; second, it may, even while lending credibility to the discussion, distort the true emphasis.

There is a kind of uncertainty principle here: it is impossible to believe that there are Communists in the project unless we identify some who have been there, but the process of identification itself means that these particular Communists are not the ones we have to worry about any longer. It is therefore a distortion to dwell upon known cases, but if we understand and allow for that, it may be instructive.

At the risk of sounding like a hypocrite, I must say I have not written this book with the intention of harming anyone, not even a certified Communist or spy, though I should be happy to assist in the frustration of his designs, which I regard as inimical to the United States, to the other justly empowered governments of the world, and indeed to his own deepest interests. Once he is defeated, however, let us abuse him no further. Some of the things published about Klaus Fuchs almost seem to me pointless sadism.

Nor can I quite understand the alacrity with which certain observers have branded Bruno Pontecorvo as a traitor. I don't believe he has been convicted of anything, or even indicted. The staff of the Joint Committee on Atomic Energy, for their part, say, in *Soviet Atomic Espionage*, p. 47: "If an innocent explanation should develop subsequent to the appearance of this report, apologies are herewith rendered in advance. At the same time . . . prudence dictates the assumption that Pontecorvo indeed went to Russia at his own volition." Then follows a rather long paragraph beginning: "By way of pure speculation it may be theorized . . ."

This book obviously has its own share of speculation and

of theory, but I have not indulged in speculation on what particular individuals may have done. I have speculated—prudence seemed to dictate it—on what may have been done, may be now in process, or may be yet to be done, by persons unknown.

Three kinds of persons are included among those whom it would have been more agreeable not to name:

(1) Persons convicted of crimes. For example, David Greenglass, who confessed he had acted as a spy for the Soviets; and Dr. Sanford Simons, who pleaded guilty to the charge of illegal possession of fissionable material.

(2) Persons who admit former membership in the Communist Party. For example, David Hawkins, Robert R. Davis, Frank Oppenheimer, and Philip Morrison.

(3) Persons whose historically important judgments have, in my opinion, been mistaken. For example, Leo Szilard in opposing the use of the A-bomb against Japan, J. Robert Oppenheimer in opposing development of the hydrogen bomb, the late Senator Brien McMahon in opposing the establishment of the Military Liaison Committee, and David Lilienthal in advocating reliance on the concept of "strategic balance."

These three kinds of persons obviously should not be confused. Those in the third group are not Communists and are not criminals; perhaps they were not even mistaken, though it seems to me that they were; perhaps I was and am mistaken. Persons in the second group presumably were Communists, since they have said they were, but they are not criminals, and they are no longer members of the Communist Party. Persons in the first group were convicted of crimes of very different degrees of gravity, and have paid or are now paying the penalty imposed. One thing the members of the three groups have in common in my mind, and that is that I do not intend to impute motives to any of them, for I do not know what their motives were.

The words and deeds which I have attributed to persons known and named are indeed their own to the best of my knowledge and belief. The evidence for my belief is cited or quoted in the main text or in the appended notes. Documentary notes have a tendency to be at once tedious and inadequate. I am sure the ones I have furnished are no exception, but to readers who find there are too many notes and to readers who think there are too few I have one reply: More are available.

* * *

Two sources of great importance I have scarcely touched. One is the work of Major George Racey Jordan, reported in his book, written in collaboration with Richard L. Stokes, *From Major Jordan's Diaries* (Harcourt, Brace & Co., 1952). The fact that I have not gone into Major Jordan's story is not due to any desire or intent to obscure its very great importance. On the contrary, I think he ought to be read in the original.

He saw uranium and heavy water being shipped to the Soviet Union during World War II, via Lend-Lease route through Great Falls, Montana. He does not pretend to give a technological evaluation of what he saw, but he knows what he saw. On this case the staff of the Joint Committee on Atomic Energy has made a study which—whatever other defects may be charged—is entirely free from bias in Major Jordan's favor. The Summary of this study reads as follows (*Soviet Atomic Espionage*, pp. 191–92):

Review of the data examined and interviews conducted in connection with this inquiry indicates that two shipments totaling 1,420 pounds of uranium salts and one shipment of 2.2 pounds of uranium metal were made to Russia under lend-lease with the knowledge and consent of all agencies and parties concerned in

1943 and 1944. In addition, two shipments of heavy water, totaling 1,100 grams, were made to Russia during the war within
existing legal provisions for such exports.

The Joint Committee staff could find no indication that documents, maps, blueprints, or classified papers other than those
authorized in connection with the wartime agreements with
Russia were shipped during the war through Great Falls, Montana. At the same time, the volume of material in transit and the
existence of channels covered by diplomatic immunity through
which unauthorized shipments might have reached Russia preclude any positive statement that nothing ever went to Russia
without approval via Great Falls.

Is there an implication there that if the shipments were
"within existing legal provisions" they were O.K.? I'm just
asking.

I have heard the objection raised to Major Jordan's account that technically uninformed people might draw wrong
conclusions from it. A more likely danger, I should think,
was that technically informed people should fail to draw
any conclusions at all.

"Have you," I was asked, "actually seen any material
being diverted?"

No. And that may be supposed to be the end of me.

But Major Jordan did.

Oh, well—half a ton of uranium compounds, a kilo of
uranium metal, and a little over a kilo of heavy water—
laboratory toys!

Explain it away to your heart's content. The Soviets
wanted the stuff. They got it. Fissionable material is far
more convenient to transport (in quantities of comparable
value), and by now probably more plentiful than heavy
water was in 1943.

Major Jordan saw some men taking the piano out the
door. I think one of them had some of the sterling in his

pocket. No, I didn't actually see what was in his pocket. Why don't we count the spoons? Oh, we don't know how many we are supposed to have? That does make it tough.

*   *   *

Another source which I have neglected is of monumental importance. It is the Report of the Canadian Royal Commission, based on the intensive investigation which eventually followed the defection to our side of the former Soviet code clerk Igor Gouzenko. Gouzenko deserted the Russian Embassy in Ottawa in September 1945, carrying with him the files on which is based ultimately nearly all our current knowledge of Soviet atomic espionage.

Gouzenko almost failed to make contact. The Canadian press seems to have been about as alert as the faithful dog in *Pogo*. The Prime Minister recommended that Gouzenko be sent back to his superiors in the Soviet Embassy. Good form, you know.

What does it take?

In that case it took Soviet stupidity. If the NKVD had just let it alone, Gouzenko would probably have been forced back into their hands by the Canadians. But the NKVD had to go breaking in doors and attracting the attention of the police.

"I could not receive an official from a friendly embassy bearing tales of the kind he had described to my secretary," said the Rt. Hon. Louis S. St. Laurent. "It was only after he was brought in contact with the police through the ordinary course of police work that they were permitted to listen to his story and take notes from him." (Quoted from Richard Hirsch, *The Soviet Spies;* Duell, Sloan & Pearce, 1947; p. 13.)

Finally, Gouzenko got someone to read the papers he had brought along. Finally, the Canadian Government estab-

lished the Royal Commission, which in June 1946 published
its Report. The Canadians were slow.

But they were lightning compared to us.

Howard Rushmore wrote the first published atomic-spy
story for the New York *Journal-American* in December 1945.
He told about the Arthur Adams case (see *Soviet Atomic
Espionage*, pp. 163–70). It was denied as untrue until it
could be dismissed as old stuff. A standard maneuver.

This Arthur Adams case is another one—an important
one—which I have not gone into in this book. There are
more.

But back to Gouzenko for a moment. He wrote an article
for *Coronet*, March 1953, called "Stalin Sent Me to Spy
School." In it he tells (p. 89) how he asked his "section
chief" in Moscow "how it was that American and English
authorities were unable to uncover our agents when there
were so many of them.

"He smiled wanly. 'Our strength is in those very numbers,' he answered. 'The authorities nip one and think they
have "cleared up the situation"—but nine stay free to continue our work. Moreover, some of our most valued agents
are in such high places that they could scarcely be suspected
of treason.'"

          ❋   ❋   ❋

I have been asked several times if I "really think" the
situation is so grave and so critical. Do I "really think" the
Communist infiltration of the U.S. atomic energy project has
been so thorough that Soviet agents have now in secret
hideouts in our own cities atomic-weapon components manufactured in our own plants and laboratories, available for
use against us at a time of their own choosing?

I really think it is probable.

The Communists, remember, did not have to puncture
the hide of the atomic-bomb project. They were already

represented in the international scientific group which in 1939 constituted the original germ cell. We know Manhattan District was unable to eliminate all of them. AEC has been unable to find many of them. From what we conjecture of Communist vitality it seems altogether likely that a significant number have successfully hibernated during the cold war.

Assuming this continual presence of disciplined Communists in the project (and in various policy shops, such as the State Department), I do not know what would have prevented their making just such a past record as has obviously been made by somebody. No one besides the Communists so clearly had reason to instigate the three campaigns of:

1. Opposition to a quick A-bomb victory in Japan,

2. Promotion of security-stripped legislation (the original McMahon Bill) for national control of atomic energy, and

3. Promotion of an international plan (Acheson-Lilienthal) for equalization of U.S. and Soviet atomic potential.

Nor do I know what would have prevented them, disappointed in the outcome of each of these campaigns, from coming at length to the realization that their best strategy consisted of co-operation with the U.S. project in basic atomic production, inhibition of any military use by the United States of that production, and preparation for use of the production eventually by Soviet agents.

Certainly the increase in production has been marvelous, as witnessed by the tests in Nevada.

Certainly no military use since Nagasaki has injured one hair of a Communist head.

Possibly there are those in the U.S. atomic bomb project who have not forgotten Lenin's injunction "to organize new organizations and *utilize* these so useful weapons of death and destruction" against the United States.

An American spokesman in Paris, the Associated Press

reported on April 26, 1953, "said atomic weapons were 'running out of our ears.'"

Why, I believe there is no doubt about it. And it seems altogether too likely that in our coma from this surfeit we are attended by some who during the night shift may take the plethoric issue and shove it back down our throats.

. Yes, I "really think" the situation is grave and critical.

But there are dozens of political and scientific authorities better informed than I am. An AEC representative at Oak Ridge told a Knoxville *Journal* reporter, according to the Associated Press, that I was "not at the tiptop but a man of some stature." The second half of this characterization is kind; the first half is incontrovertible.

The Oak Ridge AEC man was further reported as saying that my suggestion (in the *Freeman,* January 12, 1953) of the possibility that Soviet agents might secretly assemble stolen U.S. A-bomb parts in the U.S.A. was "a speculative thing that is interesting."

It would certainly be interesting to know the speculations on this subject of those who are at the tiptop.

Part Three

FUTURE HOPE

Chapter XVI ⌁ Atomic Proportion

Two dangers exist:

(1) An acute vulnerability to an atomic Guy Fawkes plot, made possible by radical deficiencies in security, notably in the interval 1945–50.

(2) Chronic susceptibility to Communist propaganda, due to confusion among the intellectuals and apathy in the population at large.

The acute danger must be met largely by professionals, particularly the AEC and the FBI, supported by public understanding of the extreme gravity of the situation.

For the chronic danger we are all to blame. We have got to get a clearer understanding of the world political crisis in general and of the particular role in that crisis of the U.S. atomic energy project.

Public apathy as a source of misunderstanding has been widely discussed, but if confusion among the intellectuals were cleared up the apathy would soon disappear, as it results in large measure from a silent conviction that the intellectuals either do not know what they are talking about or else are inveterate liars.

Most of the fashionable denouncers of official secrecy

have never shown any real willingness to be candid. Writers and editors who will not discuss frankly what is already in the public domain can hardly justify their demands for more official handouts. The only way to preserve free speech is to speak freely.

Dr. Frank Oppenheimer is an unusual intellectual in that he once formally joined the Communist Party and became leader of a cell, but he was typical of many in 1947 in that he was simultaneously pleading for the elimination of secrecy while carefully maintaining a secret of his own, and accusing the Washington *Times-Herald* of "complete fabrication" when it published what he later admitted was the truth.

Scientists meeting to plan a campaign against secrecy have kept secret the minutes of their own meeting.

Fundamental to a decade of drivel has been an exaggeration of the level of importance of atomic energy. "This is the atomic age and everything is different" is a sorry motto for numerous theoretical and practical reasons, including the reason that such a premise of total revolution obscures the nature of particular things that really are different.

It also happens that the theory that the discovery of nuclear fission alters the basis of our educational and political institutions is Marxist, and hence, in a non-Communist country, gives aid and comfort to the Communists. We should not reject a concept merely because it is Marxist, but we ought not to accept it without some estimate of what use doctrinaire Communists may try to make of our acceptance.

* * *

So far, atomic theory has been more important than atomic practice—and this in the land of supposed pragmatists, the U.S.A. The only major practical accomplishment to date has been the bombing of Hiroshima and Nagasaki.

That was epic, providing simultaneously the *coup de grâce* to the perpetrators of Pearl Harbor, and crushing in the egg the Soviet plot for the postwar government of Japan.

Even here the conclusive effect was produced in part by the plausibility with which President Truman could say to the Lords of the Rising Sun, "The force from which the sun draws its powers has been loosed against those who brought war to the Far East."

From the start the mythological element has been an essential ingredient in the political force of atomic energy. Similar destruction by more familiar means, or by any means more prosaically explained, would not have had similar consequences in Japan, in the West, or in the Soviet Union.

I do not think it either desirable or practicable to eliminate this essentially poetic quality. I for one have felt a constant fascination through a decade of revolutionary discoveries and multitudinous developments. At Oak Ridge in 1944, to walk through the great room of a race-track building in Y-12, particularly to stand in the subfloor of one of these structures in an everglade of wire and piping keyed with myriad valves and switches, was an experience at once stimulating and chastening. Surely, if the war was not going to be won here, then the Government was mad.

The paradox of the titanic out of the infinitesimal teases us out of thought "as doth eternity." The whole range of imagination is enlivened. I remember first looking at K-25 under construction. My companions and I "looked at each other with a wild surmise," for in an abrupt clearing in the Tennessee wilderness there loomed the skeleton of leviathan.

And in intellectual resonance many octaves up the scale, the magic invocation, "$E = Mc^2$."

Some kind of romanticizing such as this will not be dismissed by the scientists and administrators of the atomic energy project, for on it, rather than on demonstrable accomplishment, depends the assured flow of what they value so much—the money.

I would not if I could and could not if I would debunk the legend of atomic power. Nor does it seem advisable to be dogmatic in drawing the line between what is legendary and what is historical, much less between vagrant fantasy and authentic prophecy.

Still, it is not necessary to abandon our minds.

Among the early views of the atomic scientists were one that the law of diminishing returns set in very early in the case of an atomic arsenal, even for an aggressor; and one that against the use of atomic bombs by an aggressor there was simply no defense.

The late Senator Brien McMahon was scornful in 1945 when General Groves spoke of "keeping ahead" of other nations in atomic armaments.[278] McMahon was then at one with the *Nation,* whose opinion was that "the *reductio ad absurdum* of the nationalistic attitude is the New York *Daily News* editorial suggesting 'two atomic bombs for one.' " [279]

In June 1952 Senator McMahon said, "No matter how many [atomic weapons] we might come to possess, we would need and could profitably use far more—in the event we were attacked." [280]

We Americans are an extravagant people, but is it necessary that we leap at once from a position where the very concept of atomic superiority is ridiculed to the contention that *no matter how many bombs we had* we would need more?

Similarly with the concept of defense. The One-World-or-None-Minutes-to-Midnight-Modern-Man-is-Obsolete approach held it as dogma that "There is no defense." Had the possibility of defense been acknowledged, there would have been no need to organize the scientific lobby for the McMahon Bill and the Acheson-Lilienthal Plan.

Today all that is changed. Now we hear, from Dr. Ralph

E. Lapp and Stewart Alsop, "of a rebellion of American scientists against the assumption that there is no real defense against nuclear weapons in Soviet hands." [281] Against whom the "rebellion" is directed is not clear, but its momentum is terrific, for we are urged to spend great sums on what we were previously told flatly was impossible.

The alternate extremes—(1) no military application of atomic energy because both technical monopoly and effective defense are categorically declared to be impossible (the 1945–46 line), and (2) converting the United States into a monstrous fissionable-material magazine surrounded by paranoiacally elaborate defense mechanisms (the 1952–53 line)—exhibit a lack of proportion, if not psychopathic suggestibility.

* * *

No one doubts any longer, if anyone ever doubted, that atomic energy poses grave national and international problems, or that the atomic weapons of the world may in the aggregate determine an epoch.

But the atomic bomb is not the gravest danger to mankind or to Western civilization, and the peaceful uses of atomic energy are not their greatest hope. The bomb is a salient technical achievement which is susceptible of tragic misuse. Yet, obviously, it is not so liable to misuse as a revolver or a hypodermic, since it can be employed not by an individual, but only by an organization. The menace of Communism is older, broader, and deeper than the menace of the bomb.

To transfer our hopes and fears from a political apparatus to a nuclear gadget is merely to lapse further into the mental and moral sclerosis which gave rise to Communism in the first place. The world political crisis, in which atomic energy may prove a decisive instrumentality, was nevertheless not caused by atomic energy, and will not be solved by projection of atomic theory into history.

Illustrative of how not to think about atomic energy is a booklet called *Almighty Atom* by John J. O'Neill, Science Editor of the *New York Herald Tribune,* and once winner of the Pulitzer Prize for science writing.

"The act of creation which brought the universe in its present form into existence involved an atomic-energy explosion of infinitely great magnitude. In the pre-universe stage, the cosmos consisted of a single atom gigantically vast. . . . It is difficult to comprehend the extent of this almighty atom," says Mr. O'Neill.

After this, how salutary to turn to the words of the hillbilly song:

> "Atomic power—
> It was given by the mighty hand of God!"

Remembrance of the distinction between the gift and the Giver is fundamental if we are going to think about the atom and not worship it.

Chapter XVII ～ Rational Patriotism

It must not be forgotten that if Communists exist they exist in time and space. The secret war is not subjective. It is not a psychoneurosis to be solved with a good cry.

But the hard-core Communists have to work through others, and on occasion they have to secure at least the tacit consent of a working majority of us—you and me. The division of forces, therefore, extends into our own minds.

For example, the majority of us condoned the actions of Alger Hiss, for we permitted Dean Acheson to remain in office three years after he expressed his continuing loyalty to Hiss. It is nonsense to say we could not help it. We could not have helped it without going to some trouble, but we could have helped it.

That does not mean you and I are Communists, it does not mean Dean Acheson is a Communist. But it means the Communists influence us. If they did not influence us they could not survive as Communists. Our first duty is therefore plain. It is simply to plan and take action independently of Communist influence.

As soon as we do that, the remaining power of the Communist conspiracy will appear quite manageable. The hypnotist with whom we do not co-operate is not so formidable.

The removal of a dozen men, if we were lucky enough to select the right dozen—*and if we simultaneously clarified our own outlook*—would effectively eliminate the danger of atomic treachery. But the removal of a hundred certified traitors would not save us if we continued to act like fatheads.

What do you mean act like fatheads?

I'll tell you what I mean from personal experience. In May 1946, as I said at the beginning of this book, I took part in a CBS radio show called "Operation Crossroads," [282] which was a pretentious united-front propaganda job on the "One World or None" theme.

I was the only person on the show to take a view that was even superficially realistic. I said we ought to build atomic armaments, and I was pretty proud of myself for being so clear-sighted and courageous (for the view was not generally accepted till a year later).

Actually I was a fathead.

Why?

Well, Archibald MacLeish was on the same show, and as a former small-time English teacher I fell all over myself to meet and pump the hand of the author of "You, Andrew Marvell."

I was a fathead.

MacLeish had just said on the show, "The best chance for survival that I can see is United Nations control of atomic energy." If he was so myopic as that, I was a fathead to take that moment to congratulate him on his verbal felicity.

I assure you I was not the only fathead on that show.

* * *

It is difficult to be temperate about this matter. It is hard to think of the Senate of the United States *unanimously* passing the McMahon Bill *without* the security measures added by the House of Representatives. It is hard to think of the eminent men on that CBS radio show—General George C. Kenney, Dr. Harold C. Urey, Senator Brien Mc-Mahon, Mr. Harold E. Stassen, Mr. Joseph E. Davies, Justice William O. Douglas, Dr. Albert Einstein, Mr. Henry A. Wallace, and others, including, of course, Mr. Archibald MacLeish—it is hard to think of these men in a concert of foolish rhetoric against the concept of national sovereignty, permitting Mr. MacLeish in the final rhetorical flourish to say with mock simplicity to the radio audience, "*You* must decide. . . . The danger is not that we will make the *wrong* decision. The danger is that we will make no decision"—as if on a proposal to make an irreversible subtraction from the sovereignty of the United States "no decision" were not in practice indistinguishable from a positive decision to retain sovereignty, and therefore *as if the danger lay in the sovereignty of the United States.*

It is as if you said to a man standing on a cliff: the danger is not that you will jump the *wrong* way; the danger is that you will not jump. If you say this it is hard to believe you have any intelligent concern for the man on the cliff.

To illustrate the fact that it was not the stars or historical determinism that enabled CBS to prostitute so much collective intelligence to the utterance of such fatuous verbiage, I should like to offer in evidence a sample of rational discourse composed, delivered in a lecture, and printed in the year 1945. The author is Ernest Llewellyn Woodward, Montague Burton Professor of International Relations, Oxford.

"Finally," said Professor Woodward, "we have to consider the international organization [for the control of atomic energy] as a body . . . with the powers . . . of deciding whether this fearful sanction shall or shall not be employed. This power of decision must be given to it if its inspectors are not to be flouted by the street arabs of an aggressor nation. Any body of persons, any organization to whom such power is entrusted has in fact the mastery of the world. There were intrigues enough at Geneva, but the League had not one lead bullet of its own. Unless men have changed since yesterday, and we know that they have not changed, what can we expect of this international body holding the greatest of prizes? Either it becomes at once, and almost by definition, a world government, or it is the battleground of rival Powers." [283]

The participants in "Operation Crossroads" were not incapable of understanding that kind of reasoning. They were incapable of refuting it. They simply ignored it. What was the matter with them?

James Burnham wrote in 1946, "Any hope . . . that some kind of United Nations sleight of hand is going to provide an easy, short-cut solution to the problem of atomic weapons will in due course . . . end in disillusion." [284]

In June 1951, "Everyone knows," wrote Professor Richard L. Meier in the *Bulletin of the Atomic Scientists*, "the disillusionment that accompanied the lack of international agreement on atomic energy. . . . For many the fun has gone out of physics, they feel stale and unproductive." [285]

Why could 5,000 organized atomic scientists and 96 United States Senators not see what Woodward and Burnham could see in 1945 and 1946?

Not Communists, just fatheads.

*   *   *

We speak of Western Civilization, and of its threatened destruction by the East, or by the atomic bomb. But if history is a serious subject, then it would appear obvious that the East was conquered by the West some time back. Even before the great political triumphs of Communism, every Eastern leader of substantial power had a Western education. It is through Communism itself, however, that the West has most skillfully exploited the East.

For Communism is, of course, a product of the West, and this is true whether we are thinking of the theory or the practical organization. The principal contributions of the Russians seem to have been uncritical enthusiasm and nostalgia for absolute authority. The plans were laid in London, Paris, New York, and, of course, Switzerland.

This is not to say that the Communist empire in its present form was fully anticipated by anyone, East or West. It is merely to insist that Russia, and China, would probably have continued their older forms of society if it had not been for Western education.

Unfortunately, it was not the legitimate Western tradition on which the oligarchies of Moscow and Peking were founded. The Earl of Gloucester had a son who said,

"Thou, Nature, art my goddess."

This involved him in the commission of such unnatural acts as the blinding of his father, the temporary dispossession of his legitimate brother, and—at length—his own destruction. A genius at dissimulation and a ruthless materialist, Edmund pursued a train of havoc to catastrophe.

It is not the East which threatens the West, but the West's own bastard offspring.

Nor can the atomic bomb itself threaten the West, or of itself threaten anything, being insentient despite cybernetics—except through the fearful power of suggestion by which a fatal instrument *seems* to invite use. The steel itself draws men on, said Homer, and this is an illusion of great practical consequence.

The temptation to use a weapon can visit only those who are able to lay their hands upon the weapon, and who know or think they know how to manage it. This is the origin of the ancient common suspicion of the professional military clique. The members of the junta do not need to be morally worse than ourselves; they are dangerous because they are presumably not much better than we, and they have access to the magazine.

This is today the position of the atomic scientists. They are our Praetorian guard. How many of them say,

"Thou, Nature, art my goddess"?

Unless they disavow that, you and I are in for a very rough time.

The capital—the accumulated wealth—of the West, and its culture, and many of its inhabitants, are threatened not by the East and not by the atomic bomb, but by the ideological instability of the designers of the atomic bomb.

*   *   *

"Man is by nature a political animal," said Aristotle. "He who is unable to live in society, or who has no need because he is sufficient for himself, must be either a beast or a god." Is it not an observable danger of those who would, godlike, rise above all political society that they fall into bestial savagery? Have not morally ambitious men renounced loyalty to their native or foster land, only to end by attaching themselves to the Soviet state—preferring to rejoin humanity even as traitors and slaves rather than to remain aloof?

André Malraux told James Burnham: "We had believed that in becoming less French a man became more human. Now we know that he becomes simply more Russian." [286]

"Patriotism," said Nurse Edith Cavell, "is not enough." No, it is not enough. It is one of the minimum requirements.

I have no right to preach to the atomic scientists. But I have a right to speak if anyone will listen, and as a citizen the duty to cry out against what I see as a great danger to the republic. I see or seem to myself to see a very great danger in the fact that the physical scientists have command

and that they have no tradition of responsible command.

A former executive secretary of the Federation of American Scientists, Professor Richard L. Meier, who interviewed more than a thousand scientists for the express purpose of drawing some general conclusions about scientists, has said:

"The physicist by nature is politically radical. His mind is schooled in the proposition that progress is made by discarding various assumptions and premises and thereby making it possible to create a more powerful theory upon a simpler underpinning. The physicist, more than any scientist, deals with abstractions which make nonsense out of observations based upon the commonplace; he is educated in doubt and can disregard evidence which to the ordinary observer is both convincing and conclusive. Thus many physicists chose a vague leftist political philosophy, partly as the only relatively rational set of value premises which was offered at the time (1936 to 1940) in the world of ideas." [287]

The most disturbing feature of this—if it be accepted as approximately accurate, and I think it is—is not the characterization as "radical" or the evidence of a "leftist" trend.

What is disturbing is that these aristocrats of the intellectual world (and there is no doubt of the superiority of their intellectual gifts) should have chosen any "vague . . . philosophy" at all in the belief that it was "the only relatively rational set of value premises . . . offered" in the years 1936 to 1940. This is disturbing on at least three counts:

(1) Since the philosophy was vague the physicists did not know what they were choosing.

(2) It is simply not true that a "leftist political philosophy"—whether vague or precise—was the only "relatively rational set of value premises offered at the time," for vague "rightist" and vague "centrist" philosophies were also "rela-

tively rational," depending in each case—left, right, and center—on certain irrationally adopted premises.

(3) Whatever degree of rationality vague leftism had in the period 1936–1940 it still has. Anyone who does not know what was wrong with vague leftism in 1936 or 1940 does not know what is wrong with it in 1953.

Remember that Dr. Kenneth May, qualified as an expert on Communism at the University of California, has sworn that at Berkeley in 1940 there were in the Campus Branch of the Communist Party 100 members. Ninety-five of those are still anonymous, presumably for one of two reasons: either they are still Communists, or else they still have toward Communism and toward political philosophy in general the dilettante attitude indicated by Professor Meier.

The authorities on "Operation Crossroads" said the United States should be willing to give up its sovereignty. We have given it up. We have given it up to the ninety-five assorted Communists and dilettantes of whose existence, but not identity, Dr. May informed us.

But that is hasty and exaggerated.

I hope it is more than that. I hope it is altogether mistaken. I do not think it is altogether mistaken.

* * *

A condition of temporal hope is rational patriotism, of which the most sustained and abundant historical expression has been found in the United States of America. It should be noted that rational patriotism is not at all the same thing as patriotic rationalism. The former is a vital principle of will, guided by reason; the latter is a fad of professional intellectuals. I shall not attempt a dissertation on sovereignty, but we may observe that will, not power, is its essence, for a nation which accepts destruction rather than subjection is sovereign. The issue is determined in each case in the manner and by the authority recognized

by those experts on sovereignty whose signatures are recorded under the words:

"And for the support of this declaration, with a firm reliance on the protection of divine providence, we mutually
pledge to each other our lives, our fortunes, and our sacred
honor."

A national policy which is not a continuation of that is
not, I believe the current word is, viable. Here is where the
"isolationists" have been strong. But increasing strength in
a contracting world has brought us into conflict with those
who view our strength as the last obstacle in the way of
their one world. If the potentialities of atomic weapons are
on the order we think they are, then the conflict is not to
be avoided, for the Communists find it completely unendur-
able that we should have such weapons at our disposal.

If they are aware that among our technical experts in the
atomic energy project are many whose will is not single in
this matter, many who are not sure that the words "sacred
honor" have any operational value, then we may be sure
they will fasten there, like a leech upon the heart.

＊　　＊　　＊

G. Wilson Knight wrote in January 1946:

"A world-order is in process of formation; but hitherto no
established order has—not even in the British Isles or the
United States of America—developed without conflict. We
have just concluded what might be called an architypal war,
and may indeed hope that it be our last, though the fruits
of it are yet uncertain. It must, however, be remembered
always that the greater organism cannot be created by planning alone; what has organic life can alone transmit organic
life; and we must therefore build on what already exists,
what has maintained itself in war and peace and asserted its
beliefs and principles across the globe. A sound international order must as surely be created by or through a sound

patriotism as a sound patriotism is based on family piety and that, finally, on the individual's self-respect. Now, since sound patriotisms have a way of themselves conflicting, there may be, on occasion, the need for force. In the last resort, action may be, or seem, arbitrary. Here no reasoning is of avail, we are thrown back on the imagination, on faith. There is such a thing as righteous power." [288]

* * *

Edward Teller is a living example of the fact that a man of generous spirit feels patriotic devotion to his foster country as well as to his native country—while a man corrupted by the doctrine of the class war, to which exaggerated professional pride may furnish an introduction, has no firm loyalty to any country and may consider the very emotion of patriotism itself as beneath the threshold of response of the sophisticated. Teller may take his place in history with Kosciuszko, as a man of multiple but untangled national loyalties, a man who benefited every country he visited, a true internationalist who did not think the way to peace among the nations consisted in betraying one to another but in serving each with fidelity and all with understanding.

Dr. Teller has written: [289]

"I do not believe that the hydrogen bomb or the whole arsenal of technological warfare will save the United States unless we accept the fact that the United States and all the freedom-loving people of the whole world must be saved."

Notes

1. Alan Moorehead, *The Traitors* (Scribner's, 1952), p. 93.
2. Ralph E. Lapp, *The New Force* (Harper, 1953), p. 214.
3. Atomic energy costs should scarcely be mentioned without repeating the classic statement of Dr. Lawrence R. Hafstad, AEC Director of Reactor Development: "Figures in the literature on estimated costs for atomic energy vary by at least a factor of 10. I am not going to try at this time to give you more accurate cost figures for three very good reasons:

"1. They do not exist even within the Atomic Energy Commission.

"2. If they did exist, they could not be released for security reasons.

"3. If they did exist and if they could be released, I wouldn't believe them anyway." From "Remarks Before American Petroleum Institute, Los Angeles, Calif., November 15, 1950," published in *Atomic Power and Private Enterprise*, Joint Committee on Atomic Energy. Government Printing Office, 1952. Passage here quoted from p. 132.

4. "A Reporter at Large. Seven Men on a Problem," pp. 45–56. The same material appears in Daniel Lang's *Early Tales of the Atomic Age* (Doubleday, 1948), p. 109.
5. *Congressional Record.* Vol. 92, Part 7, p. 9253.
6. *Investigation into the United States Atomic Energy Project. Hearing Before the Joint Committee on Atomic Energy* (herein-

after cited as *Investigation Hearing*) (Government Printing Office, 1949), p. 389.

7. *Ibid.*, p. 391.

8. *Congressional Record.* Vol. 92, Part 7, p. 6082.

9. *Investigation into the United States Atomic Energy Project, Report of the Joint Committee on Atomic Energy* (hereinafter cited as *Investigation Report*), released October 13, 1949 (Government Printing Office, 1949), pp. 7–11.

10. Bernard Pares, *Russia* (Copyright, by the New American Library of World Literature, Inc.), p. 66.

11. Valeriu Marcu, *Lenin* (Macmillan, 1928), p. 394.

12. T. Zavalani, *How Strong Is Russia?* (Frederick A. Praeger, 1952), p. 10.

13. Pares, *op. cit.*, p. 89.

14. The capacity of the Dnieper Dam and the Soviet electrical energy output are from Zavalani, *op. cit.*, p. 13 and p. 57 respectively. Grand Coulee capacity is given in the 1953 *World Almanac*, p. 185. U.S. output is interpolated from a table in the 1953 *World Almanac*, p. 483.

15. Zavalani, *op. cit.*, pp. 142–43.

16. *The Forrestal Diaries*, edited by Walter Millis (Viking, 1951), p. 266.

17. Zavalani, *op. cit.*, p. 147.

18. *1953 World Almanac*, p. 483.

19. *Fortune*, Feb. 1953, p. 119. Copr. by Time Inc.

20. *1953 World Almanac*, p. 287.

21. Appropriations for atomic energy, from the beginning of the project through November 1952, are recapitulated in *The Atomic Energy Act of 1946*, Joint Committee on Atomic Energy (Government Printing Office, 1952), pp. 50–72.

22. David E. Lilienthal, *Big Business: A New Era* (Harper, 1952), pp. 100–103.

23. The *1953 World Almanac*, p. 476, gives the U.S.S.R., "including all Asiatic territory," 1,500,000 telephones; Chicago 1,526,156. U.S. telephones total 43,003,832. In support of Mr. Lilienthal's view that a flourishing telephone industry can make a unique contribution to the production of atomic weapons in quantity, is the following statement of Dr. Mervin J. Kelly,

Executive Vice President, Bell Laboratories, Inc., made before the Joint Committee on Atomic Energy, July 7, 1949, shortly after completing a survey of AEC's Los Alamos and Sandia operations: "This is indeed a complex operation; probably as complex as any single operation in applied science. . . . It is an area in which I have spent my whole professional life." (*Investigation Hearing*, p. 809.)

24. Current Soviet production may be as high as one-tenth the U.S. rate. See *Fortune*, Feb. 1953, p. 119. But the *1953 World Almanac*, p. 287, estimates the Soviet production goal for 1955 as only 7.2% of U.S. production in 1951. Any reasonable allowance for U.S. accumulation due to past productivity, freedom from invasion, and superior maintenance readily yields the 15 to 1 ratio favoring the United States.

25. *1953 World Almanac*, pp. 317–18.

26. *Fortune*, Feb. 1953, p. 211.

27. *Ibid.*

28. *The Atom, 1951, A Business Week Report* (McGraw-Hill, 1951), p. 5.

29. *Look*, March 16, 1948, pp. 27–34.

30. The following is from the *New York Times* of June 8, 1949 (p. 1): "Washington, June 7.—A Federal Bureau of Investigation Report disclosed today that Russia received a shipment of atomic research devices from the United States in 1947 and that two other shipments were blocked in 1948 and 1949. . . . The FBI report was brought into the open at the espionage trial of Judith Coplon. . . . Robert J. Lamphere, an FBI agent, testified he had prepared the document about the shipment of atomic implements to Russia. Mr. Lamphere said the report was 'authentic'—and thus not to be confused with a 'decoy' paper . . . deliberately planted where Miss Coplon would find it. . . . Mr. Lamphere's report said no export license had been issued for the shipment of atomic equipment that reached Soviet Russia aboard the steamship Mikhail Kutuzov in August 1947. It said a shipment of similar secret instruments was found aboard the steamship Murmansk in New York harbor Sept. 2, 1948, but American authorities removed the shipment because it had not been authorized. Then a third shipment was found on a dock in Claremont,

N. J., Jan. 14, 1949, and this also was confiscated, the report said. Amtorg bought the equipment that reached Russia from the 'Cyclotron Specialties Company,' the report continued. . . ."

31. Moorehead, *op. cit.*, p. 136.

32. *Investigation Hearing*, p. 292. Dr. Oppenheimer had previously stated, however (p. 284): "I do not know anything about Russia."

33. *Science Bulletin, American-Soviet Science Society*, October 1945, p. 4.

34. *Hearings Before the Special Committee on Atomic Energy, 79th Congress, 1st Session, Pursuant to Senate Resolution 179* (hereinafter cited as *Hearings Pursuant to S. Res. 179*) (Government Printing Office, 1945–46), p. 118.

35. Washington *Post*, Jan. 31, 1953, p. 1.

36. Washington *Daily News* (United Press), Jan. 29, 1953, p. 35.

37. Houston *Post* (Associated Press), Jan. 31, 1953, p. 8.

38. James Burnham, *The Struggle for the World* (John Day, 1947), p. 93.

39. *Ibid.*

40. *Ibid.*, p. 118.

41. Houston *Post*, Jan. 29, 1953, p. 12.

42. *The Atom, 1951*, p. 8.

43. *Fortune*, Feb. 1953, p. 120.

44. Reported in an editorial in the *Bulletin of the Atomic Scientists* (hereinafter cited as *BAS*), Dec. 1949, p. 326.

45. The authority for this is, I must confess, in the realm of "common knowledge." I first learned of Beria's reported responsibility in the column of Joseph and Stewart Alsop.

46. Vishinsky's use of Blackett's *Military and Political Consequences of Atomic Energy* (Turnstile Press, 1948, Rev. 1949); American title: *Fear, War, and the Bomb* (Whittlesey House, McGraw-Hill, 1948, 1949)—is reported in *Current Biography*, 1949, entry for Blackett, P. M. S.

47. Dr. Hafstad's speech is given in *Atomic Power and Private Enterprise*. The passage here cited appears on pp. 148–9.

48. The characterization of James S. Allen, identified as Solomon Auerbach, is from *Report on the Communist "Peace" Offen-*

sive, by the House Committee on Un-American Activities (Government Printing Office, 1951), p. 88. The connotations of "literary hack" should not be allowed to obscure available evidence that Auerbach-Allen is a figure of some importance in Communist circles. Whittaker Chambers in *Witness* (Random House, 1952), pp. 241–2, writes of "Sol Auerbach, better known by his party name of James Allen. Auerbach succeeded me as foreign-news editor at the *Daily Worker.* Later, he became the chief editor for International Publishers, the official Communist book-publishing house, whose manager, Alexander Trachtenberg, was a member of the party's Central Control Commission." Sol Auerbach testified before the Senate Internal Security Subcommittee February 21, 1952, where he stated, "My pen name is James S. Allen. My real name is Sol Auerbach." See *Institute of Pacific Relations, Hearings Before the Subcommittee to Investigate the Administration of the Internal Security Act and Other Internal Security Laws* (hereinafter cited as *IPR Hearings*) (Government Printing Office, 1952), p. 2876.

49. *Loc. cit.*

50. A dissertation could be written on the influence of the *Bulletin of the Atomic Scientists (BAS).* In an interview with the *Bulletin's* staff the late Senator Brien McMahon said, "I have always given the scientists a good deal of credit for the results that were achieved in 1946 in the way of atomic energy legislation. I believe that if we—those few of us in the Senate—had not had at that time the support of the scientists, the atomic energy bill could not have been made into law." (*BAS,* Jan. 1952, p. 9.) The Board of Sponsors of the *Bulletin* consists of J. Robert Oppenheimer, Chairman; Harold C. Urey, Vice-Chairman; H. A. Bethe, Detlev W. Bronk, A. H. Compton, E. U. Condon, F. Daniels, L. A. DuBridge, Albert Einstein, James Franck, S. A. Goudsmidt, T. R. Hogness, F. W. Loomis, Philip M. Morse, H. J. Muller, Linus Pauling, G. B. Pegram, I. I. Rabi, Julian Schwinger, Cyril S. Smith, Leo Szilard, Edward Teller, V. F. Weisskopf, Hugh C. Wolfe, Sewall Wright, and J. R. Zacharias. The *Bulletin* was founded in 1945 by Hyman H. Goldsmith and Eugene Rabinowitch. Dr. Goldsmith died in August 1949. Dr. Rabinowitch is the editor.

51. The substance of Dr. May's testimony is here given from personal recollection. I was a spectator at the trial. A transcript may be purchased from Mrs. Chloe MacReynolds, Court Reporter, Room 4800-E, United States District Court House, Washington, D. C.

52. Washington *Post,* April 9, 1951, p. 1.

53. See *New York Times,* Sept. 30, 1952, p. 1.

54. *Investigation Hearing,* for June 6, 1949. The Chairman, Senator McMahon, said, "I would like to ask this question, Mr. Lilienthal: Has the Commission at any time overruled a recommendation of the Roberts Board?" Mr. Lilienthal replied, "In two instances the recommendation of the Roberts Board was not followed. . . . One is the case of Dr. Edward Condon. . . . The other . . . was the case of Dr., now Senator, Graham. . . ." (p. 161. See also pp. 171–5.)

55. *Security, Loyalty, and Science* (Cornell, 1950), p. 50.

56. *Investigation Hearing,* p. 152.

57. Oliver Pilat, *The Atom Spies* (Putnam, 1952), p. 177.

58. *New York Times,* Apr. 6, 1950, p. 2.

59. Blackett, *op. cit.,* p. 81 (Turnstile edition).

60. *Hearings Pursuant to S. Res. 179,* p. 193.

61. Quoted from *Report on the Communist Party of the United States as an Advocate of Overthrow of Government by Force and Violence,* Committee on Un-American Activities (Government Printing Office, 1948), p. 15.

62. Washington *Post,* Apr. 11, 1952.

63. *The Social Task of the Scientist in the Atomic Era,* A Symposium. Emergency Committee of the Atomic Scientists, Inc., 1946.

64. See Note 66 below.

65. *Report on the Communist Party,* etc. (see Note 61 above), pp. 19, 25, 27.

66. *New York Times* (United Press), Oct. 15, 1945, p. 4.

67. *Life,* Oct. 29, 1945.

68. *Nation,* Dec. 22, 1945, p. 702.

69. *Soviet Atomic Espionage,* Joint Committee on Atomic Energy. Government Printing Office, 1951, p. 193.

70. "The New Technique of Private War," by E. U. Condon.

In *One World or None,* edited by Dexter Masters and Katherine Way (Whittlesey House, McGraw-Hill, 1946), p. 40.

71. *Ibid.*

72. *Ibid.,* p. 41.

73. Einstein said this in his historic letter to President Roosevelt, urging Government support of the atomic energy project, according to testimony of Dr. Alexander Sachs. See *Hearings Pursuant to S. Res. 179,* p. 7.

74. *Ibid.,* p. 330.

75. *Ibid.,* p. 191.

76. *Ibid.,* p. 194.

77. *A Report on the International Control of Atomic Energy,* Department of State Publication 2498, Second Reprint (Government Printing Office, 1946), p. 42.

78. Dr. Victor Weisskopf told the Nation Associates Dec. 1, 1945, "The atomic bomb will not be developed successfully by scientists unknown to the rest of the world." *Nation,* Dec. 22, 1945, p. 704.

79. *Scientific Information Transmitted to the United Nations Atomic Energy Commission by the United States Representative* (hereinafter cited as *Scientific Information*), Prepared in the Office of Mr. Bernard M. Baruch, United States Representative, Vols. VI and VII (Vol. VI, except Foreword by John M. Hancock, appears in *BAS,* Dec. 1, 1946).

80. *Ibid.,* p. iii.

81. *Ibid.,* p. 18.

82. See also the statement of AEC Chairman Gordon Dean, quoted on p. 40 above (Note 35). The point is made emphatically in the First Report of the United Nations Atomic Energy Commission, Part II B, where it is stated, "The detection of clandestine bomb manufacture as such is almost impossible; it is, therefore, vital that any unauthorized accumulation of essential nuclear fuels be prevented." Quoted from *Minutes to Midnight,* edited by Eugene Rabinowitch (Educational Foundation for Nuclear Science, Inc., 1950), p. 53.

83. *Scientific Information,* Vol. VI, p. 2.

84. *Ibid.,* p. 12.

85. *Scientific Information*, Vol. VII. Mr. Kelley wrote: "Because of the size and complexity of the electromagnetic plant diversion is possible at many places. There were over 175 buildings in the electromagnetic plant area at Oak Ridge, each one containing a maze of piping and equipment. It was part of my job during the early days of operation to supervise the accountability for uranium materials within the plant. Adequate controls were secured only with the whole-hearted cooperation of the management and workers, when they were convinced that it was their patriotic duty to help reduce losses. I am certain that had my group been the inspectorate in a plant operated by a nation intent on diversion, we could not have stopped the diversion from taking place." (p. 21.)

Of the gaseous diffusion plant (the type used now exclusively, and on a scale several times greater) Dr. Felbeck wrote: "Due to the size and complexity of the present plant, the withdrawal of material by the operating agency could be done with extreme ease from any number of places by any number of methods with little risk of immediate detection by any inspection agency. Such withdrawal could be made by taking oversize samples, by storing up material in equipment which was subsequently taken out during maintenance procedures, by not immediately discovered secret withdrawal connections, or by other more or less obvious methods. Diversion of material could be concealed by an unreported improvement in the process, since recovery and operating efficiency of any process plant are continually being improved by the operating organization. Diversion could also be covered up by very minor falsifications of isotope analyses used in calculating material balances. The detection by an inspection agency would take months to accomplish, since the accuracy of a plant material balance depends on the statistical study of a large amount of data. The operator could explain such diversions by stating that any discrepancies that might show up in the material balance were due to material remaining on the inner metal surfaces of the plant. Real inspection and control can be exercised only by the operating agency and even here absolute assurance rests on the loyalty of the members of such an organization." (pp. 25–26.) Dr. Felbeck's position in the Union Car-

bide and Carbon Corporation, operators of the U.S. gaseous diffusion plant from the start, gives his testimony the most extraordinary weight.

86. See p. 17 above (Note 6).

87. *Investigation Hearing,* p. 596 ff.

88. *Scientific Information,* Vol. VI, p. 17.

89. *Ibid.*

90. See p. 12 above (Note 4).

91. Quoted from *U.S. News,* May 3, 1946.

92. *Minutes to Midnight,* p. 38.

93. *Investigation Hearing,* p. 305. Dr. Oppenheimer's testimony on this point is, more fully, as follows: Senator Hickenlooper: "Dr. Oppenheimer, the production of weapons and the
application of materials, for instance, at Los Alamos is not done
by the Commission, is it? It is done by a contractor—the University of California?" Dr. Oppenheimer: "It is also not done by the
contractor. It is done by some fellows. The contractor during
the war years was an extremely helpful and able contractor, but
was really distinguished primarily by his absence. Since then
the university has been allowed to take a somewhat more active
part. But the Commission is dealing with technical people who
are paid and protected by the University of California, but who
are not normal employees of the University of California, who
are not doing a normal thing for the University of California to
be doing. And the policies under which the laboratory is run,
the technical directives for the laboratory, the employment policies, the conditions of work, are not determined by the contractor. They are determined by the Commission." Senator Hickenlooper: "You mean to say that the University of California does
not have a contractual responsibility for the completion of those
activities out there?" Dr. Oppenheimer: "I do not know. During
the war the University of California never saw the directives
and had no idea what the directives said." Senator Hickenlooper:
"We are talking about now [i.e., 1949]." Dr. Oppenheimer: "I do
not know the answer to that question. But my guess is that the
directives are agreed to by the laboratory staff and the Commission, that they are written out, and that the role of the contractor
is very minor." Senator Hickenlooper: "And that the laboratory

staff is paid by the University of California. Is that correct?"
Dr. Oppenheimer: "It is paid through the university." Senator
Hickenlooper: "Reimbursed by the Commission." (pp. 304–305.)

94. *Scientific Information*, Vol. VI, p. 55.

95. *Ibid.*, p. 57, and p. 56, where certain control measures are
judged adequate, "provided that the scale of authorized operations were low enough so that a small percentage diversion did
not represent a serious military hazard."

96. *Investigation Report*, pp. 7–11.

97. Moorehead, *op. cit.*, pp. 142–3.

98. *Soviet Atomic Espionage*, p. 73.

99. *Ibid.*, p. 153.

100. *Ibid.*, p. 158.

101. *Ibid.*, p. 99.

102. Pilat, *op. cit.*, pp. 158–9.

103. *Soviet Atomic Espionage*, p. 182.

104. Material relating to David Hawkins appears in *Soviet
Atomic Espionage*, p. 183; Pilat, *op. cit.*, pp. 162–4; the Denver
Post, Feb. 4, 1951; and the Boston *Daily Globe*, May 9, 1953.

105. *Hearings Regarding Communist Infiltration of Radiation
Laboratory and Atomic Bomb Project at the University of California, Berkeley, Calif.* (hereinafter cited as *Hearings on Radiation Laboratory*), House Committee on Un-American Activities
(Government Printing Office, 1951), pp. 3417–52. The passage
here quoted is on p. 3425.

106. Pilat, *op. cit.*, p. 83.

107. Dr. Hawkins repeated the substance of this testimony in
Boston on May 8, 1953. "Q.–When did you leave the Communist
Party? A.–I discontinued membership in early 1943. There was
no definite act of termination. I simply left. I believe it was in
March. I simply stopped going to meetings and paying dues."
From the Boston *Daily Globe*, May 9, 1953, p. 2.

108. Washington *Times-Herald*, June 15, 1949.

109. *Soviet Atomic Espionage*, p. 181.

110. *Ibid.*

111. Pilat, *op. cit.*, pp. 149, 154.

112. *Hearings on Radiation Laboratory*, p. 3435.

113. In Boston on May 8, 1953, Dr. Hawkins testified as follows: "*Q.*—Did you tell any authorities in 1943 that you had been a member of the Communist Party? *A.*—I did not, I wasn't asked. . . . *Q.*—Didn't they ask you if you were or had been a Communist? *A.*—They asked about subversive organization. I did not regard the Communist party as a subversive organization. They did not ask about Communist party affiliation. . . . I was given to believe that my past membership in the Communist party was known to those high up." Boston *Daily Globe*, May 9, 1953, p. 2.

114. Pilat, *op. cit.*, pp. 155–6.

115. *Hearings on Radiation Laboratory*, p. 3427.

116. *Ibid.*, p. 3441.

117. From the Boston *Daily Globe*, May 8, 1953, p. 10: "The following is the text of testimony given yesterday by Dr. Philip Morrison, visiting professor of physics at M.I.T., to the Senate Internal Security Subcommittee:

"Just after Prof. Morrison had identified himself, committee counsel Morris asked him, 'Have you been a member of the Communist party?'

" 'I joined the Young Communist League when I was 18,' said the witness, 'and at the age of 21 I became a member of the Communist party in Berkeley, Calif.'

"*Q.*—And you left the Communist party in late 1939 or 1940? *A.*—Yes, or perhaps a little before.

"*Q.*—Did you attend a meeting April 17 of this year [1953] in New York city under the auspices of the American Peace Crusade? *A.*—I attended a meeting a couple of weeks ago; I'm not sure of the exact date. . . .

"Here committee research director Benjamin Mandel read from a list issued by the Attorney General citing the American Peace Crusade as a Communist organization. . . .

"*Q.*—While you were a member of the Berkeley Campus section of the Communist party, did you deliver a series of lectures entitled 'Imperialism,' by V. I. Lenin?

"*A.*—They were in small discussion groups, and were held under Communist auspices, but many who attended were not Communists.

"Q.—You were a Communist yourself? A.—I did not conceal it.

"Q.—Have you been active in our atomic energy program? A.—I have been.

"Q.—When did you first hear about the atomic energy program? A.—I was approached and asked to join the Manhattan Project in late 1942. . . . I didn't ask. I was sought out. . . . In the late summer of 1944 . . . I . . . went to the University of California Laboratories in New Mexico, and I worked there until after the test of the atom bomb in New Mexico. . . . I was one of the group which assembled and tested the bombs that were used in combat. I later went to Japan to inspect the damage, then returned to New Mexico, and finally left the project in the late Summer of 1946, and became a professor again.

"Q.—You had access to every secret? A.—Every secret necessary to my job.

"Q.—Well, wouldn't that mean virtually every secret? A.—Only those connected with my job. I did not ask to see any others.

"Q.—Did you tell Gen. Groves, your superior, that you had been a member of the Communist party? A.—I did have good reasons to believe my superiors knew of my past connections. . . ."

118. The cases of Van der Luft and Wallis are two of six cases listed in *Soviet Atomic Espionage*, p. 195, and there described as all relating "to the theft of classified documents and photographs by enlisted men serving with the United States Army at the Los Alamos Laboratory, during the war."

119. Washington *Post*, July 10, 1947.

120. See statement of Dr. Walter Zinn, quoted on p. 13 above (Note 7).

121. *Hearings on Radiation Laboratory*, pp. 3438–9. "I am afraid," said Dr. Hawkins, "I was a disgrace to the pulpit, because I definitely felt on the high side."

122. *Ibid.*

123. An account of Steve Nelson's acquaintance with Mrs. J. Robert Oppenheimer, and of his unsuccessful attempt to exploit this acquaintance for purposes of espionage, was given (without naming the Oppenheimers) by the House Committee on Un-American Activities in a *Report on Atomic Espionage* in

September 1949 (reprinted in *Soviet Atomic Espionage,* p. 174). The story is given by Pilat (*op. cit.,* p. 154) with names. See also *Coronet* magazine, January 1951 (pp. 138–42), "When Mrs. A-Bomb Proved Her Loyalty."

124. Pilat, *op. cit.,* pp. 154–5.

125. *Ibid.* The following is from the testimony of Dr. Kenneth O. May, one-time Communist Party organizational secretary for Alameda County, California, given December 22, 1950, before the House Un-American Activities Committee, and published in *Hearings on Radiation Laboratory,* pp. 3494–3500:

Mr. Tavenner (Counsel for the Committee): You were asked questions yesterday regarding Haakon Chevalier, Dr. Frank Oppenheimer, and George Charles Eltenton. Were you also acquainted with J. Robert Oppenheimer?

Dr. May: Yes; I was.

Mr. Tavenner: I want to read you an excerpt from the testimony of Louis J. Russell, now senior investigator of this committee, relating to these individuals and also Louise Bransten. Did you know Louise Bransten?

Dr. May: I met her. I think perhaps I saw her once or twice. . . .

Mr. Tavenner: I will read a part of Mr. Russell's testimony to you. . . . This testimony is taken from volume 2 of the Hearings and Reports of the Committee on Un-American Activities for the year 1947, and appears on page 520:

"Mr. Stripling: Do you have any information regarding further association between Bransten, Louise Bransten, and Eltenton?

"Mr. Russell: Yes; it is known that Louise Bransten at one time attempted to secure employment for Dolly Eltenton with the American-Russian Institute through Gregory Kheifets. Also Louise Bransten requested Eltenton to send a telegram of congratulations to a Russian scientific society in the Soviet Union, and during the month of July 1940 it was sent. The person in charge of this scientific gathering in Soviet Russia was an individual known as Peter Kapitza.

"Mr. Stripling: Mr. Russell, tell the committee whether or not Eltenton was ever contacted by an official of the Soviet Government regarding espionage activity.

"Mr. Russell: Yes; during the year 1942, the latter part, Eltenton was contacted by Peter Ivanov, whom I have identified as a vice consul of the Soviet Government and a secretary in its consulate in San Francisco. Ivanov requested Eltenton to secure information concerning some highly secret work which was being carried on at the radiation laboratory at the University of California. Ivanov offered Eltenton money in return for his cooperation in securing information regarding the secret work which was being conducted at the University of California at Berkeley in its radiation laboratory.

"Mr. Stripling: Do you know whether or not Eltenton, in furtherance of this offer, contacted anyone else?

"Mr. Russell: Yes; in order to cooperate with Ivanov he approached Haakon Chevalier, who was a professor at the University of California . . . and requested him to find out what was being done at the radiation laboratory, particularly information regarding the highly destructive weapon which was being developed through research. Eltenton told Chevalier that he had a line of communication with an official of the Soviet Government who had advised him that since Russia and the United States were allies Soviet Russia should be entitled to any technical data which might be of assistance to that nation.

"At the time of this particular conversation Chevalier advised Eltenton that he would contact a third person who was working in the radiation laboratory and attempt to secure information regarding the type of work conducted there or any information which he could regarding technical developments which might be of assistance to the Soviet Government.

"Mr. Stripling: Mr. Russell, can you tell the committee whether or not Mr. Chevalier did contact a scientist employed in the radiation laboratory?

"Mr. Russell: Yes; Chevalier approached this third person.

"Mr. Stripling: Was that third person J. Robert Oppenheimer?

"Mr. Russell: That is right; Chevalier approached this third person, J. Robert Oppenheimer, and told him that George Charles Eltenton was interested in obtaining information regarding technical developments under consideration by the United States and also that Eltenton was interested in obtaining information regarding the work being performed at the Radiation Laboratory of the University of California. This third person—

"Mr. Stripling: Just a moment. Did Chevalier tell J. Robert Oppenheimer that he had the means of communication whereby he could transmit such information to the Soviet Union?

"Mr. Russell: Yes he did. He told J. Robert Oppenheimer that Eltenton had a source through which he could relay the information to the Soviet Government.

"Mr. Stripling: What did Mr. Oppenheimer reply to this approach on the part of Mr. Chevalier?

"Mr. Russell: He said that he considered such attempts as this to secure information a treasonable act and that he certainly would not have anything to do with such a thing."

Tavenner [resuming questioning of May]: Is it not true that Steve Nelson mentioned the subject of this testimony regarding the aborted effort to obtain information from Dr. J. Robert Oppenheimer to you? . . .

Dr. May: Steve Nelson has mentioned this, not as a fact, but he has mentioned this allegation to me on one occasion.

Mr. Tavenner: Tell us about that.

Dr. May: Well, sometime—I am not sure of the exact time, but it was probably in 1947 or 1948—Steve Nelson phoned me from Minneapolis [Dr. May was at Carleton College, Northfield, Minnesota], and I hadn't heard from him, really, since the war, and so I went up to see him, and we just sat and talked for a little while, and he said something about—this was after some newspaper reports had come out along the lines you have just read, and he made some reference to this. I assumed, when I read this in the newspaper, that it was just someone romancing. . . .

Mr. Tavenner: Did you gain the impression that the purpose of his calling you was to discuss this matter with you . . . the matter of Eltenton and the approach to J. Robert Oppenheimer?

Dr. May: This possibility has not occurred to me until now, that that is why he wanted to see me. I just assumed he wanted to see me because he liked me and so on; we were friends. . . . I think I should explain to the committee that my relation with Steve Nelson, although I have no contact with him now, he was for a time the closest thing I had to a family, and I felt a certain personal attachment to him. He had always been very nice to me, and when I came to his house to live I was in poor health and underweight, and his wife fed me well and I was in good shape to go in the Army; and if I were to see him now I feel I should greet him as a former friend, at least. I don't feel I am his friend now.

Mr. Tavenner: I wish you would tell us what he told you, as nearly as you can remember, about the reported effort to approach Dr. Robert Oppenheimer.

Dr. May: The only reason I remember it is that it seemed to me a little strange that he said anything to me about it at all. I cannot remember exactly what was said but the conversation may have gone something like this. He asked if I had noticed certain reports in the paper, and I said I had read about it, and shrugged my shoulders. He said, "Well, someone must have given this story to whoever it was given to, the FBI or whoever it was given to." Then he said, "As far as I can see, it must have been Eltenton, since he has left the country."

I didn't know Eltenton had left the country, and I didn't see any particular reason why that would indicate he had told somebody, but I didn't want to get involved, so I made some remark such as, "So what?" or "What could he say?" and let the subject drop.

Mr. Tavenner: Did you gain the impression that Steve Nelson was trying to ascertain the extent of your knowledge concerning the incident?

Dr. May: I didn't think of it at the moment, and didn't see it until now. I can see now maybe he was fishing. . . .

Mr. Velde: You are acquainted with Mrs. J. Robert Oppenheimer; are you not?

Dr. May: I was acquainted with her. I haven't had any contact with her for a long time, but I met her.

Mr. Velde: Were you acquainted with her former husband, her deceased husband, who died in the Spanish civil war?

Dr. May: I have heard of him, but I wasn't acquainted with him.

Mr. Velde: Did you know her as a member of the Communist Party?

Dr. May: No.

Mr. Velde: She was a close friend of Steve Nelson also; wasn't she?

Dr. May: I understood that she was a close friend. Steve Nelson and I never sat down and talked about it, but I gathered from things he said that he knew her because he knew her husband well; and, also, I gathered that her husband was killed in Spain at a time when Steve Nelson was present; that there was some close personal bond between Steve Nelson and her husband. I am not sure of her husband's name. Steve Nelson talked of close friends in Spain and mentioned that Mrs. Oppenheimer's husband was a close friend.

Mr. Velde: Did Mrs. J. Robert Oppenheimer make a trip back to Spain during 1940 or 1941?

Dr. May: That I don't know. I don't think I had met her at that time. I met her through Professor Oppenheimer.

Mr. Velde: Did you ever discuss with Steve Nelson his acquaintanceship with Togliatti?

Dr. May: No. I didn't know that he knew Togliatti.

Mr. Velde: You know who Togliatti is?

Dr. May: I know who Togliatti is.

You asked me a question to which I did not complete the answer, whether I had ever discussed the importance of Prof. J. Robert Oppenheimer with Steve Nelson. I don't recall any conversation, but let me say this: My conception at the time of the importance of J. Robert Oppenheimer was simply that he was a very brilliant man, a very brilliant man, and I have gone to see him, and have discussed things with him at social gatherings. I have gone to his home specifically to talk to him. My purpose was more to learn than anything else, because he was very brilliant, and what he said was always very interesting. And it was for such conversations that on a couple occasions I went to his home with Steve Nelson. We discussed political problems and such things, and even when we disagreed with him, it was always stimulating to talk to Dr. Oppenheimer.

Mr. Tavenner: Did you gain from some other source a knowledge or belief that he was a member of the Communist Party?

Dr. May: No, I didn't. He spoke to us as an independent person.

126. Quoted from *Soviet Atomic Espionage,* p. 174.

127. Pilat, *op. cit.,* p. 156.

128. *Newsweek,* June 2, 1952, p. 92.

129. See *This Week,* Sept. 7, 1952, p. 7.

130. Mr. Wallace wrote: "There is . . . a fatal defect in the Moscow statement, in the Acheson (Lilienthal) Report and in the American plan recently presented to the United Nations Atomic Energy Commission. That defect is the scheme, as it is generally understood, of arriving at international agreements by 'many stages' . . ." Quoted in Blackett, *op. cit.,* p. 167. Prof. Blackett comments: "Mr. Wallace had undoubtedly put his finger on one of the major defects, not only of the American plan, but of the wording of the original Moscow agreement."

The scheme of "stages" of installing a plan of international control had been proposed at Moscow in December 1945 by then Secretary of State Byrnes, who writes in *Speaking Frankly* (Harper, 1947), p. 268: "The only paragraph of our proposal to which Mr. Molotov raised serious objection provided: 'The work of the Commission shall proceed by separate stages, the successful completion of each of which will develop the necessary confidence of the world before the next stage is undertaken.' Mr. Molotov argued that this was a matter to be determined by the commission. I told him it went to the heart of our whole proposal and that without it we would not offer the resolution. . . ." This controversy over "stages" of applying international control, along with that over abrogation of the veto, was to remain for years as a fundamental point of disagreement between the U.S. and the U.S.S.R.

The full text of Mr. Wallace's letter of July 23, 1946, to President Truman was published in the *New York Times,* September 18, 1946. "We should not pursue further the question of the veto in connection with atomic energy," wrote Mr. Wallace, "a question which is irrelevant and should never have been raised." (For views of other Americans on this subject see Note 240 below.)

The *New York Times* of September 20, 1946, carried the following (p. 3): "The official American Communist line in connection with the present controversy over American foreign policy, as raised by Secretary Henry A. Wallace, was laid down last night by William Z. Foster, national party chairman. He addressed 16,000 at a rally in Madison Square Garden marking the 27th anniversary of the Communist party.

"The party line, as pronounced by Mr. Foster, is that Mr. Wallace was right . . ."

September 21, 1946, the *New York Times* carried the following, by Lewis Wood: "Washington, September 20.—President Truman forced Henry A. Wallace, Secretary of Commerce, out of the Cabinet today because the latter's views on foreign policy clashed fundamentally with the Administration's international program, and issued a strong endorsement of that policy as evolved by Secretary of State Byrnes."

131. The views of Norman Cousins and Thomas K. Finletter appeared in an article in the *Saturday Review of Literature,* June 15, 1946. The Baruch Plan was presented June 14, 1946. Reviewing the Acheson-Lilienthal Report, Cousins and Finletter spoke of certain conditions imposed upon the authors of that report, and asserted that the "condition . . . that the United States would still be allowed to manufacture its atomic bombs after a plan of international control was put into operation although 'at some stage' such discontinuation would probably be required" was one of two "impossible conditions." Thus Cousins and Finletter in effect supported the Soviet position in the controversy over "stages." They also indicated that their approval of the Acheson-Lilienthal Report was given "despite conditions of unilateralism favoring the United States."

132. *Forrestal Diaries,* p. 95.

133. See *BAS,* April 1952, p. 126.

134. Quoted from *BAS, loc. cit.*

135. Mr. Lilienthal testified before the Joint Committee on Atomic Energy June 6, 1949, that in the case of Dr. Frank Graham, "The Commission felt then that here was a case where honest men could differ. We differed with the members of the Roberts Board in this particular case." *Investigation Hearing,* p. 173. See also p. 41 above (Note 54).

136. Public Law 585, 79th Congress, Section 10(b)(5)(B)(i).

137. *New York Times,* Jan. 23, 1948, p. 7.

138. Washington *Post,* "Atomic Supplement," Aug. 3, 1947, p. 8B.

139. *Scientific Information,* Vol. VI, p. 2.

140. Numerous accounts have been given of the origin of the atomic energy project. Chapter III of Henry D. Smyth's *Atomic Energy for Military Purposes* (Princeton, Revised 1948), and Dr Alexander Sachs' testimony in the *Hearings Pursuant to S. Res. 179* are particularly important.

141. *Nation,* Dec. 22, 1945, pp. 718–19.

142. *Ibid.*

143. See *Current Biography,* 1951. Also *New York Times,* July 17, 1950 (p. 5), Aug. 3, 1950 (p. 17), and Aug. 7, 1950 (p. 12).

144. This is a matter of inference from a number of published statements. I do not know of any simple authoritative statement that this is correct, nor do I know directly that it is correct.

145. *Nation, loc. cit.*

146. Prof. E. A. Shils has written: "The initiator of the discussions among the scientists on the political implications of the atomic bomb, and the man who took the first steps to raise the question of international control with the late President Roosevelt, was Prof. Leo Szilard, to whose personal efforts the establishment of the atomic bomb project may be attributed." *The Atomic Bomb in World Politics* (National Peace Council, London, 1948).

147. "The Bomb Secret Is Out!" *American Magazine,* Dec. 1947.

148. *Minutes to Midnight,* p. 13.

149. *Ibid.*

150. *Ibid.*

151. Dr. Sachs testified (*Hearings Pursuant to S. Res. 179,* p. 7): "Dr. Szilard in consultation with Prof. Wigner of Princeton and Prof. Teller of George Washington, sought to aid this work in the United States through the formation of an association for scientific collaboration, to intensify the cooperation of physicists in the democratic countries—such as Professor Joliot in Paris, Professor Lindemann of Oxford, and Dr. Dirac of Cam-

bridge—and to withhold publication of the progress in the work on chain reactions. . . . Bear in mind that this world community was already functioning and included Prof. Joliot, married to a daughter of Madame Curie; Prof. Lindemann of Oxford, who afterward became Lord Cherwell . . ."

152. Hutchins, *loc. cit.*
153. *Minutes to Midnight*, p. 14.
154. *Ibid.*
155. See p. 118 above (Note 145).
156. *Hearings Pursuant to S. Res. 179*, p. 27.
157. See p. 118 above (Note 145).
158. Blackett, *op. cit.*, p. 127.
159. Quoted by Blackett, *op. cit.*, p. 117.
160. *Ibid.*
161. *Ibid.*, p. 119.
162. *Ibid.*
163. *Ibid.*, p. 120.
164. *Ibid.*, pp. 123–24.
165. *Ibid.*, p. 125.
166. *Saturday Review of Literature*, June 15, 1946.
167. Blackett, *loc. cit.*
168. Stimson and Bundy, *op. cit.* (Note 191), pp. 642–43.
169. Shils, *op. cit.*
170. Blackett, *op. cit.*, p. 131.
171. Quoted in Smyth, *op. cit.*, p. 253.
172. Quoted from Blackett, *op. cit.*, p. 5.
173. See *Current Biography* 1947, entry for W. R. Higinbotham.
174. Knoxville *Journal*, Sept. 10, 1945.
175. Nov. 17, 1945, at a Symposium on Atomic Energy at the Joint Meeting of the American Philosophical Society and the National Academy of Sciences.
176. Smyth, *op. cit.*, Chapter III.
177. *Hearings Pursuant to S. Res. 179*, p. 27.
178. *Ibid.*, pp. 92–3.
179. *BAS*, May 1, 1946, p. 5.
180. *BAS*, November 1947, p. 313.
181. *BAS*, Jan. 1951, p. 3.

182. P. 192.

183. Quoted from the back cover of *BAS*, March 1952.

184. *Forrestal Diaries*, pp. 123–4.

185. *Ibid.*, p. 133.

186. See *New York Times*, Feb. 11, 1949, p. 5.

187. *Confirmation of Atomic Energy Commission and General Manager. Hearings before the Senate Section of the Joint Committee on Atomic Energy* (hereinafter cited as *Confirmation Hearings*) (Government Printing Office, 1947), p. 26.

188. Houghton Mifflin, pp. 227–29. See also *BAS*, June 1952.

189. *Minutes to Midnight*, p. 23.

190. *Investigation Hearing*, p. 299.

191–194. Quoted from *Minutes to Midnight*, pp. 18–19. Used by permission of Harper & Brothers. See *On Active Service in Peace and War*, by Henry L. Stimson and McGeorge Bundy (Copyright by Henry L. Stimson), pp. 636–37, 640–43.

195. See p. 137 above (Note 134).

196. Stimson and Bundy, *op. cit.*, p. 644.

197. *Ibid.*

198. *Confirmation Hearings*, p. 106.

199. Stimson and Bundy, *loc. cit.*

200. *Ibid.*, p. 645.

201. *Forrestal Diaries*, p. 95.

202. *Ibid.*, p. 96.

203. *Ibid.*, p. 102.

204. Quoted from *Minutes to Midnight*, p. 21.

205. *New York Times*, Oct. 4, 1945.

206. See *Congressional Record*, Vol. 92, Part 7, pp. 9249 ff.

207. *New York Times*, Oct. 14, 1945.

208. *Nation*, Dec. 22, 1945, p. 718.

209. *New York Times*, Oct. 11, 1945.

210. *New York Times*, Oct. 4, 1945. Apparently Majority Leader Alben Barkley and Senate sponsor of the bill Edwin Johnson favored referring the bill to the Military Affairs Committee, while Senators Vandenberg and Connally held out for the creation of a special committee. The following from the *Times* (date cited above) is now ironic: "There was privately uttered speculation that some of the opponents of Senator Bark-

ley's plan were reluctant to have the Military Affairs Committee handle the atomic energy problem because Senator Elbert D. Thomas, Democrat of Utah, its Chairman, was deemed to be 'too internationalistic.'" It is also interesting that Cabell Phillips in a signed article in the *New York Times,* Oct. 7, 1945, could say the "May-Johnson bill was open to criticism only on three counts," which were said to be (1) that it did not give the Commission subpoena authority, (2) that its security provisions were deficient in that no power of censorship was granted, and (3) that it afforded no guarantee of the protection of secrets when the Commission should go to Congress for appropriations. These were the first objections to the May-Johnson Bill, later tagged as militaristic.

211. Blackett, *op. cit.,* p. 110.

212. *Op. cit.*

213. See Vandenberg and Morris, *op. cit.,* pp. 259–60.

214. In a radio address, October 5, 1945.

215. Knoxville *Journal,* Sept. 11, 1945.

216. The *Nation,* Sept. 1, 1945, published an article by J. D. Bernal, entitled "Everybody's Atom," forecasting important constructive possibilities, and declaring, "The control of atomic energy, however, which is already promised by President Truman, should be from the start a fully international control. . . . The maintaining of secrecy on the principles and processes involved and the limitation of their application to the use of particular nations will be doubly disastrous. . . ."

217. Quoted from *Minutes to Midnight,* p. 13.

218. *Ibid.,* p. 21.

219. For Oct. 10, 1945. Here and in several instances below the date given in the text is that of the *Times'* date-line. The date of the paper is in each of these cases one day later.

220. See p. 188 above.

221. *Ibid.*

222. For example, see the argument of Dr. Robert M. Hutchins as cited on pp. 121–22 above.

223. *Confirmation Hearings,* p. 32. Mr. Lilienthal added, "It is hard for me to be temperate in my feeling as to how difficult some of those things have made the present situation. . . . I am

sorry to be so candid about it, but this thing has been seething in me for quite a while." On February 2, 1949, however, Mr. Lilienthal told the Joint Committee on Atomic Energy, which had raised certain questions about the AEC's Fifth Semiannual Report, "You will recall that after Hiroshima, a great many photographs of the plants were released, and the Smyth Report was issued. *I myself think that was right.*" (Italics added.)—*Atomic Energy Report to Congress, Hearing before the Joint Committee on Atomic Energy* (Government Printing Office, 1949), p. 16.

224. *BAS*, Jan. 1952, p. 7.

225. *Confirmation Hearings*, p. 32.

226. In *The Private Papers of Senator Vandenberg* (Houghton Mifflin, 1952), pp. 255–56.

227. *Ibid.*, p. 256.

228. *Ibid.*, pp. 256–57.

229. Quoted in *Current Biography* 1947, entry for Dr. Robert F. Bacher.

230. Vandenberg and Morris, *op. cit.*, pp. 259–60.

231. *A Report on the International Control of Atomic Energy,* Department of State Publication 2498, Second Reprint (Government Printing Office, 1946), p. 42.

232. In the *Confirmation Hearings* (p. 428) Senator Knowland is reported as saying, "Mr. Barnard, . . . you are not proposing that the information be given to anyone who does not now have it without adequate safeguards being put around it. . . . That is a condition that would have to be met prior to any such information being given. Is that correct?" And Mr. Barnard replied, "That is correct."

233. *Loc. cit.*

234. Blackett, *op. cit.*, p. 114.

235. "Nomination of David E. Lilienthal," Speech of Hon. Robert A. Taft of Ohio in the Senate of the United States, April 2, 1947 [Not printed at Government expense] (Government Printing Office, 1947), p. 14.

236. Blackett, *op. cit.*, pp. 108, 110.

237. "Nomination of David E. Lilienthal," pp. 12–14.

238. *Ibid.*, p. 14.

239. *Ibid.*

240. P. 47. Joseph and Stewart Alsop on May 23, 1946, anticipated Mr. Baruch's addition of the no-veto provision to the Acheson-Lilienthal Plan, and observed, ". . . if put forward as U.S. policy it would create enormous problems of the utmost complexity. The first and most serious would be the embittered opposition of the Soviet Union to any tampering with the U.N. veto. . . . It must be emphasized that Baruch and his associates are only considering the idea and have not yet decided that such an extension of the Acheson report plan is essential to American security."–Quoted from *Congressional Record*, Vol. 92, p. A3516. Walter Lippmann on June 20, 1946, said of the no-veto provision, "This part of Mr. Baruch's proposal needs to be reconsidered and revised. In order that this may be done wisely and thoroughly, his staff could with great advantage be strengthened by the addition of men who are learned in the law and experienced in the practice of constitutions." On June 25, 1946, Mr. Lippmann said, "Mr. Baruch's treatment of the veto has taken this country . . . up a blind alley. . . . Let us not look [Mr. Gromyko's] gift horse in the mouth."–Quoted from *Congressional Record*, Vol. 92, pp. A3800 and A3805. Mr. Lippmann's column for June 20, 1946, appears to have been introduced into the *Record* on June 19, 1946.

241. "Nomination of David E. Lilienthal," p. 14.

242. *Confirmation Hearings*, p. 105.

243. *Ibid.*, p. 108.

244. Blackett, *op. cit.*, p. 188.

245. *Ibid.*, pp. 188–89.

246. *Ibid.*, pp. 143-44.

247. *Confirmation Hearings*, pp. 147, 165, 225 ff., 265 ff., 390.

248. *Ibid.*, p. 264.

249. *Ibid.*, p. 231.

250. *Ibid.*, p. 284.

251. *Forrestal Diaries*, p. 255.

252. *Confirmation Hearings*, p. 101.

253. *Ibid.*, pp. 280–82.

254. *Ibid.*, p. 312.

255. Public Law 269, 80th Congress. The "rider" was effective Nov. 30, 1947.

256. See Dean Acheson's letter to Chester I. Barnard, quoted on p. 217 above.

257. *Minutes to Midnight,* p. 27.

258. *Ibid.*

259. *Confirmation Hearings,* p. 281.

260. Morris V. Rosenbloom, *Peace Through Strength, Bernard Baruch and a Blueprint for Security* (American Surveys in association with Farrar, Straus and Young, 1953), p. 264.

261. *Ibid.* Perhaps the most unequivocal, though restrained, indication of the withholding of Secretary Byrnes' approval appears in the date imprinted on the Department of State Publication 2498 (the Acheson-Lilienthal Report). "Washington, D. C., March 16, 1946," reads the cover. Inside, the "Letter of Transmittal" *to* the Secretary of State is dated March 17, 1946.

262. *Confirmation Hearings,* pp. 285–6.

263. *Ibid.,* p. 287.

264. *Ibid.,* p. 288.

265. *Ibid.,* p. 306.

266. *Ibid.,* p. 438. On April 9, 1946, in a Department of State release "For the press, No. 235," twelve leading atomic scientists attempted to clarify the situation with regard to denaturing. "The [Acheson-Lilienthal] Report does not contend," they wrote, "nor is it in fact true, that a system of control based solely on denaturing could provide adequate safety. As the Report states, all atomic explosives are based on the raw materials uranium and thorium. In every case the usefulness of the material as an atomic explosive depends to some extent on different properties than those which determine its usefulness for peacetime application. The existence of these differences makes denaturing possible. *In every case denaturing is accomplished by adding to the explosive an isotope,* which has the same chemical properties. These isotopes cannot be separated by ordinary chemical means. The separation requires plants of the same general type as our plants at Oak Ridge, though not of the same magnitude. The construction of such plants and the use of such plants to process enough material for a significant number of atomic bombs would probably require not less than one nor more than three years. Even if such plants are in existence and ready to operate some

months must elapse before bomb production is significant. *But unless there is reasonable assurance that such plants do not exist it would be unwise to rely on denaturing to insure an interval of as much as a year."* (Italics added in the preceding quotation.) The statement was signed by L. W. Alvarez, R. F. Bacher, M. Benedict, H. A. Bethe, A. H. Compton, Farrington Daniels, J. R. Oppenheimer, J. R. Ruhoff, G. T. Seaborg, F. H. Spedding, C. A. Thomas, and W. H. Zinn. The Atomic Development Authority, as pointed out in the text, was intended to assure that such plants did exist "within other nations as well as within our own."

267. See pp. 204–5 above.

268. From "MDDC-1," released May 27, 1946, a declassified document published by the Technical Information Division, Oak Ridge Operations Office, U.S. Atomic Energy Commission.

269. In December 1945 Dr. J. Robert Oppenheimer testified before the Special Senate Committee on Atomic Energy, and the following exchange occurred (*Hearings Pursuant to S. Res. 179,* p. 197): Chairman (Senator McMahon): "Have you considered the possibility of a UNO ownership of such power plants as might be developed?" Dr. Oppenheimer: "I think it would be a very good thing. I think that, for instance, if in China, where I understand we are prepared to help with the generation of power in the Yangtze Valley, it were possible and sound to establish atomic power, it would be a very good thing to do that through the UN Commission." About three weeks later (Dec. 29, 1945) "the Institute of Pacific Relations and the San Francisco International Center held a round-table conference . . . on atomic energy and its international implications. . . . A few thousand scientists created this problem of atomic energy, the moderator stated, but millions of people all over the world have to participate in solving it. What can be done in the immediate future to dispel their suspicion of one another and to create both the will and the ability among them to answer these many difficult questions . . . ? For one thing, replied a scientist who had worked on the bomb, our own country can take the lead in allaying suspicion by abandoning production of atomic weapons. (There was no agreement on the timing of this move,

some holding that international acceptance of an adequate control system should precede such a step.) Secondly, the scientist continued, we might supply atomic power plants to nations who do not now have the needed power to develop their raw materials. One operating uranium pile in China might be convincing testimony to the Chinese, as well as the rest of the world, that we do not intend to monopolize atomic power for our own selfish national interests." *IPR Hearings,* pp. 5033, 5038. The "List of Participants" in this conference includes the names of Frank Oppenheimer and Joseph W. Weinberg (p. 5040). General Groves wrote of the conference, "On the whole it seems to be part and parcel with the general aims of those who would surrender American aims to those of the Soviet."—*IPR Hearings,* p. 4905.

270. *Hearings Pursuant to S. Res. 179,* p. 47.

271. *Ibid.,* p. 83.

272. *Ibid.,* p. 84.

273. *Ibid.,* p. 104.

274. *Investigation Report,* p. 13. In the *Investigation Hearing* (p. 770), Dr. Bacher is reported testifying as follows: "When we took over in January 1947, as a representative of the Commission, I went to Los Alamos to make an inventory of what we had. I made a rather complete inventory—this is at the end of December in 1946. This was directed primarily at making an inventory of the vital components of weapons and fissionable material in our stock. This was not something which I or any other members of the Commission took lightly at that time. We took it very seriously.

"I spent 2 days as a representative of the Commission going over what we had. I was very deeply shocked to find how few atomic weapons we had at that time. *This came as a rather considerable surprise to me* in spite of the fact that I had been rather intimately associated with the work of the Los Alamos project —roughly, a year before. [Italics added.]

"It might be interesting just to tell a word about how we conducted that inventory. I actually went into the vaults where material was kept and selected at random cartons and various containers to be opened. These, I then inspected myself, using suitable counters and other methods to determine to the best of my knowledge and observation that the materials were what they were declared to be.

"In addition to that, I was accompanied by Colonel Gee, Dr. Bradbury, and other representatives of the various departments at Los Alamos, whom I questioned on every piece examined as to whether, to the best of their knowledge and belief, the materials were as represented on the inventory cards which we carried with us.

"Judging by the consternation which appeared on some of the faces around there, I concluded that this must have been about the first detailed physical inventory that had been made; and I think I can say without any doubt, that this was about as thorough inventory as could be made without actually tearing things completely to pieces.

"Our work during the year 1947 was largely determined by what we found at that time."

Again Dr. Bacher said (p. 773): "With weapons, the situation was very bad. We did not have anything like as many weapons as I thought we had, and I was very deeply shocked at what I found when I made an inventory of what we really did have."

Concerning the remedy for this situation, and the essential role of members of the Laboratory, Dr. Bacher testified (p. 774): "Our first attention had to be directed toward the production of atomic weapons. . . . We felt it our first responsibility to do everything in our power to build the Los Alamos Laboratory. . . . I think I can say without being immodest, since most of the credit goes to members of that laboratory who went through that period, that success has been very marked."

In the *Investigation Hearing* (p. 801), Brig. Gen. James McCormack, Jr., is reported testifying concerning "the handful of key people at Los Alamos who had in their minds—not on paper —the know-how of weapons production."

275. *Forrestal Diaries*, p. 462.

276. Oct. 25, 1952, pp. 29, 150–54. Additional material on this subject appears in "The Hidden Struggle over the H-Bomb," *Fortune*, May 1953, p. 109.

277. *BAS*, Jan., 1947.

278. *Hearings Pursuant to S. Res. 179*, p. 65.

279. See p. 177 above.

280. Quoted from *BAS*, Aug., 1952, p. 173.

281. "We Can Smash the Red A-Bombers," *Saturday Evening Post*, March 21, 1953, p. 20.

282. I have a mimeographed copy of the script.

283. *Some Political Consequences of the Atomic Bomb* (Oxford University Press, 1945), p. 15.

284. *Op. cit.*, pp. 38–39.

285. P. 170.

286. *The Case for De Gaulle: A Dialogue Between André Malraux and James Burnham* (Random House, 1948), p. 40.

287. *BAS*, June 1951, p. 170.

288. *Hiroshima* (Andrew Dakers, Ltd., London, 1946), pp. 129–30.

289. "Back to the Laboratories," *BAS*, March 1950, p. 72.

Acknowledgments

Among the persons to whom I am indebted I will mention first those I have known as fellow workers in the atomic energy project. A great many of them were and are close personal friends. Hundreds of others are the special kind of acquaintances one makes in a great common adventure.

I must acknowledge next my indebtedness to the Tennessee Eastman Corporation, the Manhattan Engineer District, and the Atomic Energy Commission, successively my employers in the atomic energy project, invariably fair and generous employers as far as I was concerned.

My indebtedness to the published works of others is indicated in considerable detail in the notes, or in the text. Special reference is imperative to the published Hearings and Reports of several Congressional Committees, including the Special Senate Committee and the Joint Committee on Atomic Energy, the Senate Internal Security Subcommittee, and the House Committee on Un-American Activities; to the *Bulletin of the Atomic Scientists;* and to the *New York Times.* These are indispensable sources for any student of the political history of atomic energy, as are various official releases of the Atomic Energy Commission, notably its Semiannual Reports to Congress.

I wish to thank the following publishers and authors for

specific permission to quote copyrighted material of theirs: the *American Magazine,* the *Bulletin of the Atomic Scientists, Business Week,* the Cornell University Press, *Coronet,* Andrew Dakers, Ltd., the John Day Company, Doubleday and Company, Inc., *Fortune,* the Boston *Globe,* Harper & Brothers, the New York *Herald Tribune,* Dr. David L. Hill, Houghton Mifflin Company, Dr. Robert M. Hutchins, Waldemar Kaempffert, *Life, Look,* the Macmillan Company, McGraw-Hill Book Company, Inc., the *Nation,* National Peace Council (London), Oxford University Press, Cabell Phillips, Frederick A. Praeger, Inc., Princeton University, G. P. Putnam's Sons, Dr. Eugene Rabinowitch, Random House, Inc., Charles Scribner's Sons, Dr. John L. Simpson, the *New York Times,* Turnstile Press, Ltd., the Viking Press, Inc. I appreciate also the general permission for brief quotations from *Current Biography,* extended by the H. W. Wilson Company to one and all.

In several instances I have quoted editorials, reviews, etc., in order to contradict them as best I could. In these and other cases of what I believe is called "fair use," I hereby acknowledge indebtedness.

I wish to thank Suzanne LaFollette, Forrest Davis, and John Chamberlain, both for throwing me a life line once, and for their always brilliant work on the *Freeman,* a magazine for those who are neither ossified nor petrified.

For aid and encouragement I wish to thank Benjamin Mandel and Isaac Don Levine. Mr. Levine, in *Plain Talk* for February 1947, said much of what I have to say, but I am so slow in learning things that I did not know that until I had almost completed my manuscript. I think it is all still true, and it is still unfinished business.

I am grateful to James Burnham, leading intellectual antagonist of Communism. I am honored that he has been willing to write the Introduction for this book.

Finally, I will mention, though I will not try to evaluate,

the indispensable aid of my family and of certain friends. My parents, my wife, and my children have contributed specific assistance in many ways, besides comprising the *raison d'être* for a work which is intended to be patriotic.

The friend to whom the book is dedicated has been a companion, preceptor, patron, and good listener for thirty years. He has forgiven me a great deal; so perhaps he will forgive this. If the United States is to survive, it will be because of Americans like him, pragmatic in accomplishment, absolute in loyalty.

Among other persistently loyal friends are Evelyn Cherry, Ray W. Evans (no kin), Richard K. Hines, Foster Johnson, Louis P. Mueller, George B. Myers, and Eleanor Tretler. You cannot be entirely wrong if people like these think you have something.

M. E.

September 1, 1953

Index of Persons